C000128067

STARTING A BUSINESS IN

S P A I N

Guy Hobbs

Distributed in the USA by
The Globe Pequot Press, Guilford, Connecticut

Published by Vacation Work, 9 Park End Street, Oxford
www.vacationwork.co.uk

STARTING A BUSINESS IN SPAIN
by Guy Hobbs

First edition 2004

Copyright © 2004

ISBN 1-85458-307-7

Publicity by Roger Musker

Cover design and chapter headings by mccdesign ltd

Cover photograph of Toni-Lee's Bar Bistro, Benalmádena, Costa del Sol

Photography by Guy Hobbs and spanishforum.org

Illustrations by John Taylor

Typeset by Brendan Cole

Printed and bound in Italy by Legoprint SpA, Trento

CONTENTS

SETTING UP A BUSINESS IN SPAIN

RUNNING A BUSINESS IN SPAIN

EMPLOYING STAFF

MARKETING YOUR BUSINESS

SELLING ON

APPENDICES

MAPS AND CHARTS

FOREWORD

Information is an essential tool for doing business. This is the reason why *Starting a Business in Spain* will be useful to any British or American citizen or company wishing to do business in Spain for the first time.

Spain is well known to foreigners and especially to British citizens, as many millions of visitors and tourists come to our country each year. It is worthwhile mentioning that last year the number of visits by UK residents to Spain, including the Canary Islands, **exceeded those to France for the first time** and that many Brits own property in Spain whether for holiday purposes or as an investment (i.e. Buy-to-Let).

Moreover, the United States and the UK are some of the largest overseas investors in Spain (first and fourth respectively), and many leading UK and American companies are already operating in Spain through subsidiaries or in joint ventures with Spanish partners, reaping the benefits of a domestic market of over 40 million consumers and the additional demand coming from the people who visit our country every year (82.5 million during 2003).

But Spain still has a great deal to offer, and many opportunities to do business remain yet to be discovered. To exploit these opportunities, a good practical knowledge of Spain's legal and tax system as well as its business culture is needed.

This guide deals with many interesting aspects, especially for small businesses, and I am sure that it will be a valuable reference for those wishing to start a business in Spain.

José M. Morillo-León
Director
Invest in Spain
Office for Economic and
Commercial Affairs
Embassy of Spain

ACKNOWLEDGMENTS

The author would like to thank everyone who helped with this book, especially: Anna Henri, editor of *www.spanishforum.org*, one of the best websites detailing the facts about life in Spain for expatriates. Spanishforum.org provided some great photos, information on starting campsites in Spain and general help with the book.

In addition, the following have given invaluable assistance, for which we thank them: Alberto Salmerón of the *Consejo Superior de Cámaras de Comercio* in Madrid; Richard Spellman of Ambient Media and Communications S.L. (www.ambientmedia.es); Jos Arensen of Start With Us (www.startwithus.es2000.com) a multi-lingual business consultancy in Benalmádena; Tim Stonebridge of Diamond Commercials S.L. (www.diamondcommercials.com); Pilar Solana, co-ordinator of the *Ventanilla Unica Empresarial* in Madrid; Chantal Becker-Cid, a lawyer with offices in Madrid and Marbella (☎915-750544); Sarah Rodrigues and Homes Overseas Magazine for information on vineyards; Trevor Cayless of UK Trade and Investment in Madrid; the Labour and Social Affairs Office of the Spanish Embassy in London; David Searl, author of *'You and the Law in Spain'*; José Maria Morillo, director of Invest in Spain at the Spanish Embassy Office for Economic and Commercial Affairs in London.

Special thanks also to all those who provided case histories: Alison Benwell of *'The Village School,'* Salteras; Graham Smith of *'Toni-Lee's Bar and Bistro,'* Benalmádena; Liz Arthur, a registered midwife on the Costa del Sol; Michael and Vivian Harvey of *'Cortijo el Papudo,'* San Martin de Tesorillo; Peter Deth of *Happy Diver's Club,'* Marbella; Philippe Guémené of *'Crocodile Park Torremolinos'*; Rita Hillen of *'Hostal los Geranios',* Torremolinos; Peter and Ginette Lytton Cobbold of *Masia Rentals,* Barcelona.

PREFACE

People from all over the world have taken a chance and started businesses in Spain. It is hardly a surprise that the UK's favourite holiday destination has attracted so many people seeking a lifestyle change. As the average age of the emigrant to Spain continues to decrease, so the need for a means to sustain the holiday lifestyle has increased and people have begun to take advantage of the numerous business opportunities that the country offers.

Most people have a trade, profession or skill, which could just as easily be practised in Spain as in the UK. Starting a business in Spain offers not just the chance for a fresh start in the sunshine, but also the opportunity to become your own boss; to be in complete control of the number of hours you spend working, and the number of hours you spend watching the sunset from your balcony with a glass of Rioja in your hand.

The expatriate business owners that appear in this book all came from diverse walks of life and arrived in Spain with very different levels of business experience and expectations for the future. Yet what binds them together is a real passion for the new life that they have created in the sun and a pride in their own thriving ventures. It has been a challenge. Not one of them would deny that there have been times when they were utterly baffled by Spanish bureaucracy, incensed by the inconsistency of Spanish officials and frustrated by their apparent lack of urgency; but then again, not one of them regrets their decision to start a business in Spain and we believe that *Starting a Business in Spain* will make it considerably easier for you to do the same.

Guy Hobbs
Oxford, April 2004

Why Spain?

CHAPTER SUMMARY

- There are around 500,000 Britons living in Spain. Many of these seek to set up their own businesses or work as self-employed craftsmen or professionals, breaking free of the nine to five and enjoying a culturally richer lifestyle.
- Spain has an enormous amount to offer from the beautiful landscapes, and warm climate to a simpler more traditional way of life.
  - It has lower living costs and warm and welcoming people.
- In the last three decades, Spain has undergone an enormous transformation from a backward, rural country with an agriculturally-based economy, to a nation with a diversified economy made up of strong retail, property, industrial and tourism sectors.
- Spain is now Europe's fastest growing economy and consistently beats its European counterparts in terms of economic performance.
- **Tourism is booming.** Spain plays host to a staggering 50 million or more visitors every year, bringing in around €37 billion annually.
- The Spanish government is keen to attract new foreign investment to modernise the economy and has introduced new regulations to make the country more attractive to investors.
  - Small and medium-sized enterprises are particularly important to the economy, generating 80% of employment.
  - New incentives help enormously with small business start-ups.
- In recent years, a persistent rationalisation of Spanish bureaucracy has taken place and a wide range of information and advice is available to foreign businessmen to help them succeed.
  - The notoriously complicated and time-consuming procedures relating to starting a completely new

business enterprise have been simplified.

- **Residence Regulations.** EU citizens no longer need a residence permit to be self-employed or start a business but it is advisable and the procedures involved are fairly straightforward.
  - The residence procedures for non-EU citizens are more complicated. It is necessary to apply for a residence visa before entering Spain and those intending to start businesses will have to demonstrate that they have the necessary funds.
  - Acquiring a work permit will take several weeks and could cost up to €300.

INTRODUCTION

It is estimated that there are around 500,000 Britons living in Spain, as well as a huge number of Dutch and Germans and a mixed bag of other nationalities. Although a large proportion of these expatriates have chosen to retire to Spain, this is certainly not the whole story. A new breed of young entrepreneurs seeking to make money as well as enjoy a simpler lifestyle in warmer climes is gradually appearing alongside the traditional expatriate community of retirees playing golf and lazing in the sunshine. Recent estimates suggest that as many as 51% of the British moving to Spain choose to set up their own businesses or work as self-employed craftsmen or professionals. Indeed, those expatriates working for Spanish or larger international companies are very much in the minority and those who venture to Spain before retirement age seem to favour self-reliance. This is probably because there is a sense of freedom associated with making the move to Spain, of breaking free of the shackles of a nine to five working day and becoming your own boss; of working less but enjoying a culturally richer lifestyle.

There are numerous reasons to choose Spain over other warmer European countries but for many, the fact that there is already an enormous community of foreigners of which they can become a part, is a great attraction. Superficially the presence of so many ex-pats

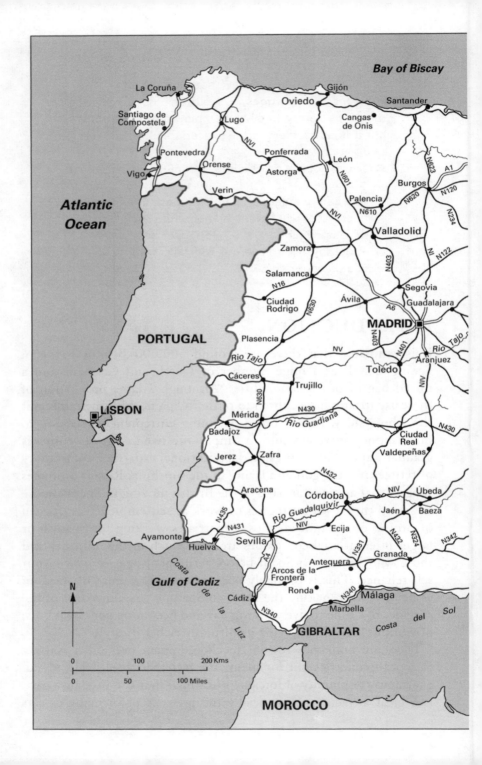

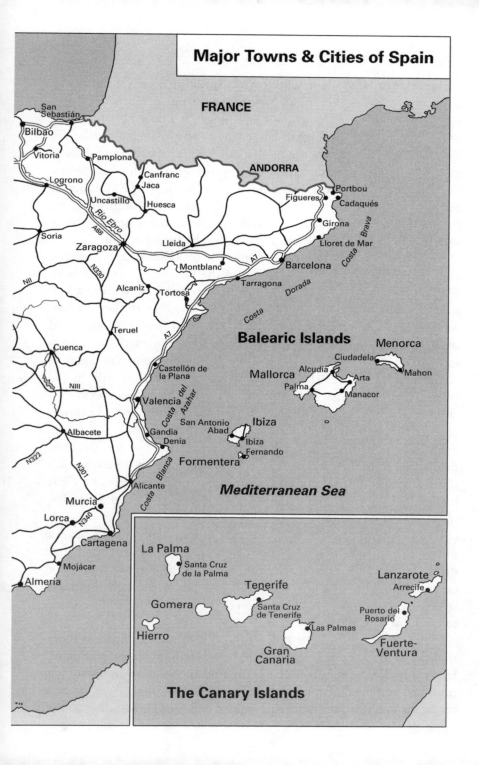

Major Towns & Cities of Spain

FRANCE

ANDORRA

San Sebastián
Bilbao
Vitoria
Pamplona
Logrono
Canfranc
Jaca
Uncastillo
Huesca
Soria
Rio Ebro
A68
Zaragoza
Lleida
Figueres
Portbou
Cadaqués
Girona
Lloret de Mar
Costa Brava
Montblanc
Barcelona
N330
NII
Alcaniz
Tortosa
Tarragona
Costa Dorada
Teruel
A7
Costa
Cuenca
NIII
Castellón de la Plana
Balearic Islands
Menorca
Ciudadela
Mahon
Mallorca
Alcudia
Arta
Palma
Manacor
Valencia
Costa del Azahar
Albacete
San Antonio Abad
Ibiza
N322
Gandia
Denia
Ibiza
Fernando
N301
Costa Blanca
Formentera
Alicante
Mediterranean Sea
Murcia
Lorca
N340
Cartagena
Mojácar
Almeria

La Palma
Santa Cruz de la Palma
Lanzarote
Arrecife
Tenerife
Gomera
Santa Cruz de Tenerife
Puerto del Rosario
Hierro
Las Palmas
Fuerte-Ventura
Gran Canaria

The Canary Islands

makes it far easier to adapt, with English-speaking friends, neighbours, clubs and societies. For those looking to set up in business or self-employment this is a tremendous advantage. You only have to glance at the classifieds of an English-language newspaper such as *Sur* or the *Costa Blanca News* to see the plethora of English-speaking plumbers, electricians, translators, hairdressers, satellite television engineers, dog groomers and every other imaginable service. The number of foreigners emigrating to Spain shows no signs of diminishing so, for the foreseeable future, there will always be a demand for those offering, in English, the kinds of services to be found at home.

For others the presence of so many British, Dutch, and German communities represents a corruption of the uniquely Spanish way of life that they have come to enjoy. Fortunately Spain is two and a half times the size of the UK and has only two thirds of the population, so there are vast areas of unspoilt beauty away from the noisy and hectic coastal resorts. Many people consider the attraction of Spain to lie in its more traditional way of life. Emigrants often cite Spanish characteristics such as the lack of violent crime, feeling safe in the streets, the respect that young people show for the elderly, the love of children that the Spanish display, the sense of community and a slower pace of life as their main justifications for having made the move. Spain has modernised incredibly quickly over the last few decades, graduating from the rural backwater of Western Europe to the world's ninth largest industrial power. Yet somehow much of the country has retained strong rural and agricultural roots and the air of a simpler, more relaxed way of life.

Traditions still play an important part in local daily life. In Spain's towns and villages, long lunches of cheap and plentiful food and drink, followed by a siesta, are customary and the evening would not be complete without a leisurely stroll (the *paseo*) through the main streets allowing collective observation of the community and a chance to catch up with the gossip.

Those looking for a simple, rural life amongst Spain's more traditional population, often with breath-taking views of Spain's fabulously diverse countryside usually find the solution in opening a rural bed and breakfast, hotel or campsite; in running a farm, garden centre, or vineyard; or in offering guided walks or horse-riding to the more discerning tourists who venture away from the beaches.

For younger residents of Spain, the attraction lies in the vitality underpinning the Spanish way of doing things. Spain has an inordinate number of festivals and fiestas and far more public holidays than the UK. Social interaction is an integral part of the lifestyle and, in the cities and coastal resorts, there are almost as many cafés and bars as there are residents. Spain's infamous nightlife usually begins with a gentle evening stroll, taking in some *tapas* and a few bars, but does not really hit full swing until the early hours. The Spanish like nothing more than to start late and then dance and drink their way through the warm summer nights until the sun comes up.

Opening a bar, restaurant, café or nightclub is probably the most lucrative method of turning these seemingly constant festivities into a way of life. It should be noted however, that some find that being on the other side of the bar does not quite meet their expectations.

Philippe Guémené - Crocodile Park, Torremolinos

I came here to the Costa del Sol for the climate. It is very similar to the climate in South Africa, so it's good for me and for my crocodiles. Good weather makes such a big difference. Work is work wherever you are, but if the sun is always shining and you are able to work mainly outside, it has an enormous effect on people's attitudes. Everybody feels happier and more relaxed. The Spanish really do have a much more laid-back way of working and although sometimes it can be frustrating, you are never going to change their mentality, so it's best just to embrace it!

Everybody has a different story as to why they first moved out to Spain, but the country really does seem to offer something for everyone. For the older generation of emigrants, Spain offers all the health advantages of a good climate and the opportunity to be more active. For younger people, the attraction lies in the fact that the sun shines more, which means there are more hours in the day and consequently people are happier and feel less constrained.

A relatively new phenomenon is that young families are now moving in their droves to Spain. Spanish estate agents are currently reporting that around half of the people that they help to relocate are families, a change that has become very apparent in the last five years. Parents are attracted by the notion that their children will very quickly become bilingual, but also by the belief that they will be much safer than in the big cities back home.

Everybody enjoys the relative cheapness of Spain. Cost of living is far lower than in the USA or Britain and crucially it is the things that make life more enjoyable that remain cheap regardless of the exchange rate – wine, beer, cigarettes, eating out and leisure activities.

Finally, the Spanish people are very warm, open and welcoming and ex-pats are able to live in harmony with their Spanish neighbours who have no deep-seated antagonism towards the large communities of foreigners. Some Spaniards, especially those who live on the *costas*, still associate the British with hooliganism, and tourists who come to Spain simply for a fortnight of lager-fuelled all-nighters do nothing to dispel this lingering stigma. However, despite the bad press that the British have received, when it comes to business the British have a reputation for fair play, honesty and hard work – a notion that has been forged by centuries of diplomatic relations between the two countries.

WHY SPAIN?

Climate. Spain is a country of climactic extremes and parts of the north-west (Galicia) can be as cold and wet as Wales. Nevertheless, it is possible to enjoy sunshine all year round, especially on the southern Mediterranean coast and in the Canary Islands. Indeed, the Costa del Sol has a celebrated 3,000 sun hours each year and it is this aspect of life in Spain that attracts the majority of foreigners.

Work. The Spanish have forty-six days holiday every year, which is thirteen days more than the average worker in the UK. Whereas the average Briton works 2000 hours per year, the average Spaniard only works 1842 hours.

Cost of living. Whilst other countries such as the UK and America may have higher average household incomes, this advantage is severely diminished by higher prices. Prices in Spain are approximately 26% lower than in the UK.

House prices. House prices in Spain have been rising almost uncontrollably for years now. Certainly on the Costa del Sol, prices continue to double every five years or so and are showing no signs of slowing down. However, the average cost of a family home in Spain is still around £60,000 cheaper than in the UK. Although Spain is rapidly catching up with the rest of Europe, you will still get far more for your money if you stay away from the most popular areas.

Culture. Spain is an incredibly diverse country with a fascinating history and a vibrant culture that shapes all aspects of life.

Communications. Although it took some time for the internet to take off in Spain, ADSL broadband access is now fairly cheap and is widely available in urban areas. Spanish transport continues to improve, with increasing investment in Spain's motorways and railways. The arrival of low cost airlines has meant that flights from the UK are now so cheap and easy that some people even choose to commute between the two countries.

Cuisine. In terms of both quality and variety, very few, if any, European countries can beat Spanish cuisine. Indeed a recent report in the *New York Times* claimed that Spanish gastronomical supremacy has displaced even France. Each region has its own speciality influenced both by the climate and the local way of life. Spain's greatest gastronomic legacy is probably *tapas* – small portions of regional specialities served in restaurants and bars and always accompanied by a glass of wine or beer.

SPAIN'S ECONOMIC STRUCTURE

The Development of the Modern Spanish Economy

Spain was exhausted by the Civil War of 1936-1939 – an internal military rebellion against the elected government which turned into an international affair. The war was brutal and when the army finally seized power, half a million lives had been lost. Among those casualties was an economy in a state of ruin worse than that of her neighbours in the aftermath of the Second World War six years later.

Spain remained neutral in World War II and even provided active aid to the Axis Powers in return for their support for Franco's dictatorship. As a result, Spain did not receive post-war aid from the Marshall Plan as the main protagonists did, and was penalised by a UN economic blockade that lasted until 1950. The extreme hardships of the post-war years came to be known as *los años de hambre* (the years of hunger), when cats and dogs disappeared from the streets and it was said that only handouts from Perón's Argentina kept the country from total starvation.

Economic isolation and disastrous mismanagement had a devastating effect on living standards throughout the fifties and it was not until the latter stages of Franco's dictatorship that there were some signs of economic progress. The period from 1961 to 1973, known as *los años de desarollo* (the years of development) saw the economy grow annually at a rate of 7%, second only to that of Japan. International companies such as Chrysler, John Deere and Ciba-Geigy set up operations in Spain and tourism became a huge earner for the country. The onset of mass tourism inevitably led on to an expatriate property buying boom, which began in the 1960s and continues to this day.

During this period, an estimated 1,700,000 Spaniards left their homes to work abroad and their earnings, sent back to swell their bank accounts at home, contributed to their country's economic expansion. At the same time, there was a mass rural exodus to the cities by craftsmen and artisans as the disparity in living standards between rural and urban areas became more apparent. The resulting depopulation of the countryside and especially the *meseta* (central Spain) caused an extreme imbalance in Spain, between the wealth and high population of the cities and the desolation and poverty of the countryside.

Franco's death in 1975 ended a period of stagnation and oppression and led to a period of rapid liberalisation of the economy. By this time, five of the nineteen provinces (Madrid, Barcelona, Valencia, Biscay and Oviedo) were producing nearly half of the country's industrial output, concentrating the wealth of the country in the North and East. Today that position is very similar, except that Navarre (in the North) has taken over from Oviedo as a centre of industrial development.

In the last three decades Spain has undergone an enormous transformation from a backward, rural country with an agriculturally-based economy, to a nation with a diversified economy made up of strong retail, property, industrial and tourism sectors. A series of radical political and economic reforms have brought the country from a dyed-in-the-wool dictatorship which lagged far behind the rest of Western Europe (with the exception of Portugal) to an increasingly liberal and open society where democracy has been firmly established. As recently as 1964, the United Nations classed Spain as a developing nation, yet today Spain takes its modernity for granted.

Recent economic developments such as the joining of the European

Monetary Union in 1998, followed by the adoption of the euro in 2002 have placed Spain in a position of strength in the world markets. Furthermore, the ongoing programme of privatisation has brought a new wave of workers skilled in areas like finance, consultancy, electronics, information technology and industrial design which have little to do with the service sector and tourism.

The Current Economic Situation

According to a recent study by the accountancy firm PriceWaterhouse-Coopers, Spain is Europe's fastest growing economy and consistently beats its European counterparts in terms of economic performance. By late 2004 the GDP growth is expected to have accelerated to 2.75%, whereas in much of Europe growth has stagnated at a meagre average of 1%.

Spain's buoyant economic growth has been fuelled in recent years by successful supply-side reforms, the growing purchasing power of consumers, service improvements and the quick pace of innovation.

Today, Spain is an industrialised country with the services sector and industry representing almost 90% of the country's GDP. In contrast, agriculture has proportionately declined as a result of the country's intense economic growth and makes up less than 5% of the GDP.

Inflation in Spain has fallen steadily since the late 1980s and fell to below 5% for the first time in 1993. It has been as low as 3%, but is currently stable at around 4%. Spain's official interest rates have also reduced massively in recent years, from around 10% in 1993 to the current 2.75%. Unemployment remains at one of the highest levels in the EU but it has come down dramatically in recent years and dropped below 10% for the first time in 2002.

British companies such as BP, Cadbury Schweppes, ICI, Lloyds TSB Bank and Unilever all now have operations in Spain and there is a British presence across a wide range of industries and business activities. However, there are few Spanish companies, other than Seat (which was bought out by Volkswagen), that are well known outside Spain.

Tourism. One of the Spanish economy's most dramatic success sto-

Regions & Provinces of Spain

The Basque Country

Biscay

Guipuzcoa

Alava

Navarre

Rioja

Huesca

Lérida

Gerona

Soria

Aragon

Catalonia

Zaragoza

Barcelona

Tarragona

Guadalajara

Teruel

Cuenca

Castellón

Balearic Islands

Menorca

Mallorca

Mancha

Valencia

Ibiza

Albacete

Alicante

Formentera

Murcia

Mediterranean Sea

Almeria

La Palma

Lanzarote

Gomera

Tenerife

Hierro

Gran Canaria

Fuerte-Ventura

The Canary Islands

ries is the tourist trade. The numbers of visitors to the country have been steadily increasing ever since the first charter flights of the 1950s opened up the Mediterranean Costas to foreign visitors. Today, Spain plays host to a staggering 50 million or more visitors every year, which is an enormous amount considering that the indigenous population of Spain is only around 41 million. The annual revenue that tourism brings into Spain is around €37 billion and the tourist trade employs 1.5 million workers, contributing over 12% to the country's gross national product. The industry currently shows no signs of slowing down and in 2002 Spain overtook France for the first time as the most popular holiday destination for UK residents.

Domestic market. People thinking of starting a business in Spain should be aware that as well as the enormous demand for goods and services created by such a buoyant tourist industry, growth in the Spanish economy in recent years has also been driven by strong domestic demand, in the context of an increasingly open economy. Spain has a domestic market of around 41 million people, with an estimated per capita income of roughly $15,000. Increased standards of living have seen raised consumer expectations and a high demand for consumer goods and services. Demand for the construction and service industries, in particular, continues to grow steadily.

Companies from outside the EU who are thinking of setting up in Spain will also find that they have access to 375 million consumers of the European Single Market, without any trade barriers. Also, the close economic, cultural and political links that Spain has with Latin America and North Africa, make Spain an obvious gateway to those regions.

Foreign investment. The Spanish government is very keen to attract new foreign investment to modernise the economy and it has created new regulations to make the country more attractive to investors. Spanish law allows foreign investment of up to 100% of equity in most sectors and capital movements have been completely liberalised. Investors are attracted by Spain's large home market, export possibilities and growth potential.

However, the government is not just looking to attract larger foreign investors. In Spain, 99% of businesses are small and medium sized enterprises (known in Spain as *pequeña y mediana empresas, PYMEs*) and these generate around 80% of Spanish employment. As a result, the legislation regarding PYMEs is fully integrated and compatible with EU standards. Various incentive plans have been designed and implemented such as a reduced rate of corporation tax for smaller companies.

Infrastructure. The last decade has seen an extensive renewal of Spain's infrastructure and the government has plans to continue investing heavily in the future. The Overall Infrastructure Plan which began in 1993, plans to have spent a total of $133 billion by 2007. Spain's motorways have more than tripled in length since 1982 and Spain aims to have one of the most modern networks in the world. High speed train-lines have become a priority and the government forecasts an investment of 40.9 billion euros in the railways between 2000 and 2007. Plans are underway to connect Madrid to France by high speed train and to build a tunnel between Spain and Morocco, joining the continents of Europe and Africa.

Spain's economic achievements of recent years are remarkable and the current economic situation shows a solid and sustained growth with no signs of diminishing. This is a great encouragement for potential investors from both large and small companies that choose to operate in Spain.

WHY START A BUSINESS IN SPAIN?

The Economy. The Spanish economy is still booming and prospects for the future are good. Spain has the eighth largest economy in the OECD with a modern network of transport and telecommunications, a highly qualified local labour force and growth above the EU average. It is also the second tourist destination in the world.

Success of Small Businesses. The number of new business start-ups is currently increasing by around 3.8% each year, whereas the number of businesses going into administration has reduced by around 10% in recent years. The large ex-pat population means a wealth of opportunities for business and self-employment.

Low Fixed Costs. Spain is a fairly cheap country in which to do business. Almost all of your fixed business costs will be lower than in the UK, including the cost of renting/buying premises, utilities, and staff wages.

Encouragement for Businesses. In 2003 123,484 new businesses were established. This is, at least in part, due to the important efforts of the Spanish government to promote small and medium-sized businesses and procure the most favourable business environment for their success. The procedures for incorporating a company have also been dramatically simplified.

SPANISH ENTREPRENEURIAL SPIRIT

With so many reasons to make the move to Spain and an economy that has emerged from nowhere to become the fastest growing in Europe, it is no surprise that so many are choosing to leave behind the monotony of a nine to five job in favour of their own entrepreneurial venture in the sunshine. Those who make the move will be in good company. A recent survey on Spanish work habits shows that over 60% of Spaniards would prefer to be their own boss than to be a salaried employee. The reality of the situation in Spain reflects this attitude. As mentioned above, 99% of Spanish businesses are small or medium-sized. In fact 94% of all businesses in Spain are *micro-empresas* with less then ten salaried workers and 52% of businesses have no salaried workers at all. Spain is traditionally a country of small companies, sole traders and family-run businesses.

There is a deep-seated entrepreneurial spirit in Spain.
The Spanish highly value public institutes such as the chambers of commerce as sources of advice and information. Spain has some of the most respected business schools in Europe and there is no shortage of young native entrepreneurs seeking to take advantage of the country's booming economy.

Despite this surge of native entrepreneurial activity, there is very little antagonism between Spanish and foreign entrepreneurs. Indeed, on the Costa del Sol alone there are over 10,000 legal foreign business owners. The Spanish have an ingrained self-reliance and an economy which runs on individual entrepreneurial spirit, and as a result they have a deep respect for successful foreign businessmen. On the costas, British bars work side by side with Spanish breweries and suppliers and the larger cities such as Madrid, Barcelona, Valencia and Seville, boast a significant Spanish-speaking expatriate population of professionals, who run businesses aimed mainly at the native population.

In order to actively encourage inward investment, the regulations regarding working and starting a business in Spain have been relaxed in recent years, especially for EU citizens. EC regulations stipulate that an EU citizen can work in Spain under exactly the same conditions as a Spaniard. 'Equal treatment' and 'non-discrimination' are the fundamental principals behind this legislation offering the consolation that although you may still become bogged down in a quagmire of red tape, at least you will be in good company.

The removal of barriers to employment and self-employment across the European Union means that visitors from Britain and other EU states do not need a work permit and it is now much easier to transfer qualifications across EU borders. North Americans considering the move will run into more difficulties and will have to satisfy a wide range of criteria before they can start a business or operate as a self employed professional or craftsman.

The procedures involved with buying a business have also been simplified and there are literally hundreds of commercial estate agencies throughout Spain specialising in guiding the entrepreneur through the legal and administrative red tape. It can take only a matter of days to finalise contracts and transfer a licence to a new owner.

Even the notoriously complicated and time-consuming procedures relating to starting a completely new business enterprise have come on in leaps and bounds, with a little pressure from EU directives. At central and regional government level schemes have emerged purporting to facilitate small business creation in just forty-eight hours. However, these schemes are still not perfect, running as they do in only selected areas of Spain and the advantages of such rapid incorporation are slightly tarnished by the fact that a local council can take up to six months or more to approve an opening licence for the premises. Nevertheless, there is no doubt that a persistent rationalisation of Spanish bureaucracy is taking place, and a wide range of information and advice is available to foreign businessmen to help them succeed.

Whether your aim is to provide a business service for expatriates or to find a more general niche in an economy that is still developing and diversifying, as long as you have a creative approach and a little business acumen, your prospects of establishing a successful business in Spain have never been better.

RESIDENCE REGULATIONS FOR ENTREPRENEURS

RESIDENCE CARDS FOR EU CITIZENS

New regulations governing the issue of residence cards came into effect on 1 March 2003. These state that British and other EU citizens intending to remain in Spain for a continuous period of more than ninety days no longer need to apply for a residence card and may reside in Spain with a valid passport as long as they come under the following categories: Employees, Self-employed, Students, EU national dependents of an EU or a Spanish national. The basic rule is if you work or earn money in Spain you no longer need to apply for *residencia*, therefore it does not matter whether you work under contract for a company, whether you own or form part of a company or whether you are registered as self employed. However, the exemption does not apply in the vast majority of cases to EU citizens who have retired to Spain and persons of independent means.

Nationals of Norway, Iceland, Liechtenstein and Switzerland are also exempt from registering for residency in Spain under a bilateral agreement.

Although no longer necessary for many, the Foreign Residents Department advises everybody to apply for *residencia* and the community card (*tarjeta comunitaria*) may be applied for on an optional basis. Voluntary applications should be made direct to the local *Comisaría de Policía* or *Oficina de Extranjeros* in the larger cities.

In fact, there are a number of advantages of being a resident. For example, it is impossible to get a bank loan unless you are a legal resident. There are also several tax benefits, such as the reduced rate of capital gains tax (15%, rather than 35% for non-residents).

Applying for a Residence Permit

You are able to apply for a residence permit as soon as you arrive in Spain. The process is fairly straightforward, although you cannot expect English or other foreign languages to be spoken by the police and taking along a Spanish-speaking friend or using the services of a *gestor* is probably a good idea if you are not completely comfortable with Spanish. It is possible to download an application form from the Ministry of the Interior website (www.mir.es).

The list of required documents can vary from office to office and from region to region, but usually you will need:

o Completed application forms.
o A full valid passport.
o Proof of residence such as utility bills, rental contracts etc.
o Marriage documents (if applicable).
o Four passport-sized photographs.
o A standard medical certificate from your doctor.
o Bank statements showing your regular income.
o Details of your health insurance (you will need a certificate from the insurance company stating that full hospitalisation and treatment are covered, or evidence of registration with the Spanish Department of Health/Social Security, the INSS).
o Evidence that you meet the requirements (as for a Spanish citizen) to operate your business or exercise your profession.

Once you have presented the above documents, your application will be processed and the authorities will contact you when the card is ready. This can take anything from one month to six months depending on how busy the civil servants are. Upon notification, you should return to the police station or Oficina de Extranjeros to collect your card and have your fingerprints taken for police records.

Residence visas may have to be renewed periodically. There are two types of residence card depending on the duration of your residence. A temporary residence card lasts from three months to one year and a full residence card lasts for up to five years. It is then automatically renewable. If you move out of Spain or back to your country of origin, once the residence permit has been handed in at the police station, your right to residency in Spain automatically ceases.

More information on all of the above and further advice is available at the Spanish Ministry of the Interior's website, www.mir.es, or may be obtained by calling the free information number (☎ 900-150000).

EU nationals do not need a work permit in order to work in Spain.

VISAS AND WORK PERMITS FOR NON-EU CITIZENS

Non-EU or EEA nationals applying to take up residence in Spain have much more red tape to cope with, although the volume and variety of the bureaucracy will vary according to nationality (and if there are reciprocal health and tax agreements for example). Non-EU citizens will require a visa to *live* in Spain, although not necessarily to visit. They should apply for a visa, the *visado de residencia,* through the Spanish Consulate in their own country before leaving for Spain. Without a visa application, they cannot apply for a work and residence permit.

There are seven types of *visado de residencia*, including a special classification of visa for those wanting to start a business. However, the regulations governing the granting of this visa are quite strict. Non-EU citizens must demonstrate to the consulate that they have the funds to invest in their Spanish business and often they must demonstrate that they will provide work for Spanish nationals. It is not unusual for the Spanish consulate to insist that the investment is made, the employees are hired and that the business is ready to operate before they will grant the visa. Given the Spanish Ministry of Labour's concern for job creation, the more Spaniards you intend to employ, the more favourably the visa application will be regarded.

As well as the more specific requirements for those starting a business, the majority of non-EU citizens applying for the *visado de residencia* will also need to present, among other things, a certificate showing that they have no criminal record (available from local police authorities), a medical certificate, a letter from the home country's consulate in Spain proving that they have registered, medical insurance with a company that has an office in Spain and payment of the fee. The fee varies according to the country but is not usually very high.

The granting of the visa is subject to the approval of the work permit by the Spanish authorities, which usually takes several weeks.

Work Permits for non-EU applicants

Non-EU citizens are supposed to complete the process legalising their work and residence status in Spain before starting work. Work permits are granted by the Foreigner's Office, *oficinas de extranjero* or by the provincial office of the Ministry of Labour. They can cost up to €300 and are normally issued for one to five years. Unfortunately the process for applying for a work permit is still rather complicated and will require time and effort. It is advisable to take some expert legal advice from a *gestoría* or a lawyer. The minimum price that a *gestor* will charge to guide you through the process is around €150, plus taxes and fees. A lawyer can cost anything from €300 upwards.

The Spanish labour authorities grant different types of work permit, depending on the type of work and its duration. There are currently ten different types of permit. However, those intending to be self-employed, or start a business, need only concern themselves with work permit classes D and E. Initially most people will receive a temporary type D permit, which lasts for one year and may limit the permit holder to a specific activity or geographical area. After the initial year this may be renewed and replaced with a two-year type D permit, allowing any work to be performed throughout Spanish territory. Finally, when this permit expires, self-employed workers may obtain a type E permit, also valid for two years.

Note that in recent years, the Spanish authorities have tightened up entry and work regulations for non-EU or European Economic Area citizens. Illegal residents run the risk of being thrown out of the country straight away and being forbidden to return for three years. It is therefore very important that you follow all of the procedures to the letter.

For non-EU applicants, the procedures for obtaining a work permit usually take several weeks. The official application form must be presented along with specific documents relating to the business activity you intend to carry out, such as a summary of the project and evidence that the permits and licences required for start-up have been applied for. Applications are not accepted by post in any circumstances and instead should always be made in person or by a representative who has written consent from the applicant to act on their behalf. The following documents are required for an application for the *autonomo* work permit. However, not all of the items on this list are required in every case.

- Title or degree. In order to practice a profession it is necessary to present certificates detailing your qualifications. Validating these in Spain may take quite a long time (see *Procedures for Starting a New Business*).
- Proof from the *Agencia Tributaria* that you have registered for the IAE tax on business activity (see *Procedures for Starting a New Business*).
- Proof of registration with the Spanish Social Security, at the local office, as a *trabajador autónomo*, a self-employed worker.
- An opening licence (*licencia de apertura)* will be required if you are operating from business premises. These are granted by the town hall (see *Procedures for Starting a New Business*).
- A written explanation of the business activity you will carry out, known as the *memoria de actividades*.
- Deed of Incorporation, if a company has been formed (see *Procedures for Starting a New Business*).
- Passport and photocopy.
- Four recent photos.

Work permits are granted, taking into account the employment situation of Spanish nationals for the same kind of work. However, there are certain preferred categories such as foreigners with Spanish family ties, workers necessary to set up or repair imported machinery, or senior executives.

Once a work permit has been granted by the Ministry of Labour, the application papers are transferred to the Ministry of the Interior, which is responsible for issuing residence permits. The Spanish labour authorities notify the local Spanish consulate that the work permit has been granted. It is then necessary to collect the visa in person, from the consulate in Spain when advised to do so. Applicants must take their passports with at least one blank page to affix the visa, the consular fee and the communication from the consulate stating that the visa is ready for collection. They should subsequently collect the work and residence permit from the Ministry of the Interior in Spain. Work permits will always be issued for the same duration as the residence permit.

A Spanish embassy or consulate can advise as to the strict rules of taking up employment in Spain. For example foreigners may be prevented from doing work that could be done by the Spanish, or undercutting wages and conditions that apply locally. They will advise you also on the specific forms that need to be filled in. It may be necessary to obtain a police certificate, from your home province or state, which proves that you have no criminal record. In order for the Spanish authorities to accept this certificate, it must be translated into Spanish and legalised. The consulate in your home country will help with these procedures. When in Spain, it is also necessary to get a health certificate demonstrating that you have no contagious diseases. This is known as the *certifcado medico* and medical centres or *gestorías* will provide the correct forms. Finally, it is necessary to provide evidence that you have registered with the consulate of your home country in Spain.

Changes to requirements.
Note that whether you are an EU or non-EU citizen, requirements can change without notice and sometimes at the whim of local civil servants. Always check with the authorities or a reputable gestoría before you apply. Comprehensive and up-to-date information

is available on-line (in Spanish only) from the Ministry of the Interior website; www.mir.es. The Ministry also runs a free help line (☎900-150000), which is open during office hours.

Tax and Residency

You will become resident for Spanish tax purposes if:

○ You spend more than 183 days in Spain during one calendar year, whether or not you have taken out a formal residence permit, *or*
○ You arrive in Spain with an intention to reside there permanently, you will then be tax-resident from the day after you arrive, *or*
○ If your 'centre of vital interests' is Spain, although this rule is hardly ever applied, *or*
○ If your spouse lives in Spain and you are not legally separated, even if you spend less than 183 days in Spain.

Numero de Identificación de Extranjeros (NIE). If you reside in Spain, or if you own a property and are non-resident then you need an NIE. This is a tax identification number and is obtainable from the *oficina de extranjeros* of the local police station. An application form can be downloaded from www.mir.es.

The NIE allows you to open a bank account, file tax returns and most other documents and to vote in local elections.

Spanish Residence. Residence in Spain is not the same as citizenship, those who wish to become a Spanish citizen will have to have lived there for ten years. Once resident in Spain, as anywhere in the world, it is also advisable to register with your embassy or consulate: a list of these is provided below. This registration enables the authorities to keep emigrants up to date with any information they need as citizens resident overseas and, in the event of an emergency, helps them to trace individuals. Your embassy or consulate can also help with information regarding your status overseas, advise with any diplomatic or passport problems and offer help in the case of an emergency such as the death of a relative overseas. However, consulates do not really function as a source of general help and advice and appeals for assistance in matters which fall outside their duties often fall on deaf ears. A full explanation of the duties of British embassies and consulates can be found at the Foreign and Commonwealth Office website, www.fco.gov.uk.

Spanish Embassies and Consulates in the UK

Spanish Embassy: 39 Chesham Place, London SW1X 8SB; ☎020-7235 5555; fax 020-7259 5392.

Spanish Consulate General: 20 Draycott Place, London SW3 2RZ; ☎020-7589 8989; fax 020-7581 7888.

Spanish Consulate General: Suite 1A, Brooke House, 70 Spring Gardens, Manchester M2 2BQ; ☎0161-236 1262; fax 0161-228 7467.

Spanish Consulate General: 63 North Castle Street, Edinburgh EH2 3LJ; ☎0131-220 1843; fax 0131-226 4568.

Consular Section: Spanish Embassy, 17A Merlyn Park, Ballsbridge, Dublin 4, Ireland; ☎+353-1269 3444.

British Embassies and Consulates in Spain

British Embassy: C/ Fernando el Santo 16, 28010 Madrid; ☎917-008200; fax 917- 008272; www.ukinspain.com.

British Consulate-General: Paseo de Recoletos 7/9, 28004 Madrid; ☎915-249700; fax 915-249730.

British Consulate: Plaza Calvo Sotelo 1/2, 03001 Alicante; ☎965-216 022/216/190; fax 965-140528.

British Consulate-General: Edificio Torre de Barcelona, Avenida Diagonal 477-13, 08036 Barcelona; ☎933-666200; fax 933-666221.

British Honorary Vice-Consul Benidorm: to be contacted through Alicante.

British Consulate-General: Alameda de Urquijo 2-8, 48008 Bilbao; ☎944-157600; fax 944-167632.

Honorary Consular Agent: Plaza San Cristóbal 3, 18010 Granada; ☎669-895053; fax 958-274724.

British Vice-Consulate: Avenida de Isidoro Macabich 45-1°, 07800 Ibiza; ☎971-301818/303816; fax 971-301972.

British Consulate: Edificio Eurocom, Bloque Sur, C/ Mauricio Moro Pareto, 2, 2°, 29006 Málaga; ☎952-352300; fax 952-359211 (Postal address: Apartado Correos 360, 29080 Málaga).

British Consulate: Plaza Mayor 3D, 07002 Palma de Mallorca; ☎971-712445; fax 971-717520.

British Vice-Consulate: Sa Casa Nova, Cami de Biniatap 30, Es Castell, 07720 Menorca; ☎971-363373.

British Consulate: Edificio Catalun[ti]a, c/ Luis Morote 6-3°, 35007 Las Palmas de Gran Canaria; ☎928-262508; fax 928-267774.

British Vice-Consulate: Plaza Weyler 8-1°, 38003 Santa Cruz de Tenerife; ☎922- 286863; fax 922-289903.

Honorary British Consulate: Paseo de Pereda 27, 39004 Santander; ☎942-220000; fax 942-222941.

Honorary British Consulate: Apartado de Correos/PO. Box 143, 41940 Tomares (Sevilla); fax 954-155018.

Honorary British Consulate: ☎986-437133; fax 986-112678; email vigoconsulate@ukinspain.com.

Spanish Education, Labour and Social Affairs Office: 20 Peel Street, London W8 7PD; ☎020-7727 2462; fax 020-7229 4965; www.sgci.mec.es/uk/. For advice on work and social security in Spain; and publishes *Regulations for British Nationals Wishing to Work or Reside in Spain.*

Employment Service: Overseas Placing Unit,, Rockingham House, 123 West Street, Sheffield S1 4ER; ☎0114-259 6000; www.employmentservice.gov.uk. Publishes information sheet on *Working in Spain.*

Other Embassies and Consulates

Spanish Embassy: 2375 Pennsylvania Avenue, NW, Washington DC 20037; ☎202-728-2330; fax 202-728-2302. There are Consulates in Boston, Chicago, Houston, Los Angeles, Miami, New Orleans, New York (☎212-355-4090), Puerto Rico and San Franciso.

Spanish Embassy: 74, Stanley Avenue, Ottawa, Ontario K1M 1P4, Canada; ☎613-747-2252/7293; fax 613-744-1224. Consulates in Edmonton, Halifax, Montréal, Québec, Toronto, Vancouver and Winnipeg.

United States Embassy: Serrano 75, 28006 Madrid; ☎915 872 200; fax 915 872 303; www.embusa.es.

Canadian Embassy: Edificio Goya, Calle Núñez de Balboa 35, 28001 Madrid; ☎914 233 250; fax 914 233 251; www.canada-es.org.

Possible Types of Business

CHAPTER SUMMARY

- ⦿ Many people feel more comfortable setting up a service for other foreigners, but you cannot afford to completely ignore the local market.
- ⦿ A new business will need to have a unique selling point to distinguish it from the competition.
- ⦿ **Starting vs. buying:** Before deciding which type of business to run in Spain, you will have to decide whether to buy an existing business or start a completely new enterprise.
- ⦿ **Tourism:** The sheer scale of investment in and promotion of tourism by the Spanish authorities suggests that now is a very favourable time to buy or establish a tourism related business.
  - ⦿ As the price of renting holiday homes rises, the popularity of camping in Spain has increased considerably. Now is a good time to open a campsite.
  - ⦿ Increasingly the trend for foreigners opening a small hotel or B&B is to opt for somewhere inland in a beautiful rural setting.
- ⦿ **Eating and drinking:** There are more bars in Spain than in the rest of Europe put together.
  - ⦿ If you lack the funds to invest in premises for a restaurant you could offer a 'dine out at home' service.
- ⦿ **Farming** is becoming more popular with foreigners as they are attracted to a simpler agricultural life and the availability of arable land at cheap prices.
- ⦿ More and more **vineyards** these days are opening themselves up to wine tourism due to its growing popularity throughout Europe.
- ⦿ If you have TEFL qualifications, you could consider opening an **English language school**, which involves little bureaucracy and has low fixed overheads.
- ⦿ **Property.** Accumulated foreign investment in the Spanish property market has seen outstanding growth, rising

107% in the last four years.

- ⊙ Given the number of foreign-owned holiday homes in Spain, there is a huge market for estate agents and property management companies.
- ⊙ The rapid expansion of the Spanish property market has created a demand for service tradesmen; **plumbers, gardeners, electricians** etc.
- ⊙ One of the more obvious routes towards business success is to set up a shop to sell goods imported from the UK to homesick Britons who miss their native products.
- ⊙ Many couples routinely offer a number of services at the same time, from house sitting and maintenance, to hairdressing and vehicle repairs.

INTRODUCTION

Recent research has suggested that there are more than 10,000 registered foreign business owners just on the Costa del Sol and many more are operating illegally. The recent spate of media interest and the proliferation of television programmes documenting the progress of would-be entrepreneurs all attest to the fact that setting up a small business in the sun is a very popular option. This is hardly a surprise. Why should it just be the pensioners who get to enjoy the gloriously predictable climate and the longest holiday of their life? Why not invest some working capital into an untapped market and take the opportunity to make a comfortable living whilst simultaneously improving your quality of life? It can be a very successful and gratifying venture.

The type of business that you choose will depend on a range of factors such as whether you decide to buy an existing business or start a new one from scratch, whether you decide to cater for the tourist market, the expatriate market, or the local market, and your own personal skills and interests. Starting a business in Spain requires a good deal of determination and initiative and making a go of it will entail thorough preparation and planning, hard work and a healthy dose of luck.

Many people feel more comfortable setting up a service for other foreigners, but you cannot afford to completely ignore the local market. There is a risk that you simply will not have enough customers during the low tourist season and even in high season any serious downturn in the tourist market could leave you struggling. Blending in with the Spanish and catering for their tastes will invariably be a more enriching experience, but it depends heavily on where you choose to establish your business. If, for example, you choose a town like Javea where around two thirds of the population are British, then you may well wish to capitalise on your 'foreignness'. Ultimately though, your business will succeed or fail on the basis of what you are rather than your nationality.

Each type of business has its own specific set of regulations and procedures for starting up. Unfortunately Spain's overly bureaucratic regime delegates overall responsibility for these procedures to the autonomous communities. As a result, the procedures involved in opening a particular type of business in Andalucia may differ enormously to opening the same business in Madrid. This chapter gives a general outline of various procedures, but for more specific regional information the *Ventanilla Unica Empresarial* (one-stop shop for business) website has a useful search engine for each region and each type of business. To access this go to www.vue.es and click on *Biblioteca de Trámites* (procedures library). Here you can enter your region followed by the type of business you wish to start and view the most recent regulations.

Be Creative

In some lines of business and in some areas of Spain, the competition for trade is so great and the number of customers so greatly reduced out of season, that businesses close within months of opening up; bar and restaurant owners can work horrendously long hours just to scrape together a living and do not have the time to enjoy the sunshine just outside their front door; and some businesses are simply killing each other off by undercutting to the point of making a loss, just to entice customers away from the competition. The expatriate community, especially along the costas will furnish you with any number of horror stories about unsuspecting foreigners who came to start a business in

Spain with the sun in their eyes and lost everything.

In order to avoid these potential pitfalls, it is necessary to be a little bit creative in your choice of business. The tourism and service sectors are the obvious business choice for most people who want to live the holiday lifestyle by the beach; to not have to learn Spanish because all of their customers will speak English; and to be able to benefit financially from the fact that tourism is still booming in Spain. All of these things may well be true, but the saturation of trades and services in resort areas is very common, and often the only people who are making money are the estate agents buying and selling businesses and the landlords taking a cut every time the leasehold on their property changes hands. There are simply too many bars, restaurants, and shops catering to the tourist market in the resort areas, and not enough customers to go around, particularly in the winter months. This is not to say that such a business is not viable, but simply that a new business will need to have a unique selling point to distinguish it from the competition, and that potential entrepreneurs should always do some comprehensive market research before rushing into anything (for further information on market research see *Procedures for Starting a New Business*).

It is important that entrepreneurs think carefully about their motives for starting a particular type of business. You should never open a rural bed and breakfast because you would like to be a guest at one, nor should you open a bar because you enjoy drinking (a shocking number of foreign-owned bars close because the landlord has been drinking the profits). If you do, the reality of the hard work involved in either venture will be a horrible blow. It is important to maintain a reasonable balance between 'living the dream' and good business sense. Many people make the mistake of going into a business which they have very little experience of, a notion which they probably would not even contemplate in their home country.

The most important consideration when deciding on the type of business you will open is whether or not it is viable. Is there a market for your product or service and will you be able to compete against similar products or services in the area? An innovative business, or a business catering to a previously untapped market in Spain will always prove to be more lucrative in the long run.

Starting a Business Vs. Buying a Business

One decision that you will have to make before deciding on the type of business that you want to establish is whether to start up from scratch or to buy an existing business. There are pros and cons to both options and these are summarised in the table below.

STARTING VS. BUYING

BUYING AN EXISTING BUSINESS

Advantages

Most businesses fail within the first two years of operation. Existing businesses have already gone through this difficult period and hopefully established a good reputation, recognised products, loyal clientele, proven management techniques, a place in the market and a clear and visible profit margin.

Existing businesses involve less paperwork. Having bought the business you simply need to transfer the licence to your name. Legal fees are therefore much lower and you should be up and running in a matter of weeks.

Disadvantages

It is very difficult to value an existing business. How do you know how much the 'intangible assets' such as client base and reputation are really worth? Many people fail to keep proper tax records and their official accounts may bear little resemblance to the reality.

Your choice of business is limited to those which are on the market. Quite often, especially in the coastal resorts, these businesses are for sale because they are struggling to survive in a saturated market.

STARTING A NEW BUSINESS

Advantages

The business will be entirely your own project – you are free to open exactly the business that you want to open, where you want to open it and you are free to run it exactly as you wish. It will not have any of the baggage that goes with buying an existing business.

All of your options are still open. There are a number of legal entities available, which allow you to minimise your personal liability.

Disadvantages

Start-ups can fail due to a host of reasons that could not possibly have been foreseen and the majority of new businesses take around a year or even more to show a profit. During the initial period, all your time energy and funds must be invested into the business. You may need to cover the business's expenses without taking a salary for yourself.

Starting a new business involves a lot of bureaucracy, paperwork and hence legal fees. Even if you decide not to incorporate a company, you could find yourself waiting six months or so for the town council to approve an opening licence.

The reality is that it is quicker and easier to buy an existing business but this has to be balanced against the fact that when buying you are limited to the businesses that are on sale, you have a greater chance of being targeted by conmen and you may buy a business that has very little chance of success because the books were pure fiction. The international legal expert John Howell argues that: *'Existing businesses come with too much baggage such as differing management styles, décor, staff policies and a possibly undesirable customer base. People find that it takes them a lot of hard work, changing things around, before they get it right. Starting a business from scratch allows you to establish the business exactly as you want it, from the outset'.* Of course, balanced against this is the fact that the legal fees relating to starting from scratch are higher and it can take much longer.

Ultimately, it will come down to a purely personal decision based on the type of business that you wish to establish. If the business you hope to start is fairly original and there is nothing like it on the market, then you will have no choice but to start from scratch.

TOURISM

Tourism is booming in Spain. In recent years Spain has overtaken France to become the most popular holiday destination for UK residents and in total 51.7 million tourists visit every year. Spanish tourism today is a solid, well-founded sector which has learnt to grow, consolidate and undertake large investments to improve quality. This boom is partly the result of a huge amount of government investment. Tourism accounts for 12% of Spain's GDP and employs 1.5 million people. It also provides the country with an annual revenue of thirty-seven billion euros, so it is hardly a surprise that the government is keen to promote its largest industry.

The *Plan Integral de Calidad del Turismo Español 2000-2006*, or the Spanish tourism integral quality plan, was established by the *Ministerio de Economia* in order to address the challenges facing Spanish tourism. It is co-ordinated by both the private sector and the public administration and is heavily supported by EU funds.

The aim of the plan is to promote business opportunities in the tourism sector in two ways. Firstly by investing in the recovery and regeneration of an already mature Spanish tourism, i.e. the traditional sun, sea and sand holidays based largely around the *costas;* and secondly by promoting alternative kinds of tourism in new destinations. It is worthwhile considering the types of venture that the Spanish government is keen to promote, as you are likely to be eligible for a number of investment incentives (see *Financing your business).* These include:

- **Sports Tourism**, consisting of new golfing, adventure, sailing and skiing ventures.
- **City and Cultural Tourism**, focusing on language courses, museums, gastronomy, heritage sites and festivals. Over 70 million euros were invested into this area of tourism between 2002 and 2004, the objective being to strengthen the cultural attractions and convert them into a tourist product.
- **Rural and Active Tourism**, focusing on guest houses in rural areas and the national parks and biosphere reserves. Rural tourism began to take off in the nineties and is growing year by year, currently at around 12%.
- **Business Tourism**. The aim is to increase the number of business meetings, conferences and conventions held in Spain. Spain is already the fifth most popular destination in the world for congresses and meetings, generating a revenue of 2,350 million euros in 2002 alone.
- **Health Tourism** is on the rise, with a seemingly unstoppable increase in demand for beauty treatment and relaxation. Such businesses generate 606 million euros a year. Spain currently boasts 130 health resorts, 22 thalassotherapy centres, 24 health and beauty complexes and 50 hotels with their own spas. Such centres are a good way to combat the seasonality of Spanish tourism.
- **Residential Tourism**. There are already three million second homes in Spain, as well as a million European, non-Spanish residents. It is estimated that in the next five years between 800,000 and 1.7 million European non-Spanish families will establish their second home in Spain, and it is hoped that this will lower the seasonality of the industry.

The sheer scale of investment in and promotion of tourism by the Spanish authorities suggests that now is a very favourable time to buy or establish a tourism related business in Spain. With millions of tourists visiting Spain each year, spending an average of 660 Euros each during their visit, there is a lot of business to go around.

Tourist Attractions

There will always be a market for keeping the growing number of visitors to Spain entertained. Tourist attractions of any kind usually require a huge amount of investment, although you may find the municipal authorities to be encouraging towards new enterprises that help to bring visitors to the area. This was certainly the experience of Philippe Guémené, a Frenchman who runs the Crocodile Park on the Costa del Sol. Seven years ago Philippe decided to import crocodiles to Spain and set up a tourist park. His new park in Torremolinos boasts over three hundred crocodiles housed in an elaborate African fortress, as well as a mini-zoo, a gift shop, a playground and a snack bar.

This park opened at Easter in 2003, but before that we had another park inland, which was quite successful. Here we expect even more visitors. Malaga province has around nine million tourists a year. Most of our visitors are British, around a third are Spanish and the rest come from all over.

If we had tried to start up initially in such a prime spot they would have laughed at us. But because we gave the town council all of the information about the previous park and the company, they thought it was a good idea. They were keen because it encourages tourism and encourages people into the area, so they gave us a fairly good deal. The land here is municipal but they have given us the lease for 50 years. In return they take a percentage of the entrance fee rather than a fixed rent.

The first park we opened was on agricultural land, so we had to have the land assessed and licenced to open a zoo. Then we had a lot of red tape to deal with because we were working with a protected species and we had to get special licences to import the animals. The animals came by plane from South Africa and it was very complicated. The authorities there wouldn't give authorisation to export until we had the authorisation here to import, but the authorities here said the opposite! It took about six months before they decided who would authorise the permit first.

First they gave us a permit on the basis of the idea, and then we had to do a technical project using an architect, of what we were going to do with the land. The architect took the project and the ideas to the municipality, and eventually they gave us the building authorisation. After that we just needed the opening licence.

We formed an S.L.(limited company) when we started. It's the best way because you are protecting yourself at the same time. We have to pay quite a high insurance premium because we have a civil responsibility. We are open to the public, so we need insurance against people falling and hurting themselves etc. People don't have direct contact with the animals, except at the end of the tour when people can hold a baby crocodile with its mouth tied up. I know that in Africa they do it with an open-mouthed crocodile. I wouldn't take the chance!

The Spanish have a very different attitude towards the animals. They are used to bull fighting and they need action. If we did a normal tour, like we could do for the English people, they would get bored and frustrated! So we have to make the crocodile move. If it looks like the crocodile is going to bite you, then they are very happy. If the crocodile actually does bite you they are ecstatic.

*A tourist attraction is quite a seasonal business. This is something that you have to take into account. **We are lucky that our rent to the council is a percentage of our takings as it means that we pay them less when times are slow.** We work with the same personnel all year round but we tell them that in the summer they have to work very hard, and then during the winter they can relax. Otherwise we would have to employ more in the summer and lay people off in the winter. The problem is trying to find the right staff with the right attitude. Altogether we have 14 staff here – guides, café, entrance etc. all of them are Spanish.*

Financing the business was difficult. We received no government incentives or grants. Nothing. Not a penny. We took out a huge loan by mortgaging the land we owned.

Banks here will only give you an umbrella when it's sunny. If it's raining they won't have any. If you have something to offer as security, then they will let you have a loan. Otherwise there's little chance.

I think it is reasonably easy to open a business here. If I wanted to start a business like this in France, I would need a special diploma for handling crocodiles and then a special licence for showing crocodiles and if I wanted people to be able to touch the animals like they do here at the end of the visit, then I would need a special permit. I have actually found the bureaucracy slightly easier.

The advice I would give to people who want to start a business here is to investigate thoroughly before starting. Find out the basics and study the market. We did our own marketing study with the customers. When you live in a country you know what will work but coming from outside you are totally in the dark and you need to put in months of preparation before you can be sure that your business will succeed.

Camping and Caravanning

The price of renting a holiday home has continued to rise in recent years and as a result there has been a distinct increase in the popularity of campsites, especially amongst the British and Germans. In 2002 and 2003 the number of guests staying in campsites increased considerably and this trend looks set to continue. Camping is a very popular holiday option in Spain and there are some 740 *campings* or *campamentos turisticos,* which receive around six million guests per year. The majority of Spanish campsites are situated on or near to the coast especially in Andalucia, Cataluña and Valencia.

In Spain campsites are divided into four categories: *lujo* (luxury), *primera categoria* (first class), *segunda categoria* (second class) and *tercera categoria* (third class). In some regions such as Andalucia there are also campings-cortijos (farmhouse campsites). Statistically most campers are attracted to the second class category of campsite but over 2.3 million campers stay in luxury and first class sites. Motorhomes and campervans are a frequent sight on the Spanish roads, and as many localities and regions in Spain have now prohibited 'wild' camping, there is certainly a market for more campsites to cater for them.

In order to qualify for third class status, a campsite must have the bare minimum of facilities, which are: at least 55 square metres of land per plot, unlimited drinking water, a reception area, a bar, bathroom facilities including toilets, washbasins and showers (second and third class campsites do not have to provide hot water), sinks and washing facilities, guaranteed medical assistance, a public phone, twenty-four hour surveillance, a free safety box for valuables, and a post collection and sending point. First class and luxury campsites provide far more space and amenities such as restaurants, supermarkets and swimming pools.

The best place to start if you are planning to set up a campsite is the Spanish Federation of Campsites (*Federación Española de Empresarios de Camping y Centros de Vacaciones:* FEEC; www.fedcamping.com). It is important to remember that in Spain campsites are highly regulated and that each region has its own specific rules. These must be followed to the letter if permission is to be granted for your venture. Full contact details for the FEEC office in your region can be found at www.fedcamping.com/asociaciones.htm.

A major consideration is the location of the land which you are proposing to use for camping. Many regions prohibit sites which are too near to roads, water supplies for the local population, monuments or historical sites or factories. Nor should they be located on riverbeds or in areas where there is a risk of flooding. This last regulation was specifically tightened up following the Biescas tragedy in 1996 when flash floods swept away a campsite on a dry river bed and killed 87 people.

The local authorities will arrange an inspection of the proposed site and will ensure that the regulations regarding the water and electricity supply, waste disposal, waste water disposal and fire precautions are strictly enforced. Once permission has been granted, the authorities must be notified of your opening dates.

Unless your campsite is in the Canary Islands, the Costa Blanca or the Costa del Sol, where there is a temperate climate all year round, your campsite will be a seasonal business. Many are only open for six months of the year – from Easter to the end of September. Even if you are able to open for a longer season, business will be much slower in the winter months. This is an important consideration, and prospective campsite owners will either need to spend the winter months back in their own country, or in some other means of employment to make ends meet during the winter. Alternatively, if you have a bit of money behind you, the winter months can be utilised to upgrade the campsite's facilities, increasing your income for the following season. One final consideration is that despite the recent influx of foreign tourists visiting Spanish campsites, the majority of campers are Spanish residents. It is therefore vitally important that you market your site not just to the foreign tourist element. Having registered with the Spanish Federation of Campsites, they will include your site on their website and also in their annual publication *Guia de Camping.* There are also a number of other guides such as the *RACE Guia Ibérica de Campings.* It is also worth registering with *TurEspaña*, the Spanish Tourist Office, who publish free brochures listing all official campsites.

Hotels and Guest Houses

A fair number of hotels, guest houses and B&Bs in Spain are run by foreigners. As with a bar or a shop, a hotel business can be bought and sold separately from the building, which is then rented. If possible, it is better to buy the building as well, in order to make sure you reap the benefits of any improvements made to the premises. Hotels and bed and breakfasts are not too expensive and with the current property boom in Spain, they are a good investment.

Visitors to Spain are often bewildered by the elaborate variety of places to stay. If you want to set up such a business, it is worthwhile getting to grips with these from the outset:

- ○ **Fondas.** Identifiable by a square blue sign with a white F, these are the least expensive of places to stay in Spain and are often positioned above bars. These are slowly disappearing as Spain upgrades its tourist facilities.
- ○ **Casas de Huéspedes/Pensiones/Hospedajes.** The distinction between these has blurred over the years. The *casas de huéspedes* or 'guest houses' literally, were traditionally for longer stays. All three are fairly cheap options for tourists.
- ○ **Hostales.** These are far more common and although slightly

more expensive, they offer good functional rooms, often with a private shower. They are categorised from one to three stars.

O **Hoteles**. Hotels are star-graded from one to five.

O **Paradores**. Usually converted from castles or monasteries, these are state-run and very expensive. These are the top end of the hotel scale.

O **Casas Rurales.** These are very similar to the French *gîtes* and are very popular in Spain. Accommodation at these varies from bed and breakfast at a farmhouse to half-board or self-catering in a restored manor.

A useful source of advice for the hostelry industry is the *Federación Española de Hosterlería* (Cº de las Huertas 18 – 1a Plta, 28223 Pozuelo de Alarcón; ☎913-529156; www.fehr.es). It is not obligatory to become a member of the FEHR, but the majority of hotel businesses do so. All hotel related businesses will need an *autorización de centros hoteleros,* which involves presenting the following documents to your local *ayuntamiento* (town hall). You should be aware however, that the exact requirements vary from region to region:

O Title deeds for the property.
O A detailed floor plan of the property, often with photographs.
O A business plan stating what sort of accommodation you are offering and the prices charged.
O A certificate stating that the building is structurally safe.
O A certificate stating that the correct fire prevention measures have been taken.
O Proof that the property has adequate waste disposal facilities.

The authorities will contact you and arrange an inspection of the property to ensure that it is suitable for guests. The whole process should only take around three months.

Rita Hillen moved to Spain to open a small hotel in Torremolinos. Hostal los Geranios has now been running for ten years.

I used to have a restaurant in Holland but I sold it. Then, when I was on holiday here, I saw the sign outside this place, and I thought I'd have a look. They told me that the owner wanted to leave, so I had a look around, went back to Holland and later came back again to look at the books. My son was 17, so I thought it was a good time for him to move out of Amsterdam. One month later I started up.

I rent the property. There is no chance of buying the freehold – he doesn't want to sell because it means paying a lot of capital gains tax. I don't mind though because I signed a good contract with him when I came and he can never change the rent. Whereas rent has gone sky high along this stretch of coast, my rental conditions stay the same. I also put in the contract that if I die, the traspaso (lease) *will go to my son, so he can basically never get rid of us. The rent is raised every year only with inflation, which is very little. I lived here for seven years, but my son lives here now. Its very helpful but quite rare to find a business with accommodation and it helps to keep the expenses down.*

This business was started fifty years ago by a Spanish lady – she only had three rooms – but that was in the time when there were no tourists here – just the Spanish. It was an advantage taking over an existing business because I already had customers who had been coming for years and years and that was very important. That is included in the traspaso (lease). *It is your responsibility to keep the clients. If they all run away, then you know that you are doing something wrong!*

I formed an S.L. (limited company) *in order to keep business finances and private finances separate. It's fairly expensive to form an S.L. but it's worth it because you never know what can happen. If you have customers and something happens like they fall down the stairs then you may be liable for damages. It was in my own name before, but I changed it because I wanted my son in the company as well, so we are the S.L. together. Insurance here is much cheaper. It is normal to pay around €300-€400 per year.*

I think that the most important thing is to find a good gestor *who speaks English. They are around and well worth it. I pay a small monthly fee to the gestor and he sorts out all of my legal and administrative problems, which is absolutely vital.*

Its also a good idea to have experience. I had a hotel in Holland – so when I came out here I knew what to do and I knew what I was looking for. The hotel in Holland had 300 rooms, so to me 14 rooms was perfect. People say to me – 'why don't you put another story on

*and make more money'? – I don't want to make it bigger because
then I would have to work harder. We live in Spain because we want
to enjoy life a little bit, have more free time – I could have stayed in
Holland and worked 7 days a week.*

*My customers here are mostly Spanish. If I were to start again I would
always choose a business aimed at the Spanish, because they live here and
they will stay here all year. Tourists only come for a few weeks of the year.*

Rural Bed and Breakfasts

Increasingly the trend for foreigners opening a small hotel or B&B
is to opt for somewhere inland in a beautiful rural setting. The traditional beach holiday will always be popular with tourists, but for
some the crowded resorts, the heavy traffic of the coastal roads and the
late-night noise of youthful revellers have lost their appeal. Radically
improved transport systems in the interior of the country have allowed
the backwaters of Spain to enter the limelight and demand for hotels
and other services in areas of natural beauty and tranquillity is increasing. To match this trend, more and more property owners are setting
up rural accommodation facilities (*alojamiento rural*). The number of
B&B and self-catering establishments increases by approximately 20
per cent each year.

Property in the country is often much cheaper than land on the
coast, with *fincas* or country farms going for as little as £20,000,
depending on their state of repair. With some work and investment,
such properties can be converted into guesthouses and B&Bs. Grants
are usually available from the local authorities for building work on
rural properties.

Although these businesses are highly seasonal, and not likely to
generate a massive income, some are able to supplement their income
by setting up as mountain-bike, hiking, fishing, or horse-riding
centres. Currently the most popular inland areas of Spain are the
provinces of Avila, Guadalajara, Granada and Madrid, as well as the
region of Asturias. An exciting location for a rural business is the River
Ebro, which runs through the north of the country. Catfish weighing
up to 100 pounds have been caught here, making it the ideal location
for fishing holidays.

Rural accommodation is highly regulated in Spain and each region has its own legislation and regulations, often with very different requirements (for regularly updated information from all of the regions visit the webpage: www.toprural.com/propietario/legislacion.cfm). Before investing in a guest house, it is a good idea to investigate the local regulations. Unfortunately, these regulations change frequently and even local town councils often give conflicting advice. For example, when Michael and Vivian Harvey decided to use part of their *cortijo* (farmhouse) as a B&B in order to generate a little extra income, they encountered a number of problems with local regulations: '*Officially, as an agrícola* (the term used to denote agricultural businesses, which have a special social security regime), *we are also able to have paying guests in up to six rooms without any extra red tape. Unfortunately, the town council don't know anything about that. At one point, the Guardia Civil even turned up and threatened to close us down because we did not have a* Licencia de apertura (opening licence) *or a* libro de reclamación (complaints book). *Eventually we had to go to the Mayoress to sort it out!'*

To qualify as rural accommodation under most local regulations, your property cannot be situated on main roads but it must have proper access and be adequately signposted. If the property is at the end of a pot-holed track then you will need to provide transport back and forth. The property must have water and electricity supplies and adequate waste disposal. Fire prevention measures are also regulated and some regions, such as Andalucia, even regulate the minimum size of the rooms. In Murcia, the number of people that you can provide accommodation for is limited.

As the owner of an *alojamiento rural*, you have certain obligations, which again vary from region to region. These include regulations regarding providing guests with a detailed map of the location, first aid kits, deposits and bills, cleaning and even breakfast. By law all accommodation establishments in Spain must keep a *libro de reclamaciones* (complaints book), which should in theory be regularly inspected by the authorities.

Further information regarding rural accommodation businesses and regional rural tourism associations can be found from the Spanish websites www.toprural.com and www.azrural.com. These are also some of the best places to advertise your business as they offer to post your details in a variety of languages with photos and prices.

Sports and Adventure Tourism

Spain's climate, its mountainous topography and 5,000 kilometres of coastline make it the ideal location for sporting holidays. On the coasts sailing, sport fishing, diving and windsurfing have been practiced for many years and in rural areas, trekking, rock-climbing, descending rivers, and air sports are all taking off. Golf can be played all year round thanks to over 200 courses, and in Spain's mountainous regions, there are numerous ski resorts. For those with an enthusiasm for sports and a little entrepreneurial spirit, there are plenty of opportunities to be found.

Scuba diving has been a real growth industry in the last twenty years and one which has been tapped by enthusiasts up and down Spain's costas. After a diving trip to the Red Sea, Peter Deth decided to open his own Diving Centre on the Costa del Sol where he identified both year-round diving opportunities and an untapped market. The Happy Diver's Club on the seafront in Marbella has been open now for eight years and is still going from strength to strength.

> Before I opened the diving business, I was an agricultural engineer so it was quite a big change. I was looking for a career change and this opportunity came up, so I thought ' why not?'
>
> The idea first came up over a beer with my own diving instructor in Egypt. Within a couple of months of coming home I had reached an agreement with a hotel here in Marbella and we went ahead.
>
> Scuba diving is booming – the industry is still developing and more and more people want to dive. At the start of the nineties there was 10% growth every year throughout the industry. Scuba diving is still very young, and it has only become popular in the last 15 years. I found a gap in the market and that was an important factor for success. Scuba diving was big on the Costa Brava and in the Canary Islands but very few people offered diving on the Costa del Sol, which is incredible because diving here is great - it offers a unique combination of the Mediterranean and the Atlantic Ocean.

I started everything from scratch. I formed an S.L. (limited company). *It was quite complicated because I did not speak much Spanish at that time and I couldn't find any professional advice back home. In the end I found a* gestor *here to help me. I let the professionals do a lot for me. It is an expense, but without it I couldn't exist. My time is too expensive. Lawyers, gestores and accountants know exactly what they have to do, whereas I would have to waste time and money finding out. It took about a year to formalise all the paperwork here.*

Most of my clients are foreigners, although in August there are a lot more Spanish. We are better known now after 8 years so we get more locals – but it took a long time. We have customers who come every year. It is very important to build up a client base. Treat the customers you have well and they will come back.

With a tourist related business you have to allow for the low season. In November for example, there are very few tourists, so for a few years we have run instructor courses. We teach people how to teach scuba diving.

The first year was horrible. We had weeks where nothing was happening, nobody knew me, I didn't really know what I was doing. I had to learn everything by experience and I didn't make any money. **When you start a business you need money to live on at least for the first year because any money you make must be reinvested.**

Inexperience costs you money. It's the same wherever you run a business. There are too many divers running dive businesses and too few businessmen running dive centres. Those who don't have much experience run into nasty surprises. I was an experienced businessman, but I was inexperienced in other areas and that cost me a lot of money.

The equipment for scuba diving is expensive, so we operated on the philosophy – start slow and let it grow. There is no need to start a massive operation. I started with very little and gradually brought in more and more equipment. It was a constant growth as the business built up.

I was a fully trained instructor when I came here and there was no problem transferring the PADI qualification because it is internationally recognised. PADI (Professional Association of Diving Instructors; www.padi.com) *is the best known dive organisation in the world and they regulate the industry. You have to be a member of a dive organisation to open this type of business.*

When I started PADI didn't exist in Spain. Now it has 150 affiliated dive centres. The competition here is good. I'm very happy that other serious centres have opened here because we cannot serve everyone – the Costa del Sol is 150 km long so there is space for ten dive centres or more. We are all busy and it helps to promote the Costa del Sol as a dive destination which is important. We all work together.

When I started, the business consisted of one dive master and me. Now I employ eight other people. It is very easy to find staff but it is harder to find qualified staff. We have to train them ourselves, to our own requirements. It takes six weeks before they can start working for us. For a long time we had a very high employee turnover and we are still in the process of finding stable staff.

In terms of promoting the business, we don't wait for the customers to find us, we go out to different hotels promoting the business, offering try-dives and that works well. We also advertise in different dive magazines. I advertise in both Germany and England. I have just got back from a diving show in Birmingham. The English market is very important on the Costa del Sol because flights here are so cheap.

These eight years have been full of lots of very rich experiences and I hope it will continue. Things have changed tremendously. Tourism has exploded in recent years which is great for business. The experience has been far better than I ever expected. I am enjoying what I am doing, and I would do it all again the same way.

Those wishing to start up a water sports business will probably have to emulate Peter Deth and start up from scratch. Established businesses do not come onto the market very often but when they do a good place to find them is the British company, Ascending Parachutes Ltd (5 Gardner Close, Hawinge, Folkestone, Kent CT18 7QJ; tel. 01303-894333; info@parasailing.uk.com; www.ascendingparachutes. co.uk), agents for the sale of water sports and parasailing businesses with licenses, in Spain and the Canary Islands. Their prices range from £25,000 to £150,000. They also sell equipment for new businesses and offer training courses in water sports (including SCUBA diving and parasailing) instruction.

EATING AND DRINKING

An enormous percentage of foreigners moving to Spain choose to make their living running a bar, restaurant, café or nightclub for tourists and expats. In the resort areas of the Costa Blanca and the Costa del Sol, it is hardly possible to take a step without encountering a British bar with Tetleys on tap or a café selling a full English for €3.50. Without a doubt, the market for such businesses in certain areas is saturated and a full study of the viability of a location must be carried out before buying.

Tread carefully. Jos Arensen – Start With Us, business consultancy, Benalmádena

People tend to misinterpret the situation out here. I have never seen a place where bars open and close so fast. The problem is that the competition is just too big to support a market which is buoyant for three months in the summer and then falls off dramatically for the rest of the year. Also, for foreigners, it is almost impossible to get the Spaniards into your bar, restaurant or café. I would say that in certain areas, 90% of new bar and restaurant businesses fail, often within months of opening up.

The businesses that survive are the ones with deep financial reserves, the will to succeed, the will to make personal sacrifices and a lot of luck.

With so many bars, cafés and restaurants in Spain, it is very unlikely that you will have to start a business from scratch and you may even find that the local authorities are unwilling to grant a new licence. However, a visit to any of the commercial estate agents (see *Acquiring a Business or Business Premises*) will yield a wide selection of these businesses for sale. Freeholds do come up for sale occasionally, but usually foreigners buy the business and then pay a monthly rent to the freeholder for the use of the premises. The price varies enormously because what you are buying is the 'goodwill', the value of which depends on factors such as the location of the bar, its established client base and the fixtures and fittings. According to Tim Stonebridge of Diamond Commercials S.L., the average amount that people pay for the goodwill of their first business is around €30,000.

One consideration for couples considering moving to Spain to start this type of business is that working together behind a bar or in a hot kitchen can put an enormous strain on a relationship and even causes marriages to fail. As Tim Stonebridge puts it, *'Couples in England are not used to spending all day working together and then suddenly they are getting under each other's feet for up to eighteen hours a day. Whether you are busy and stressed out all day, or you are worried because there aren't enough customers coming in, it's hard. You have to be nice to people and smile, even when you don't feel like it.'*

Special Licences

Every single person who works in a bar, café or restaurant, or any business where food or drink is involved needs to be in possession of the *carnet sanitario*, which is a health and hygiene certificate. In order to obtain one, it is necessary to take a fairly simple examination at the town hall, which costs approximately €50. In the coastal resort areas it is likely that you will be able to take the test in English or even other European languages, but this provision is not made in the majority of Spain.

In the past, health and hygiene laws have not been very thoroughly enforced in Spain. As with many official procedures, the authorities adopt the attitude of non-interference. Nevertheless, if they receive a complaint about your business, they will investigate and should they find your business is flouting any of the rules then you will receive little sympathy. This *laissez faire* attitude is gradually changing however, and in some areas of Spain new hygiene regulations are beginning to be enforced. For example a new system of self-regulation requires businesses to pay for a personal consultant to implement a series of regulations regarding such issues as water contamination and general cleanliness.

Bars, restaurants and cafeterias are all granted the right to sell alcohol as part of their opening licences. You will not require a separate alcohol licence.

Another consideration is music. In order to play any kind of music in a bar, be it live, recorded, or coming from a television, you need a licence from your local *ayuntamiento* (town hall). There are different types of licence in each autonomous region. As an example, the Costa del Sol has three varieties of licence. A full music licence allowing live music is quite difficult to get and requires 100 square metres of space. It is easier to obtain an *especial* licence which allows karaoke and juke boxes. Most bars opt for the normal licence available for only €10 a month, allowing the bar to have background music and television.

Finally, food and drink businesses with a terrace on a public street will also have to pay a 'terrace tax' levied by the local Town Hall. Charges vary according to the size of the terrace, but an average cost is around €600 per annum.

Restaurants

Eating out is a vitally important part of Spanish culture. Every weekend around 70% of Spaniards have lunch or dinner outside the home in one of Spain's 68,000 plus restaurants. Eating is very much a social occasion and it is common for Spaniards to entertain their friends and family at a restaurant rather than at home. Spain offers a huge variety of restaurants including *comedores,* which serve cheap but substantial lunch time meals, roadside inns known as *ventas,* that offer country cooking at bargain prices, *marisquerías,* which serve only seafood, *cafeterias* and *restaurantes*.

Despite the apparent saturation of the restaurant market, this is still a growth sector for a number of reasons. Firstly more and more Spaniards are choosing to eat out. In fact around 23% of Spaniards eat out regularly and this figure is on the increase. Work is the main reason for eating in restaurants, a trend which has significantly increased due to changing working hours. As more businesses bring their hours of trading in line with much of Europe, the traditional long meal at home with the family is disappearing and workers are opting for the convenience of eating establishments near to their place of work. Another factor is the continued strength of the tourism sector, with seasonal visitors demanding a variety of eating establishments during their stay.

The Spanish restaurant market is dominated by small independent restaurants, rather than big chains, which is good news for the entrepreneur. Of the 68,407 restaurants recently surveyed, only 483 of them belonged to chains. Spain's strong food culture and the Spanish loyalty to traditional regional cuisine have severely hampered the penetration of fast food into Spanish eating habits. Of course pizzas and burgers are popular amongst the young, but for the majority, eating is a social occasion which simply should not be rushed. As a foreigner opening a restaurant, you may also be frustrated by the locals' loyalty to traditional cuisine. However, recent surveys have suggested an increasing sophistication of Spanish consumers and opportunities for growth in alternative cuisines.

In the summer months the *costas* are of course swarming with tourists with crisp euros burning a hole in their pockets, and if you decide to open a restaurant in a resort area, it can be very lucrative, if only for the tourist season. However, it is important to remember that despite the apparent hordes of tourists, not all of them are potential customers in your restaurant. Many will be on full board packages or staying in self catering accommodation. Others are only there for a very short period and even if they venture into your restaurant once, are unlikely to return. Therefore, if you do intend to target the tourist market, it is extremely important that you also remember to get the approval of the locals. For one thing it is illegal to provide menus in foreign languages but not in Spanish. More importantly the tourist season will only last for around four months, and for the rest of the year the local residents, whether Spanish or foreign, will be your bread and butter. There is also no better advertisement for a restaurant than a regular client base. If the locals are impressed, they will come regularly and tell their friends.

The idiosyncratic method of rating Spanish restaurants bears mention here. Restaurants are issued with between one and five forks, denoting not the quality of the food it would seem, but the facilities offered within the establishment. This is a far cry from the Michelin Star system due to the fact that it is unregulated. The restaurant owner issues himself with a number of forks expressing the kind of restaurant he believes he runs, the only proviso being, the more forks you have, the more tax you pay to the local council. So, as Jos Arensen, who runs *Start With Us* a business consultancy in Benalmadena, eloquently put it, *'you can give yourself five forks, and still serve crap'*. Perhaps not an advisable long-term business strategy, but a possibility none-the-less.

If you lack the funds to invest in premises for your restaurant, or you don't want to work full time, then one possibility is to offer a 'dine out at home' service. It is fairly common in Spain for caterers to provide their customers with meals in their own homes, often complete with a chef and waiter. Reputation is everything in Spain, and offering this service would allow you to establish a reputation for good food whilst simultaneously accruing funds to buy or lease premises in your ideal location.

Bars

It is estimated that half of the registered bars in Europe are in Spain. Currently there are 145,639. With a population of around forty million, that works out at 1 bar for every 274 people. Even considering the massive significance of tourism, this seems excessive and in recent years the number has declined. If you want to make a go of it, research the area and the competition very, very carefully before buying. Though many are attracted to the idea of running a bar in the sunshine, or near to the beach, the reality often involves working incredibly long hours for very little reward.

The Spanish are a nation of drinkers, with over 80% regularly consuming alcoholic drinks. However, whilst they may drink regularly, alcohol consumption is quite low – the Spanish like to linger over conversation and a drink. Drinking is not however restricted to meal times and nights out. It is not uncommon to see Spaniards drinking beer or wine at breakfast time, or having a brandy with their morning coffee. You will therefore have to research your client base before deciding on opening hours. Some bars open all day, others open from noon until 4pm and then from 8pm until midnight, and others open only in the evenings. There are no licensing hours in Spain and bars usually close when the last customer goes home in the early hours.

As with restaurants, chains play a very limited role. Most bars are small, family-owned concerns, with 87.5% having less than two salaried workers. It is this fact which makes it very hard for foreigners to compete. Family-run bars have very few overheads as they only 'employ' members of the family, who often work very long hours. Employing staff in Spain is a costly business and the foreigner, devoid of the free labour of extended family, is therefore at a distinct disadvantage. It is for this reason that many attempt to illegally employ immigrants and travellers, without registering them with the social security office. This is a pursuit likely to end in heavy fines.

You may even have trouble finding a native workforce for bar work. According to the Spanish Federation of Hostelry (*Federación Española de Hostelería*, Camino de las Huertas 18, 1a Planta, 28223 Pozelo de Alarcó, Madrid; ☎913-529156; fax 913-529026; e-mail fehr@fehr.es; www.fehr.es) bar and restaurant work has a low social image in Spain due to poor pay, long working days and the necessity to work weekends. Some say that the lack of an available workforce is strangling the industry.

One thing to bear in mind is that it is the smaller bars which account for the bulk of the current decline. It has been suggested that smaller, more traditional bars have failed to respond to the changing demands of the consumer and as a result, do not attract clients, especially young people and women.

Location and personality make a successful bar. Tim Stonebridge, Diamond Commercials S.L., Fuengirola

Your custom really does depend on where you are. For example, if you run the only bar on an urbanisation then you are likely to have customers all year round. On the other hand if you are on the tourist strip with hundreds of other bars, then your custom is likely to be reduced in the winter months. Once you have found a bar you like, you should spend some time studying the number of people that are likely to come in.

It really is what you make of it. To work behind a bar you have to be bubbly and friendly and make people feel welcome. Often when you go into a bar, the owners are sitting out on their terrace and they ignore you. You have to have the right attitude. Make a point of saying 'hello' to people and sitting and chatting to them. Create a bit of atmosphere. You will find the winter season far easier if you have built up a good relationship with the locals.

The key to running a good bar, is simply to love what you do.

In the coastal resorts there are literally thousands of foreign-owned bars catering mainly to the tourist trade and expatriates. Many of these style themselves as English pubs with traditional names like the Red Lion. The local Spanish population very rarely venture into such places, finding them unwelcoming and pricey. On the other hand, some foreign bar owners are able to attract a mixed nationality crowd by having Spanish bar staff and offering a *menu del dia* – the cheap lunchtime set menu, usually offering several courses for less than €10.

Virtually all the catering businesses in Spain are 'free houses', which means that you can deal with as many or as few breweries as you like. Regular visitors to Spain will have sampled a range of Spanish beers such as San Miguel, Cruzcampo, Aguila, Mahou etc. However, these days it is easy to find most of the British favourites available as well, such as Guiness, Boddingtons, Tetleys, Stones, as well as draft ciders such as Olde English and Strongbow. German, American, French and Dutch beers are also available.

If you buy the freehold or leasehold of a bar, it will often come fully stocked and this will be included in the price. If not, the breweries are very amenable to new bar owners and will often throw in a few free barrels or crates. Fully stocking a bar from scratch will cost around €2,000.

Breweries will also provide free of charge beer coolers and fonts as well as umbrellas and beer mats etc. The suppliers deliver on a daily basis, sometimes until two or three o'clock in the morning, meaning that little bar space is lost to non-moving stock. Suppliers also take care of some of the more arduous duties of running a bar such as cleaning and servicing the pipes, pumps and chillers. All the bar owner has to do is change the barrel.

Graham Smith decided to buy a bar in Benalmádena on the Costa del Sol because he found the lifestyle of a retired ex-pat slightly lacking. Toni-Lee's Bar and Bistro is now a thriving business catering mainly to the huge community of British expatriates.

We came to Spain for the warm weather. I used to be a farmer in Scotland, but I retired when I was sixty-two years old. We had travelled to Benalmádena for sixteen years and we liked it and knew the people, so we moved here. But after six months I was absolutely bored to tears. My wife was working in a bar seven days a week, not because she needed the money, but just for something to do. I thought – this is ridiculous – so I said to her, 'how do you fancy your own bar?'

This place was advertised in the paper, so I rang up and came to see the owner. I liked what I saw, came back again and made him an offer – two days later he accepted it. Simple as that. I knew the guy who owned the place but we got the gestoría *to check that everything was OK. The offer was accepted, we paid 10% and when the legal work was all done we paid the rest. You'd be a foolish man to buy a bar without having your gestor check that all the bills are paid. If you took something on where the bills haven't been paid, then you would be liable for them.*

I bought a traspaso *– I tried to get the freehold, but the guy who owns this place wouldn't sell it. Freeholds are difficult to come by because the landlords don't want to sell them. They like the bars to change hands every three months because they get around 15% of the leasehold money. So if it changes hands 3 or 4 times a year he gets a nice quarterly income. The fact that so many people come over here and open up bars without knowing the first thing about running one, means that they are on to a nice little earner as the majority will fail very quickly.*

The bar has only been going a short time but it is doing reasonably well, although we're now coming to the time of year where it is definitely quieter. Running a bar or a hotel is a very seasonal business. November through to February is very quiet. Then we should start to build up and it should start to take off until the end of September. It is hard to deal with the amount of competition here. Some businesses are killing each other by continually undercutting until they're selling at prices on which they can't make a profit. I would never do that, but what I have got is a beautiful place here, good food and very clean premises – there are a lot of dirty bars here. And to be honest we're not struggling. It is difficult to get customers, but once we get them here we keep them. We talk to the residents, we get to know them and we now have a good clientele who will be here all year round.

Another thing that people do to save money is to employ bar staff and kitchen staff illegally. The fines for this are horrendous. All my people are on contract and the price isn't that much more. People who are struggling are prepared to take that risk for a minimal amount of social security. It's a cut-throat market.

I am delighted with the way it is going but I think my story is completely different from 90% of people here. Most people come over with anything between fifteen to twenty-five thousand pounds, with which you can by a poorly positioned bar, and they don't have any reserves. What they don't cater for are taxes and the slower months. There are so many things on top. The transfer of the licence is about €600. People don't take all of these things into consideration. Then you've got your stock to buy. It's not cheap to stock a bar. It's cheaper over here than in the UK, but it's still not cheap.

Our suppliers are all Spanish. They may have British people working for them, but they're Spanish owned. And I find the Spanish much easier to deal with and more honest than the British out here. The Spaniards will work twice as hard, twice as long for less money – but again its because I've got lots of friends here, who will direct me to the best people. I do think it is essential for people to learn Spanish before coming over here to start a business.

At the moment we are doing far better than I ever expected. We do a little bit of advertising, but the best advertising here in Spain is word of mouth. It does take about two or three years to establish a bar properly. Next year, we'll have people who came here this year coming back and so the business will grow that way.

INFORMATION TECHNOLOGY AND E-COMMERCE

The improvement in communications in Spain in the last ten years has made a huge difference to the I.T. industry. Whilst Spain has a reputation for being a little behind in terms of technological developments, billions have been invested in communications and Spain is now a sophisticated, well-equipped and modern country. In fact in some areas it is a world leader. For example, the small, medieval, walled city of Zamora in the north is one of the first cities in the world to offer wireless internet connection wherever you are in the city. ADSL broadband access is now fairly cheap and is widely available in urban areas.

The Information Technology industry is so vibrant in Southern Spain that, according to John Howell & Co. Solicitors & International

Lawyers, the Costa del Sol is set to become the California of Europe. Some surveys suggest that as many as thirty per cent of the British working in Spain are involved in I.T. Of course not all of these people are involved in creating a shiny new silicon valley, the majority probably work in PC sales and repairs, but for those with an interest in technology there are a range of opportunities.

The lure of living in Spain is even greater for those who have the luxury of being able to operate their business from anywhere in the world. Many people who settle in Spain do all or some of their business via websites (information regarding the setting up of websites can be found in *Marketing Your Business*). These days, with broadband internet connections, ISDN lines, mobile phones and video conferencing, it is possible to be connected to the rest of the world at all times. It really does not matter where you are based. Self-employed expatriates who do all of their business on-line are able to concentrate on their businesses without being distracted by endless meetings, lunches and paperwork.

Recent laws in Spain have established certain regulations regarding Information Services and Electronic Business. The new attempts to regulate e-commerce related activities are fairly complex and likely to change very rapidly. As they stand at the moment there are several issues that the potential e-entrepreneur should take into account.

Firstly, internet businesses should consider the protection of their rights with regard to the web page and its contents. The most common methods of protecting these rights in Spain are firstly registration of the copyright with the Register of Intellectual Property, and secondly, depositing the content, design or font code with a Notary Public. In the event of these rights being prejudiced the copyright holder can then file legal proceedings.

Secondly, any personal data obtained as a result of mercantile activity via the web must be appropriately and securely stored and notified to the Data Protection Agency.

It is possible to start and operate an internet business anywhere in the world, so if you already run an internet business in the UK, it would be fairly simple to relocate to Spain. In Spain, suppliers of services offered on web pages are not generally obliged to obtain prior authorisation and may offer their services in free competition.

The only proviso is that suppliers of services should be registered in the public registries in the locality where the domain name has been assigned. They should provide the registries with the name of the entity or person providing the service, the registered office, e-mail address, tax identity number and copies of the deeds of incorporation where applicable. According to JQ International, financial advisors (☎+33 687-830758; www.jqin.co.uk), if you wish to continue paying taxes in Britain, but spend most of your time abroad, it can be done but requires a little care. If the Spanish authorities think you should be paying more, they have the right to demand that you pay a top-up tax directly to them.

The tax issues that e-commerce raises are complex and as a result, the Spanish have not yet seen fit to adopt unilateral measures, preferring to wait until a consensus is reached either regionally or worldwide. All of the most up-to-date information on the legal framework and the tax implications of e-commerce can be found, in English, on the website of the Spanish Economic and Commercial Affairs Office in the United States (www.spainbusiness.com).

FARMING

Although not the most common of activities for foreigners to become involved in, there is a lot to be said for farming in Spain. Those tempted by a simpler agricultural life and spurred on by the sheer variety of crops that grow in Spain's warmer climes and the availability of arable land at cheap prices are beginning to make the move. Despite the massive shift to urban areas that has taken place over the last forty years, agriculture is still a mainstay of the Spanish economy and employs around seven per cent of the labour force. Spanish final agricultural production amounts to about 12% of all EU Member State production.

The image of farming in Spain is quite different from the UK or USA. The countryside and farms are still a fundamental aspect of the Spanish identity, with 35% of the population living in rural areas. There is a sense of great pride that Spain is still, for example, the world's largest producer of olive oil (50% of all olive trees grown in the EU are in Spain), and that Spain's vineyards are the largest in the world (60% larger than France's in fact). The leading agricultural products, after grapes and olives include a huge variety of fruits as well as cereals, vegetables and root cops. Those looking to grow olives will find that eighty per cent of all olive production occurs in just two provinces in Andalucia; Cordoba and Jaen. For further information on growing olives, visit the Olive Oil Agency (*Agencia para el Aceite de Oliva*) website: http://oracle2.mapa.es/pls /aaoliva/inicio. There are also opportunities to be found in forestry, with help available for the re-forestation of formerly productive agricultural land.

Farming in Spain will probably not reap vast financial rewards. Farmers have been particularly badly hit in recent years by falling prices and drought. For those with a little entrepreneurial spirit however, running a farm gives rise to a number of possible sidelines. Take for example, Michael and Vivian Harvey (see below), who as well as growing crops have turned part of their *cortijo* (farm house) into a bed and breakfast, have set up a plant nursery, and also supplement their income with landscape gardening.

Even if farming will not make you rich, at least you have the chance to buy farm land at a reasonable price. Land is very cheap by British standards and can start at as little as €2,000 a hectare, although the price varies according to the area, the type of land, the availability of water, access routes and so on. If the land comes with a *finca* or farmhouse that is habitable, then the price will increase.

There are a number of estate agents dealing specifically with rural properties and farms. Country Estate España S.L., for example, has a range of properties on its books and also offers to try and find a property to your exact requirements (UK office: Country Estate UK Ltd., Omega House, 6 Buckingham Place, Bellfield Road West, High Wycombe, Bucks HP13 5HW ☎ 01494-435309; Spain Office: Country Estate España S.L., Calle Armagura 13, 29180 Riogordo, Malaga; ☎ 952-506268; fax 952-506543; www.countryestatesspain .com). Another English-speaking organisation with a range of farms for sale is Eurofarms (www.eurofarms.com), run from France. Their Spanish department is fairly new but is growing day by day.

AVERAGE PRICE OF LAND IN SPAIN ACCORDING TO REGION

Autonomous community	Average cost of land (€/hectare)
Andalucia	13,930
Aragon	2,666
Asturias	10,367
Balearic Islands	14,790
Canary Islands	78,073
Cantabria	8,740
Castilla-La Mancha	5,420
Castilla y Leon	4,022
Cataluña	8,381
Extremadura	3,852
Galicia	14,191
La Rioja	7,461
Madrid	5,666
Murcia	12,958
Navarra	7,246
País Vasco	12,410
Valencia	20,733
Total average for Spain	**8,001**

Farming in Spain is a long-term investment and the country has a great deal to offer those wishing for a new direction. The government is in the process of developing the commercialisation, transformation and modernisation of agricultural products. Current information on developments in the agricultural sector as a whole can be found at the following websites: www.infoagro.com; www.agricultura.org; www.agroterra.com; www.agrodigital.com.

One interesting recent development is organic farming. Spain has become Europe's fourth largest organic food producer. Organic production has been so successful in Spain because the natural conditions of the land allow for a higher diversity of production, there is a favourable climate for early cultivation, numerous ecosystems and a relatively moderate use of agro-chemicals in most parts of the country. Currently 666,000 hectares of Spanish land are farmed organically, generating produce worth €173.9 million. Andalucia is the area most dedicated to organic farming with 225,600 hectares under organic cultivation, followed by Extremadura, Valencia, Navarra, Murcia, Catalonia, Aragon and the Canary Islands. Each of the autonomous communities has a regulatory body for organic crop production (*Consejo Regulador de la Agricultura Ecológica*). The address of your local organisation can be found at the website: http://www.vidasana.org/autoridades.html.

The Spanish government and the farming community are very open to people from Northern Europe seeking to move to Spain, who can bring with them agricultural skills, a sense of entrepreneurial spirit and a commitment to live in and contribute to rural communities. Spain is certainly one of the less bureaucratic states when it comes to integration into the farming system.

Overall responsibility for the agriculture sector in Spain lies with central government's Ministry for Agriculture, Fisheries and Food (*Ministerio de Agricultura, Pesca y Alimentación: MAPA*). All enquiries relating to documentation and information should be directed to *Servicio de Información Administrativa*, (see address below). That said, all of the paperwork needed to set up an agricultural business of any kind in Spain has to go through the authorities in the seventeen regions (*Comunidades Autónomas*) and the provincial and local authorities.

There are a range of grants available to farmers. Each autonomous region has its own Department of Rural Development, the first port of call for finding out what is available. Currently there is a real drive for agro-tourism and such businesses in areas of longstanding agricultural importance should be able to obtain financial aid. For young farmers a range of special grants, such as low interest loans for those undertaking a first farm installation, are available. Free assistance is also available for preparation of viability studies. The MAPA website has links to each autonomous community office which keep a database on all subsidies available on both a national and a local level. To access this, visit www.mapa.es and select *ayudas al sector*. Any enquiries regarding subsidies should be directed to *Departamento de Desarollo Rural* (see address below).

Social Security and Insurance in Agriculture. The Spanish social security system establishes a special regime for agricultural workers and farmers of any sort, *Régimen Especial Agrario*. This differs from the general programme in that there are no minimum and maximum contribution bases. Agricultural workers must pay contributions according to a set base, which depends on the type of work. The special regime has certain advantages for farmers, including the fact that they are able to employ workers on casual contracts and pay them a daily wage with lower social security contributions. Further information regarding the Special Agricultural Social Security regime can be found at the website: www.seg-social.es, or by phoning the twenty-four hour information line (☎901-502050).

A final consideration for potential farmers is insurance. Because agricultural insurance needs to cover a wide range of considerations such as climatological risks, crop production and livestock production, there is a special insurance system in place. The Combined Agricultural Insurances System established the joint participation of the State and private insurance institutions in insuring all forms of agriculture. Subscribing to the insurance is voluntary but if you do subscribe the cost is subsidised by the state.

The Spanish government annually approves the Agricultural Insurance Plan which sets out the insurable risks as well as the state contribution. The governing body of Spanish agricultural insurance is ENESA (*Entidad Estatal de Seguros Agrarios*). In order to access the latest information from ENESA, in English, visit the MAPA website (www.mapa.es) and select ENESA from the *organismos autónomos* toolbar.

FINCAS

The term *finca* is generally used in Spain to describe a large plot of land or estate in a rural location. This land often includes orchards, olive groves, outbuildings and a farmhouse. Catalonia contains a wealth of large farmhouses called *masiás*, and in Andalucia such properties are known as *cortijos*. If you intend to run a farm or vineyard, you will probably find yourself living in a finca.

For many years the Spanish had very little interest in old rural properties and were looking to move into modern properties complete with all mod cons. This led to a wealth of cheap inland properties, which were often fascinating and usually beautifully located. As a result foreigners swooped in and began to snap them up. The ideal of living in blissful tranquillity and surviving only on the freshest of Mother Nature's produce is an irresistible dream for many and books such as Chris Stewart's *Driving Over Lemons* (Sort of Books; 1999) have shown, that it is in fact achievable.

Today however, the picture is somewhat different. Spanish tastes are changing and there is renewed interest in properties with character. As wealth increases, many Spaniards are buying second homes in the country as places to escape to at weekends and in the summer. The demand for fincas has therefore increased dramatically, and the supply is beginning to dry up. The fincas in the best locations have mostly been found and renovated, and the remaining properties are often either dilapidated and overgrown, or they are situated in poor locations. Those looking for fincas would be well advised to look inland, as any near to the coast will either have already been sold or will be prohibitively expensive.

Any renovation work will require permission from the local council, planning permission and a great deal of bureaucracy, so think carefully before committing yourself to any derelict ruins.

Useful Addresses

MAPA information service: Servicio de Información Administrativa, Area de Documentación e información, Vicesecretaría General Técnica, Pº Infanta Isabel 1, 28014 Madrid; ☎ 913-475368; fax 913-475412; www.mapa.es.

MAPA Department of Rural Development: Departamento de Desarollo Rural, Paseo de la Castellana 112, 3ʳᵈ Floor, 28046 Madrid.

Asociation of Young Farmers: Asociación Agraria Jóvenes Agricultores, C/ Agustin de Bethencourt, 17 – 2º, 28003 Madrid; ☎ 915-336764; fax 915-351102; e-mail asaja@asaja.com; www.asajanet.com.

Union of Small Farmers: Unión de Pequeños Agricultores, Agustín de Betancourt 17,3º, Madrid; ☎ 915-541870; fax 915-542621; www.upa.es.

Spanish Federation of Associations of Producers and Exporters of Fruits, Vegetables, Flowers and Live Plants; La Federación de Exportadores de España, Miguel Agnel 13, 4º, 28010 Madrid; e-mail fepex@fepex.es; www.fepex.es.

Institute of Agrarian Investigation: Insituto de Investigaciones Agrarias, Ministerio de Ciencia y Tecnología, Paseo de la Castellana 160, 28071 Madrid; ☎ 902-446006; fax 914-578066; e-mail info@myct.es; www.myct.es.

Cortijo el Papudo

Michael and Vivian Harvey bought 70 acres of farmland in rural Andalucía in 1981 for about £80,000. Nowadays, with a shortage of land in the area, the property is worth about £40,000 an acre. Originally they intended to grow avocados but they have diversified to running a garden centre, landscape gardening business and Bed & Breakfast.

In 1981 farming in England was going through a bad spell and the government was telling people to diversify. So we did. We diversified out here in Spain. We had visited our cousin in Portugal who had set up a citrus farm – he had some avocado trees which were huge and falling off with fruit and I was very envious. Land in Portugal was very expensive so we began looking in Spain for a farm with lots of water. That was what we bought – there's an underground lake supplied by the river and it's very clean. That's why we bought the farm, we didn't really look in the house – it was uninhabitable.

Initially we made plans to build a house somewhere else on the land, but we had nowhere else to stay, so we started to do little bits to the farm. We knew building a house would take some time, so we put a bathroom and kitchen in, and then once we'd done all that we fell in love with it. We did everything slowly because we didn't have much money, so whenever we didn't have any gardening work to do we would work on the house.

Much of the land we rent out to farmers for sheep grazing but we still keep an orchard on an acre of land near to the house. Things grow so well here, we are able to produce a huge variety of fruit. We have mangoes, bananas, lemons, limes, grapefruits and oranges. The oranges are all sold to the village. There are three or four firms packing oranges and they pay a fixed amount for the whole lot. They come and pick them and look after them – they have to do everything and if they all rot, it's their hard luck.

It all started with a contract to grow camellias for a New Zealand firm. But it was a bit of a disaster and the company stopped paying us the rent after six months. So we started selling the camellias and I brought some other plants in from New Zealand although they got stuck in Malaga airport for a while. They wouldn't let them out because not all of them had Latin names! – One was a fig for example.

We then bought some babacoas (a type of fruit) *from the New Zealand firm and put about fifty plants in. We used to go to the markets selling babacoas and camellias and a few other plants. We went to various local markets on different days of the week. We had to have a plate full of babacoa for them to taste – because they didn't know what it was. At most of these markets you needed a licence to sell, which we didn't have. We asked for a licence, but they said there was no space, so we continued going illegally. There were gypsies who were doing the same thing and they would whistle when the police were coming, giving us warning to follow them around the corner!*

The sales in the nursery soon built up to a very big level because there was only one other nursery in the area. We were getting seeds and cuttings and introducing new plants which weren't already here. Mostly we grow plants that aren't native, plants that people can't get anywhere else.

We had no money when we arrived and the only way we could get a loan was to form a Spanish company. So we formed an S.A. (a limited company) and that's been going ever since we started. The S.A. owns everything here, and we don't – we are just shareholders, unpaid directors of the company. We are taxed in England on our personal income because we still have a farm there, but here the company puts the tax returns in. This creates a clear distinction between our personal finances and the company's finances.

We have had very little luck with grants. The town council offered us a grant to renovate the house but we never received it. Then, when we started putting in the transformers, water pipes, pumps, greenhouses etc. we were accepted for an EEC farm improvement grant. But after we had done all of the work they decided we couldn't have it after all. They said we had 66% of the workers we needed – we should have had nine but we had six. Because of this they didn't let us have the grant even though we went up to Madrid with the asesor fiscal *to argue our case. In Spain, even when something has been agreed, they often go back on it. They like to tell you what you want to hear. The subsidy encouraged me to spend more and I'm jolly glad we did, even though we never received any money.*

*The place is a paradise now, as a result of lots of hard work. But I
enjoy working hard, I couldn't come here and do nothing. I was fairly
bored in England just growing wheat and looking at it all winter.
The decision to move out here was not affected by a romantic dream
of living abroad, it was a practical business decision and it has been
very successful.*

Vineyards

If you are thinking of leaving the rat race for the quiet rural life in
Spain, you could do far worse than running a vineyard. Until the
1980s, the wines of Spain were better known for their quantity and
low price than for their quality, but in recent years Spain has shed its
cheap plonk reputation and earned international recognition. Indeed,
the harvests of 1994 and 1995 produced some of the highest quality
wines in Rioja and the Ribera del Duero and the 1994 harvest is considered the best vintage of the century.

Spain has over fifty per cent of the European Union's vineyards.
There over 5,400 square miles of vineyards producing a range of both
young and aged reds, crisp whites and rosés. La Rioja continues to be
the major wine area, with an annual production of over 400 million
bottles and Navarra is also famed for its quality wines. There are over
50 different recognised denominations and many regions are up and
coming such as the Costa del Azahar, which has the advantage of
being less remote than Rioja, but with very fertile land producing
good grapes. For a detailed analysis of Spain's different wine growing
regions, visit www.filewine.es.

In order to survive on a harvest from a vineyard, you will need about
10 to 15 acres of land. However, many people find that they need to
have an alternative income, especially in the short term. Producing
wine for pleasure on fewer acres requires less work and is more likely
to live up to the dream, but if you want to run a commercially viable
vineyard it will take a lot of time and money.

When buying a vineyard, it is very important to consider exactly
what you are getting for your money. For example, farming equipment
will not necessarily be included in the purchase price, nor will the
stock of wine, the price of which depends on its stage of production.

Many vineyards belong to co-operatives, which produce wines from grapes supplied by all of its member vineyards. Therefore another potential cost, if you wish to produce wine independently, will be compensating the co-operative for the years left on the agreement. One final consideration is when to buy. If you buy a vineyard midway through the crop cycle, you will have to compensate the owner for the work he has already done on a crop which you will eventually harvest.

Buying and running a vineyard is certainly not going to be cheap and rewards cannot be reaped quickly. A vineyard is very much a long-term investment and to be avoided if you are likely to have a cash flow problem. Many people do not understand the amount of time needed to get the production process up and running. A great deal of time and money must be spent on replanting vines, new methods and equipment, ageing the wine in barrels and reducing quantities to achieve higher quality (the higher the density of vines, and the fewer bunches of fruit per vine, the higher the quality of the wine). Of course, estates that are already selling the product in bottles and have an established client base will come at a much higher price.

Replacing old vines with new ones is a particularly slow and expensive process. It involves ripping up the old vines, preparing the ground and then replanting the following spring. It then takes a further three years to produce the first crop and another year after that to get grapes which can be used. With the cost of a new plantation at around £20,000 per hectare and no return for at least four years, this is a very long term investment indeed.

One way of lessening the burden of such a long-term investment is to combine your winery with a more immediate source of income. More and more vineyards these days are opening themselves up to wine tourism, due to its growing popularity all over Europe. Although a sideline, such a venture would have obvious benefits to the winery, as guests who sample the product may well end up being regular customers.

When you do come to actually sell your product you will find that the most viable ventures are those which bottle and sell their own wine for the retail price, rather than using a chain of distributors and middle-men. Many people choose to sell their wine in bulk to merchants to be used in blends, but this is much less profitable.

Finding a suitable vineyard in your ideal location may take quite a lot of perseverance, but there are a number of companies who can help. A company which deals solely in the sale and purchase of vineyards in Spain, as well as France, Italy and Chile is Vinea Transaction (1475 Avenue Albert Einstein, 34000 Montpelier, France; tel. +33 (0)4 67 22 55 55; e-mail info@vineatransaction.com; www.vineatransaction.com). They have a number of Spanish vineyards on their books. Another possibility for finding your ideal vineyard is the Spanish company, Country Estate Spain S.L. (Calle Armagura 13, 29180 Riogordo, Malaga; ☎952-506268; www.countryestatespain.com). Although Country Estate do not deal exclusively with wineries, they often have properties with vineyards on their books and if they do not have anything suitable, they will attempt to find a specific type of property.

ENGLISH TEACHING AND TRANSLATION

Teaching English is a well-trodden path for newcomers to Spain. Most EFL teachers come to Spain primarily to travel and experience the culture for a few years, but for those who decide to make a career of it, opportunities abound to start up your own school, or to work from home as a freelance (*autónomo*). Despite the fact that almost every back street in every Spanish town has an *Academia de Ingles*, the Spanish interest in and need for English continues unabated.

When the industry first started to take off in Spain, it was as a side effect of Spain's unprecedented economic growth and entry into European markets. The majority of learners were adults seeking employment in business and industry. These days however, the emphasis has shifted to the teaching of children and even the preschool age group. There is a national push to introduce English early and it is compulsory within state schools to study English from the age of nine. For years now the Spanish Ministry of Education, Culture and Sport (www.mec.es), in conjunction with the British Council has been recruiting experienced EFL teachers to work in primary schools. This trend has filtered through to private language providers and schools which dealt more or less exclusively with company personnel for a decade are suddenly asking their teachers to organise sing-songs and games for young children.

One of the main advantages of making a career out of English language teaching is that it requires only the ability to speak English as a first language and an EFL qualification. Most EFL teachers hold an internationally recognised qualification such as the Cambridge CELTA (www.cambridgeesol.org) or the Trinity College TESOL (www.trinitycollege.co.uk) qualification. It is possible to take either of these intensive four-week courses almost anywhere in the world at a cost of around £1000. With increasing numbers of teachers possessing these qualifications it is becoming more and more difficult for the unqualified to find work as a teacher in Spain. Having gained an EFL qualification and a few years experience teaching, you have the basis of a profitable and rewarding business.

If you are tired of working under contract (which, with less reputable organisations, can involve low pay, long hours and exploitative conditions), but lack the funds to set up your own school, an alternative is to work as a freelance teacher (*autónomo*). Private tutoring pays far better than contract teaching because there is no middle man. It can be difficult to build up enough clients at first and there is often heavy competition, but with good marketing it is possible to make a reasonable living. Most freelancers charge a minimum of €20 per hour. The only down side is that it can be difficult to earn a stable income due to the frequency with which students cancel. This problem is particularly apparent in May when school pupils concentrate on preparing for exams and other activities fall by the wayside.

There are many advantages to opening your own English language school. It will take a bit of work to find the right area as in the larger towns the market is fairly saturated. Most town halls will be able to provide you with information regarding the demographics of an area. Once you have set up, the overheads are fairly low – there is no stock to buy. All you really need is somewhere to teach, teachers, books and stationery. The only disadvantage is that you are limited to certain hours of business. Many of the private English schools run courses in line with the official school term, meaning that students can only come after school. It also means that the summer months may be very quiet. Nonetheless, this can be countered by running adult classes and perhaps branching out into related activities such as running TEFL courses.

Opening your own school is a far easier option than opening many businesses. There is little bureaucracy involved. Once you have found a suitable location, the only red tape you need concern yourself with is an opening licence. The *licencia de apertura* is a necessary requirement for any business premises and is basically authorisation from the local council that the premises meet certain health and hygiene standards and are appropriate for the type of business. Further information on this can be found in *Procedures for Starting a New Business.* You must also have a *libro de reclamación* (complaints book), as with many small businesses and a notice announcing that you have one.

Most private schools are not regulated by any education authority, so there will be no inspections as to the content of your courses. The only stipulation for such schools is that any certificates which are issued must state '*enseñanza non-regulada*' (unregulated schooling).

A final consideration for such a business is the insurance. With any business where clients visit the premises, you need cover for public liability. The premiums for this will almost certainly be higher when there are children involved and insurance companies often require that they are fully informed of the number of students that may be on your premises. Be sure to furnish your insurance company with a name and date of birth each time you enrol a new student.

In July 2001, Alison Benwell opened *The Village School* with her brother in the traditional village of Salteras, Andalucia. The school has been such a success that they have recently opened a second school in the adjacent village of Olivares.

My brother, Rob, had been teaching English in Seville for some time and I decided to come out to Seville to do my TEFL qualification because it was a bit cheaper in Spain. I loved Seville, so I found work in one of the English schools but after a while I found it quite frustrating that I wasn't able to teach how I wanted to teach and to do exactly what I wanted to do. I think a lot of teachers working for someone else think they could just as easily work for themselves if they only had the facilities. Rob and I both love teaching, we didn't want to become business people but we did want the freedom to be able to do our own thing. I felt that the time was right to open our own school, although we discussed the idea for about a year before opening the school in Salteras.

Setting up the school was not very difficult, although it was a bit nerve-wracking.

One of the biggest problems was finding a suitable property. A lot of the premises we looked at had huge difficulties. Many were on the first floor of buildings and needed lifts putting in. Often the buildings were simply shells without floors or ceilings and the expense was going to be enormous. We nearly dropped the idea, but then in June 2001 we found that the bread shop had closed down and had a for sale notice on it. The property was perfect for our needs and it took just two weeks from finding the property to opening the school. The only work that needed to be done was to divide the one large room up into two classrooms and a reception area.

For legal and financial help we used local people and they have been really helpful. The local bank manager was great and helped provide us with a secured loan to fund the business. In terms of our legal status, Rob operates as self-employed (autónomo) *and he employs me and our other staff. We are quite small so it didn't really make sense for us to form a company just yet.*

I came up with the name – The Village School – while sitting in a bar. We had a list of names like 'institute' and 'centre' but they all sounded wrong. We wanted something that everybody would understand. We have tried to cultivate a certain sort of atmosphere, a small village culture which fits in with the name. Certainly the locals have been very supportive of the idea and it was really important that we are brother and sister and operate as a family business.

We had done little market research, but we knew that parents would be keen to help their children to feel confident in English from an early age. Our youngest pupil is three years old! Attracting people was quite difficult at first, after all there are only four thousand people in the village and learning English is not a cheap activity. But we offer a complete package, we have small class sizes, we speak in English to the children all the time – from the moment they enrol and even when we see them in the street. The fact that we are actually English has encouraged a lot of parents to send their children to us. We also do a little bit of advertising with posters and flyers.

One of the most important decisions we made was to have a secretary who is Spanish. She is our link with the community. The children need someone who can deal with their problems and we need someone who can deal with the parents. That way, when the students are here, we are able to concentrate on being teachers, which is what we love doing.

The business is going really well, and this time last year we decided to branch out and open a second school in the neighbouring village of Olivares. The only real difficulty we have is the seasonality of the business. The summer months are difficult because we still have to pay rent on the premises. In August we shut down completely, just like the rest of Andalucia but in July we have started to run a course for kids who have failed their school exams and also a few workshops.

What makes it so enjoyable to run the school is the support of the community and also the enthusiasm of the children to learn. They have really made the place their own and they often call in to visit outside of class hours. My advice to anybody thinking of starting a similar business is – just go for it!

If languages are your forte, you need not restrict yourself to teaching English. Many language centres also offer courses in EFL teaching and if your Spanish is very proficient and you are based in an area with a high number of expatriates, you may be able to turn your hand to teaching Spanish. There are of course many native teachers, but expats often find it easier to learn from those who can empathise with their difficulties.

Translation

Another possibility is translation. Most translators have been English teachers at some time or another. This is one type of work that can be done anywhere. The translation business has developed from the old days of the typewriter and fax machine into a virtual market place that never sleeps.

Unfortunately, the translation market place is very competitive and unless you can understand everything that you read in Spanish – making allowances for the odd obscure term or phrase – it is not worth kidding yourself that you can make a living as a translator. Unless you are completely bilingual, you will usually need a degree in Spanish and a masters degree in translation. Most translators choose to specialise in one area, such as law, finance, engineering, medicine, pharmaceuticals, patents etc. Qualifications in one of these areas in addition to very good Spanish should suffice.

If you think that your language skills are really up to it, then the first step is to register yourself with the websites where translation work is put up for bidding, such as www.proz.com and www.translatorscafe.com. If this proves to be unsuccessful then you can try bombarding agencies and potential customers with your CV. Many find that it is a bit of a catch 22; you need experience to get work, but it is very difficult to find work without experience.

As a self-employed translator, it is a legal requirement that your register with the local social security office as an *autónomo*.

PROPERTY RELATED BUSINESSES

Foreign demand for housing in Spain has been increasing continuously over the last few years, and in the first quarter of 2003 it really took off. Accumulated foreign investment in the Spanish property market has seen outstanding growth, rising 107% in the last four years. There are three million second homes in Spain with 1,200,000 belonging to foreigners. In the next five years, between 800,000 and 1,700,000 European families are expected to buy a second home in Spain. These families will come mostly from the UK and Germany, but also from Scandinavian countries.

Many foreign investors from mature domestic markets are coming to Spain to obtain expected returns, particularly in the 'buy to let' sector. With the UK pensions industry in crisis there is a growing trend for people to turn to property abroad as an investment for the future. This has of course led to an expansion of the real estate and construction sectors, as well as individuals investing in property and sidelines such as property management companies.

For those interested in a property related business, the two most promising alternatives are: emerging areas with prices that are still comparatively low such as Murcia and Almería, or mature but internationally renowned areas such as the Costa del Sol, Costa Brava, Costa Blanca or Costa de la Luz.

According to John Howell and Co., International Lawyers, around fifty per cent of new businesses being set up by foreigners relate to the holiday home and property trade.

Estate Agents

The law regarding estate agents (*inmobiliarias*) has been completely overhauled in recent years. Previously the profession was well regulated and only those who were qualified APIs (*Agente de la Propiedad Inmobiliaria*) could sell real estate. These agents belonged to the association of real estate agents in Spain and were made up of university graduates and those with specific training. In the early nineties however, a new breed of less qualified agents appeared in Spain, known as GIPEs (*Gestoría Inmobiliaria Propiedad España*). After long standing disagreements and legal battles between the two groups, the restrictive laws were removed altogether. The proliferation of estate agents all along the coast bears testament to the ease of setting up as an estate agent. Literally anyone can become an estate agent in Spain without training or qualifications and as a result there are a number of agencies with dubious reputations. Whether or not the law will change in the future is still a matter of some debate.

The number of estate agents especially along the costas is extraordinary. Many are part of a chain but the majority are one-office businesses. It is fairly usual for these smaller outfits to work together in a network, sharing contacts and splitting the commission.

Usually estate agents' commissions are between 5% and 15%. They are often on a graduated scale depending on the value of the property, so cheaper properties demand a higher commission percentage. Rates also vary from region to region, with higher rates being charged in the more popular resort areas, although the commission recommended by the API is, in most regions, 3%.

Running an estate agency involves large sums of money and many carry professional indemnity insurance, which is certainly a good idea. For information on insurance for estate agents, contact the *Consejo General de los Colegios Oficiales de Agentes de la Propiedad Inmobiliaria de España* (Gran Via 66, 2a planta, 28013 Madrid; ☎ 915-470741; fax 915-593255; cgcoap@consejocoapis.org; www.consejocoapis.org). It is also worth having a bonded client bank account that any monies can be put into until the sale of a property has gone through.

With the current foreign interest in starting up businesses in Spain, there is certainly money to be made as a commercial estate agent. As Jos Arensen of Start with Us points out: *'For every bar and restaurant on the Costa del Sol, you will find a broker. It's big business. In fact, the biggest business here is selling and re-selling restaurants, not the restaurants themselves'.* This is exactly what Tim Stonebridge and his wife Leslea decided to do. They set up *Diamond Commercials S.L.* in Fuengirola, selling a range of businesses, mainly to British clients.

We have been running the business for nearly four years now. It takes a while to get established here and get your name known, but once the word has got around, there is a huge demand. Buying a business out here is very popular, especially with the British.

It all started when we came to Spain on holiday. We were both fed up of working in the UK, so we decided to make the move and we put our house on the market.

We set up the company from scratch. We formed an S.L. (limited company), which was fairly straightforward and only took us about a month, and then we started looking for premises. Our licence was dealt with by a local gestor who speaks very good English and we built up a good relationship with him. He is now vital to the business. I take all of my contracts to him and he checks them out for me. I will not take a bar on unless he has given it the go ahead. He also does our accounts and we recommend him to our clients for licence transfers, NIEs and residence permits.

In the beginning, we had to work fairly hard going round to all the local businesses and getting them on the books and advertising, but at the moment we are sending out over a hundred brochures a week to people in England. Most of this business comes from the website, which has a very good response rate. We also advertise in Dalton's Weekly *and* The Publican.

We now have a large selection of businesses on the books, although most people want a bar, and they want it for about €30,000. There is a trend for people to run a bar for one or two years and then go back to the job they did in England, often starting their own company. Lots of people see a bar as a first investment. There are quite a few bar owners who are now estate agents!

Our commission on a sale is 5%, although we are quite flexible. We are very happy with the way things are going and being in this business has made us a lot of friends in a lot of bars in the area!

Property Management Companies

Given the sheer number of foreign owned holiday homes in Spain, there is a huge market for letting agents and companies who manage the properties of absentee landlords. Many non-resident property owners rent out their holiday properties for the months of the year when they are back in their own countries and need someone to take care of the property, organise bookings and collect the rent. Even some resident property owners who have other business interests, or little time to manage their properties will turn to such companies. As long as the demand for second homes keeps rising in Spain, there will be a demand for property management companies.

There are huge numbers of these along the Spanish *costas* and many estate agents also offer management services. These companies deal with the nitty gritty of letting. For example, they pay all routine bills such as electricity, water, community charges, insurance, local rates etc. from their own funds and then bill the landlord at the end of the month. They also monitor the landlord's local bank account and send statements out every month. Other services offered include looking after the general maintenance of the property, for example routine and emergency painting and plumbing etc., pool cleaning, gardening, security, all year round supervision of the property, spring cleaning, laundry service, providing maid service during holiday-let tenancies, welcoming holiday-let tenants and being on hand to offer tenants advice or in case of emergencies. They also find and vet tenants and many offer a marketing service for the property.

Property management companies usually charge an agent's commission of 15-20% of gross rental as well as a monthly charge, regardless of whether the property is occupied. Further charges are made for extra services such as laundry and cleaning. It is therefore possible to create quite a lucrative business out of this very simple idea.

One advantage of this kind of business is that no particular skills and qualifications are needed other than good business sense. You will need a lot of energy and a good contact book of reliable plumbers, electricians, carpenters and so on. It is by no means an easy option. Hazards of the trade include being woken up in the middle of the night by guests who have lost their way or had a power cut, having to deal with difficult guests and working very long hours in high season.

One of the biggest problems faced by people starting this kind of business is the high level of competition for clients. Although more and more foreigners are buying property in Spain with a view to letting it, in some parts of Spain there is already a surfeit of agencies, and outside of high season, there simply is not enough business to go around. It is therefore imperative that new businesses research their location thoroughly, use a good marketing strategy and offer a unique or superior service.

The most crucial factor in this business is gaining a reputation as a trustworthy and reputable company. People are not going to hand over the keys to their property and the management of their rental income unless they have a lot of faith in your abilities. It is necessary to build up close client relationships and to keep them informed every step of the way. The majority of work will probably come via word of mouth once the business and your reputation are established so building a trusting client base will be your bread and butter.

Gardening and Maintenance Services

There is an enormous demand for landscape gardening services. With a horde of foreigners buying new and resale houses that shows no sign of diminishing, there will always be a demand for decorative gardens. But it is not just the expats who create a flourishing market for this kind of service. Ten or twenty years ago, the Spanish would have balked at the idea of having a garden with no purpose other than to look pretty. Gardens were there to provide food. These days however, with increasing numbers of Spanish either moving back to their rural roots, or perhaps buying a second home in the country, the Spanish are discovering the aesthetic virtues of the productivity of their native soil.

Michael Harvey, who runs the farm (*cortijo el papudo* – mentioned above) also runs a landscape gardening business as a sideline.

> *We started doing the landscape gardening because we saw a gap in the market. I always said that this would be the California of Europe and it's turning out to be so. Obviously, when we did our garden, we saw how amazingly things grow here and if people are interested in gardens, it's much better gardening here than in England. Things grow quicker, there's a great deal of variety. We are able to grow all sorts of exotic plants in the nursery which can be used to create beautiful gardens. I think gardens should have lots of colour and be full of surprises.*
>
> *Most of our customers are people who have just bought brand new houses. Either that or they have bought a resale property with just a bit of grass and a few trees and they want their gardens prettying up. There is so much demand that word of mouth is the only advertising tool I need. I don't really want any more gardening jobs as I already have more than I can handle.*

Private Rentals

There is a genuine boom in buying property to let at the moment. Analysts are agreed that property prices in Spain are on the increase. Indeed a recent report suggested that property prices on the Costa Blanca are set to double in the next five years. This is hardly surprising considering the steady stream of Britons and other northern and eastern Europeans entering the Spanish property market and increasing demand. As a result, buying property can be a very shrewd investment in the long run, and in the mean time a steady additional income can be made from renting your property out. It is perfectly legal for owners of private villas, houses or flats to rent out their property and many people find that letting their property is a good way of accruing income on an investment or paying off the cost of a second home especially in the light of the current climate of low interest rates and high rentals.

As with any business operation however, it is important to be aware of the potential pitfalls. Landlords should be very careful about the terms of contracts and the quality of tenants. In the majority of cases, people have very few problems when letting property, but problems can arise with difficult tenants and unreliable letting agents, so it is always best to act cautiously.

Holiday Letting. Most holiday homes are occupied for less than three months of the year so it can be a very wise move to turn an otherwise dormant property into an asset, hopefully generating hundreds of pounds a month. Whilst it may be a wrench to consider allowing unknown quantities into your beautiful home, the potential income is quite high and some owners manage to make a decent living solely from letting their holiday homes. Villas in a good location, with their own pools will often command rents over £1000 per week at the height of the summer season.

As always in the property game, the importance of location cannot be underestimated, especially when it comes to holiday letting. It is worth bearing in mind that in northern Spain the holiday rental period is really only July and August, whereas further south the season extends into spring, autumn and sometimes winter due to the warmer weather. If you are looking to maximise your rental income, an interesting option might be the Canary Islands where the year-round temperate climate allows for a 52-week letting year.

Easy access to the beach, shops and nightlife are all prime concerns for holiday-makers, as is a private or communal swimming pool. The property must also be within easy reach of an airport with regular charter flights as most visitors will not wish to endure a long and complicated drive along unfamiliar roads at the end of their journey. Golf complexes are very much in demand and tend to attract people with the ability to pay higher rates. However, these properties are usually much more expensive to buy.

If your property is in a major tourist hotspot, such as the Costa Blanca or the Costa del Sol, then demand will be much higher. Conversely, inland retreats and lesser known resorts do not have the same commercial appeal. The more discerning visitor may well be attracted to a mountain hideaway far from the madding crowd, but the more lucrative investments are on or near to the coast. Property management companies can be a good source of information when deciding where to buy. They will be able to tell you the areas of Spain where there is the most need for holiday properties, as well as property for long-term rental.

There are of course downfalls to renting your Spanish home out as a holiday home. Short-term lets require a great deal of management time spent on them as tenants may be arriving weekly, especially during high season. If you are resident in Spain and live near the property then you can be on hand to clean, welcome visitors, hand over keys, provide local information and so on. However, if you have other business interests, or are away from the property then you will have to consider a property management company (see above). If you do decide to use a property management company, it is worth shopping around, as although they mostly charge a similar commission at around 15% of the gross rental, the monthly charge can vary considerably and there are often a number of hidden charges. Visit a number of agencies in the area and ask for a complete breakdown of their services and charges, and find out what penalties there are if you decide to terminate the contract. It is also worth asking around for recommendations and checking the references of prospective agencies.

You will, unfortunately, find yourself having to make a few compromises in order to accommodate guests. It is therefore important to make firm decisions at an early stage as to which dates you yourself will want to be there and whether for example, you will allow children and pets into your home.

Perhaps one of the biggest compromises will be in the furnishing and equipping of your home. Short term rentals often mean a great deal of wear and tear as holiday tenants, as a rule, take less care of the property. It must be equipped practically because things will undoubtedly get broken and you should therefore use robust furniture and low maintenance surfaces, and keep any valuables or breakables locked away.

Long term rentals. Many people invest in property purely as a source of income, or perhaps as part of a long-term plan to make the property pay for itself before moving in themselves. Long term rentals are only a good idea if you are not looking to make personal use of the property for at least several years.

Long-term letting is a different ball game to holiday letting. Whilst holiday letting offers a lucrative, high-turnover of tenants, tenancies lasting from a couple of months to a few years offer a reduced weekly return but a steadier source of income. It also requires commitment to a longer period of investment, suiting owners who are not in a hurry to release the capital.

If you are buying property for the sole purpose of letting it out then it is very important to seek professional and independent advice on its marketability. You will need information on everything from future development in the area to crime levels. There are a number of factors which will affect letting potential. People who are looking for somewhere to live longer term are often more flexible than those who are looking for the perfect two-week break, and quite often properties that do not meet the criteria for holiday accommodation make good longer-term rentals. One possibility, though expensive, is to buy in one of the larger cities, especially Barcelona or Madrid where the demand for property is high and regular tenants are guaranteed.

An advantage of long-term letting is the lower degree of maintenance required. Tenants are expected to pay the rent on time, to maintain the property in a good state of repair and to pay their own utility bills and cleaning costs. As a landlord, you have the right to inspect the property at any time providing you give your tenant plenty of notice. It is recommended that you inspect your property every few months in order to check the general state of repair. It is the landlord's obligation to carry out repair work and general maintenance to the property.

The disadvantage of renting out your property on a long-term basis is that it can be difficult to get rid of an unwanted tenant. Long term contracts in Spain last for five years, no matter what the contract actually says. Therefore even if you have agreed a one or two year period with a tenant, he is well within his rights to renew the tenancy annually for up to five years. The rent can only be revised upward by an inflation factor each year during the term of each contract. It is perfectly legal to demand an advance deposit of one month's rent against damage, a *fianza*, which will be held by the housing department of the regional government.

A landlord can only evict his tenant, which may take many months, for failure to pay rent, damage done to the property, the use of the property for immoral purposes, subletting without permission and for causing a serious nuisance. It is therefore recommended that tenants are carefully vetted before entering into a contract with them.

Rental Contracts. There are two types of rental contract in Spain. The *alquiler de temporada* (short term) and the *alquiler de vivienda* (long term). The short term contract covers any period under a year and the long term contract covers tenancies of five years. Bizarrely, pre-printed contracts can be bought from tobacconists and kiosks but before signing any contract as a landlord, it should be checked over by a lawyer. If you decide to use a property management company, you should also take a copy of their contract to a lawyer to have it checked for legality before signing anything.

Any long term rental contract should state who is responsible for the payment of rates, the property tax and community charges. The normal practice is that the landlord pays the rates and the tenant pays the community charges.

Masia Rentals

Peter and Ginette Lytton Cobbold have lived in Spain for three years. They own a seventeenth century Catalonian *masia* (a country farm house) near to Barcelona, once used for winemaking. The size of the property allows them to live comfortably in one part of the house whilst renting out the rest to holidaymakers.

We came to Spain because we used to live in Madrid years ago and absolutely loved it. The house is amazing; it was built in the seventeenth century and has been added to over the years as it became a larger wine producer. All of the vineyards down the valley were once a part of the estate and there are still wine vats where the grapes were fermented and two old wine presses. We rent half of the masia as a five-bedroom holiday house with access to the swimming pool, which we share. The guests are totally self-sufficient, they have their own entrance, kitchen and garden and their own path to the swimming pool. Generally we expect the house to be full all summer and empty all winter. That is what happens in this kind of business. We have found the website (www.masiarentals.com) to be a very useful resource that has generated a lot of interest.

It is a lot of work to maintain the house and I have had to learn how to be a builder, plumber, electrician and gardener in the last three years, though we do employ someone to do all the cleaning for a few hours a day.

Seeking good professional advice is a must. We have used lawyers, accountants, architects, builders and so on, and have been impressed by all of them. Unless you have a lot of money to throw at getting the best people (note that what you pay for is what you get does not necessarily apply) you need to spend time getting to know people. In Spain you get a much better service if you build up a relationship with the people you are going to employ, so learning the language is a must (although we have found Catalan to be far more important in this region than we were expecting!). One of the beautiful things about living in Spain is that money doesn't have the same pull. It is still important how you treat people.

We haven't had many problems setting up, although getting permission to build the swimming pool was very difficult. There was a block on any building permission at the time due to a local urbanisation project. We went to the ayuntamiento (town council) *and told them exactly what we wanted to do, but they refused. We kept going back to try to persuade them and in the end one of the people we saw told us to stop making so much noise, close our gates and get on with it. So we built the swimming pool. Once we had finished we received a letter from the* ayuntamiento *saying that we should stop building the pool immediately or they would confiscate our building materials. As it was already built, we went to a local gestor for advice who told us to apply for permission locally and pay the fee for a licence application. The council refused this stating that the pool was in a state of illegality. However our gestor told us that this was a positive reply as being in a state of illegality was not the same as saying it was illegal, so the chances are we will not be asked to fill it in!*

SHOPS AND SERVICES

Shops

One of the more obvious routes towards business success is to set up a shop to sell goods imported from the UK (or another English speaking country) to homesick Britons who miss their marmite and digestive biscuits.

There is also a market among the local population for everyday British items which appear quite exotic to the Spanish so there is no need to limit yourself to the expat market, although as Pilar Solana of the *Ventanilla Unica Empresarial* (one-stop shop for business) in Madrid points out: *'the Spanish have very different tastes to the British and it would be foolish to assume that just because something is popular in the UK that it will sell here. A good deal of market research should be carried out before introducing a new product. The Spanish are very price conscious, but they also appreciate quality'.*

Spain's growing economy is in part fuelled by a continued increase in household consumption, helped by low interest rates, a steady decrease in unemployment and rising wages. The retail sector is therefore a particularly buoyant part of the Spanish economy and offers a wealth of business opportunities.

Despite the influx of chains and supermarkets, Spain still has one of the highest percentage of independent retailers in Europe, especially when it comes to food. This is because of the emphasis on fresh rather than frozen produce in Spain. Many housewives still shop daily in Spain, not usually out of necessity, but rather for enjoyment and the chance to socialise. Small local grocery shops and specialised outlets such as butchers, bakeries and fishmongers have therefore not yet been completely superseded by supermarkets.

The non-food sector has continued to grow in certain areas. For example the clothing and footwear sector has received a boost in recent years, due to increased disposable incomes for women. However, it must be noted that the Spanish consumer still has some way to go in reaching the high frequency purchase levels of clothing items as other European consumers.

The majority of people starting retail businesses tend to take over an existing shop because it is so easy. It is possible on the coast to buy fully-stocked, fully-licensed supermarkets for as little as €50,000 with a monthly rent on the premises. Such a purchase would include all of the contracts with suppliers and all you would have to do is transfer the licence into your name.

Services

The pages of the English language media in Spain are filled with advertisements for every imaginable expatriate service in English, including **car and van hire, builders, carpenters, electricians, piano tuning, international removals, sign-writers, insurance, antiques, world-wide shipping, central heating specialists, lawyers, car sales and mechanics, kennels and catteries, hairdressers, and plumbers** to name but a few. If you have experience providing a service elsewhere, there is no reason why it should not translate to the expatriate market in Spain, many of whom are uneasy about employing the services of the Spanish due to the language barrier. Once you have established a reputation and begun to grapple with the language then you should also be able to offer such services to the local population.

Many couples routinely offer a number of services at the same time, including house sitting. Some of this work is done by people who are not registered with the authorities. Spain has a huge illegal labour market and this is the kind of work which is easy to hide from the authorities. Illegal workers are not covered by social security and do not make any payments into the system. Nor do they declare the work on their annual income tax returns. In Spain, the law states very clearly that all workers must be covered by social security. As a self-employed worker, this involves paying social security contributions under a special scheme as a *trabajador autónomo*. Further information regarding this can be found in chapter 8, *Tax, Social Security and Other Matters*.

Liz Arthur, a registered **midwife**, moved to Spain to offer a much needed service to both the expatriates and the Spanish on the Costa del Sol.

When we decided to move out here, I had never even been to Spain before, so we came out to research the market and to find out if there was going to be any work for me. I very quickly decided that I didn't want to work within the Spanish State System because childbirth is not seen as a natural event but a medical procedure. In some hospitals they are still practising in a way that we did in England back in the 60s and 70s. It just wasn't for me. So I decided to practise privately. I had to look at the number of English people out here and try to estimate if there was a market for what I do. Then I called all the local GPs and went to the clinics asking about their maternity services. Post-natal services are something which we are very used to back in the UK but which do not exist here, so I decided to give it a go. I do feel that there is a huge need for qualified people in childcare.

I am trained as a midwife in England, but I am now registered to work both in Spain and the UK. I have worked in the NHS for a long time so I know the ins and outs of it. In England they are heavily promoting choice in childbirth, but in Spain the options are very limited. There is no homebirth in this region and although things are changing, they're not changing fast enough. There are a lot of expat women here and hence a demand for greater choice. Some Spanish regard me as a little strange as I offer homebirth, which they consider to be quite radical.

The majority of my clients are English, but I've had a couple of Spanish clients for homebirths and it has made me realise that they do want something different – they do want some choice – so the sooner I can give it to them the better. My Spanish is coming along and I plan to employ bilingual staff in the future, so I hope to attract even more Spanish women.

Those patients that don't want a homebirth come to a private hospital in Malaga for the delivery. I approached them with an offer to bring patients in and they were very friendly.

Being self employed is good because you are your own boss – but you are always on call. It is difficult because people don't have babies at regular times. There are periods when I hardly have any work and then it all becomes frantic again. As an autónomo *(self employed), I didn't have to form a company. You can if you want, but for me it is much easier just to have everything in my own name.*

Setting up a business out here is hard work. You have to do a lot of independent research to check there's a market for it, how much you're going to charge, all those kinds of things. But even with all the hard work, it has been very challenging and very interesting. I don't have much spare time but it really has been worth it.

Procedures for Starting a New Business

CHAPTER SUMMARY

- **The Spanish government** actively encourages inward investment and there are several good sources of information and advice available to the potential entrepreneur.
- The prospective businessman will at some point during the setting up, buying or running of an enterprise need to consult a lawyer or *gestor* for specialist legal advice.
    - There are huge numbers of English speaking lawyers in Spain.
- **Spanish Chambers of Commerce**: offer a variety of information-based services to the entrepreneur, such as the Business Creation Service, the Institute of Business Creation and Development and the *Ventanilla Unica Empresarial*, the so-called 'one stop shop for businesses'.
    - The VUE is an innovative service offering all of the facilities for business creation in a single location.
- Good market research is necessary for the entrepreneur to ascertain who are the potential consumers for his product or service and is the best way to avoid failure and disappointment. Producing a business plan is not obligatory but it will force you to examine the viability of the business proposal.
- EU nationals and permanent residents of Spain can be self-employed in a profession or trade. The General System for Mutual Recognition of Professional Qualifications enables fully qualified professionals from one EU country to join the equivalent profession in Spain without having to re-qualify.
    - British crafts and trades people who wish to work in Spain can apply to have their experience documented under the UK Certificate of Experience scheme.
- All self-employed people must register for income tax, social security and VAT.
- It is perfectly acceptable to register a business at your own residence or at rented accommodation as long as

the landlord agrees. Operating a point of sale business from your home would require permission from the local council and an opening licence.

O Incorporating a new business will require a lot of time and patience but the process will be rendered more palatable by seeking the advice of an experienced professional.

   O The deed of incorporation must be signed before a notary public.

   O The new company must be registered at the central companies' registry within thirty days of incorporation.

O Before a new company can begin operations, there are a number of legal and fiscal obligations which must be fulfilled, such as obtaining licences, registering for taxes and legalising the company books.

TALKING TO THE RIGHT PEOPLE

Sources of information

The bureaucracy associated with starting a business in Spain can be both onerous and tedious. With a complex array of documents and procedures, and a dreary wait of around four months, it is no surprise that in previous years only 10-15% of those who started the procedure managed to successfully incorporate their company. It is also not surprising that so many businesses choose to operate outside the law. However, the consequences of doing so can be extremely costly and the difficulties involved in establishing a business presence in Spain can be minimised simply by taking professional advice and talking to the right people.

The Spanish government actively encourages inward investment.

There are several good governmental sources of information available to the potential entrepreneur, who will be happy to deal with initial enquiries and provide general orientation, for example the General Directorate for Trade and Investment at the Spanish Ministry of Economy (*Ministerio de Economia*, Dirección General de Comercio e Inversiones, Paseo de la Castellana 162, Planta 7, 28071 Madrid; ☎ 913-493983; fax 913-493562; e-mail buzon.offici al@sgiex.dgcominver.sscc. mcx.es).

From the UK, the Commercial Office of the Spanish Embassy is a good source of advice and information (Invest in Spain, Office for Economic and Commercial Affairs, Spanish Embassy, 66 Chiltern Street, London, W1U 4LS; ☎020-7467 2387; fax 020-7224 6409; e-mail buzon.official@londres.ofcome s.mcx.es). Finally, those intending to set up a slightly larger company will find the official publication *'A Guide to Business in Spain'* very useful. This book is published by the Spanish Insititute for Foreign Trade (ICEX) and is available for €27.05 (including postage) from ICEX (Instituto Español de Comercio Exterior, Departamento de Asesoría Jurídica y Administración, Paseo de la Castellana 14-16, 28046 Madrid; ☎913-496100; fax 913-496120; e-mail icex@icex.es). Alternatively the guide is available to view on-line at www.investinspain.org.

The Spanish Embassy Office for Economic and Commercial Affairs in the USA also has a helpful website for potential investors in Spain; www.spainbusiness.com. The website is packed with information such as market information, trade statistics, information on Spanish companies and it also lists trade fairs and events in Spain.

Once in Spain, a good source of information is the commercial section of the British Embassy in Spain, known as UK Trade and Investment. Although their main remit is to help British companies who are looking to trade with Spain, or to set up a branch in Spain, they will be happy to help individual businessmen. This help will usually consist of providing information and contacts and generally directing people towards relevant associations, trade fairs and publications. They can be contacted at UK Trade and Investment, British Embassy, C/ Fernando el Santo 16, 28010 Madrid (☎ 917-008200/ 913-190200; fax 917 008272; www.uktradeinvest.gov.uk).

On a more local level, there are numerous organisations offering advice on business creation and setting up in a self-employed capacity, including employment services, autonomous community authorities and even your local *ayuntamiento* (town hall). However, it is always a good idea to take legal advice specific to your business idea either from a *gestor* or a lawyer. It is also advisable to contact the local Chamber of Commerce in order to benefit from their expertise on the economic conditions of the local area.

If you are thinking of buying an already established business then you will have far less red tape to deal with, but you are running a completely different set of risks and will benefit enormously from professional advice, especially in light of the recent changes to leasehold law (see *Acquiring a Business or Business Premises*) and the rate at which businesses change hands on the costas.

Useful Official Websites

www.ceoe.es: Spanish Confederation of Entrepreneurial Organisations.

www.cepyme.es: Spanish Confederation of Small and Medium-Sized Enterprises.

www.ipyme.org: General Directorate of Policy for Small and Medium-Sized Enterprises.

www.cscamaras.es: High Council of the Spanish Chambers of Commerce, Industry and Shipping.

www.camaramadrid.es: Chamber of Commerce, Madrid.

www.investinspain.org: General Directorate for Trade and Investment at the Ministry of the Economy.

www.spainbusiness.com: Spanish Embassy Office for Economic and Commercial Affairs in the USA.

www.investinmadrid.es: Madrid Development Institute.

www.icex.es: Spanish Institute of External Trade.

www.vue.es: Ventanilla Unica Empresarial (one-stop shop for business).

www.mir.es: Ministry of the Interior.

www.mcx.es: Trade and Tourism Secretary of State.

www.map.es: Ministry of the Public Administrations.

www.mineco.es: Ministry of the Economy.

www.europa.eu.int: European Union.

Gestores

The peculiar Spanish love of bureaucracy has created the need for an equally peculiar and quintessentially Spanish institution known as the *gestor*. Spanish bureaucracy is so labyrinthine that it is necessary for ordinary people to be guided through it by a special official. Admittedly this profession dates back to the time of mass illiteracy, when ordinary folk needed help with official paper work. However, the need still exists in Spain as even straightforward procedures can require three or four different pieces of paper, all with small print and fees that have to be paid at different counters, probably in different towns. If you have fluent Spanish, limitless patience and no time restrictions then you may save some money by wading through the quagmire of red tape yourself. Otherwise, it is recommended that you consult your local *gestoría* (the office of *gestores*) of which there are several in any town.

The gestor is less qualified than a full lawyer but also far less expensive. His fundamental role is to take on the burden of bureaucracy for you in any dealings with officialdom be it employment and residence permits, obtaining a driving licence, registering a car or social security. They are particularly useful for negotiating the procedures relating to starting and registering a business. If you go to them with any questions regarding permits, licences, insurance etc., they will explain the correct procedures to follow and often suggest shortcuts that you may not otherwise have found. With a signed letter of authorization, the gestor will also act in your name to carry out tortuous procedures such as presenting necessary papers at relevant departments.

Similarly a *gestor* is very useful when buying a business as they can pass a qualified eye over the contract and also investigate whether the business has all of the necessary licences and whether there are any outstanding debts in the name of the business which would be transferred to the new owner.

A good *gestor* can be a valuable asset and it is very worthwhile to establish an on-going relationship with them so that you have a useful contact whenever a problem arises. *Gestores* can also offer a range of other useful services such as accounting and book-keeping. Some even act as small business advisors.

The fees of a *gestor* are generally reasonable, especially considering the amount of confusion they will save you. However, the quality of the service that they provide can vary considerably and they do not always do a professional job. It is therefore worthwhile asking around for recommendations.

Legal advice

Inevitably the prospective businessman will at some point during the setting up, buying, or running of the enterprise, need specialist legal advice from a qualified, English-speaking lawyer. This applies no matter how large or small the business is. Do not confuse the lawyer (*abogado*) with the notary public (*notario*). The *notario* is a public official in charge of officially registering certain events such as property purchases and the incorporation of a company. The notary's fees are fixed by law.

> **Take professional advice early. John Howell & Co. Solicitors and International Lawyers.**
> *The earlier you seek professional legal advice regarding your business venture, the better. If you don't, the consequences can be terrible. A client of ours came to us with what he thought was a small legal problem. He had been on holiday to the Canary Islands many times and noticed that there were no ice cream vans there. Spotting a potential money spinner he bought a fleet of vans and a warehouse to store the ice creams and then entered into supply contracts with Italian and Spanish ice cream distributors. When he came to us, he was having problems obtaining the licence. We did some investigation and found that the reason that he couldn't get a licence was that it is in fact illegal to sell ice cream from vans in the Canaries. As a result he lost a lot of money.*

If you are willing to spend the money, it is possible to give a lawyer power of attorney to deal with all of the necessary procedures involved in establishing a business presence. Lawyers such as Chantal Becker-Cid, who has offices in Madrid and Malaga and specialises in helping foreigners to set up businesses (see address below), will take care of all of the paperwork for you. She delivers what she calls 'key companies' to clients which means that she will deliver a company with all of the necessary licences and documentation and which is ready to start trading. All you need are the keys to the office. It is well worth investing the money in seeking professional advice, because the authorities are becoming increasingly vigilant and will not hesitate to close down or heavily fine a business that does not have the correct papers to trade.

Lawyers' fees can vary enormously in Spain, depending on the amount of work involved. It is best to ask in advance and try to agree on a fee or a percentage before choosing a lawyer.

There are a number of UK law practices with knowledge of Spanish law and some international law firms with offices in Spain. However many small businesses will be best served by a local Spanish practice and although these are numerous, English-speaking lawyers are still fairly rare. What follows is a selection of UK lawyers and English-speaking lawyers in Spain who deal with commercial law. A full list for your local area can be obtained from the British Consulate.

UK

Bailey Gibson Solicitors, 5 Station Parade, Beaconsfield, Bucks HP9 2PG; ☎01494-672661; www.bailygibson.co.uk.

Baker & Mckenzie, 100 New Bridge Street, London EC4V 6JA; ☎020-7919 1000; fax 020-7919 1438; www.bakerinfo.com; Spain office: Paseo de la Castellana 33, Edificio Fenix Planta 6, 28046 Madrid; ☎ 912-304500.

Bennet & Co. Solicitors, 144 Knutsford Road, Wilmslow, Cheshire SK9 6JP; ☎01625-586937; fax 01625-585362; www.bennett-and-co.com; Associated offices throughout Spain.

Florez Valcarcel, Lawyer and Notario: 130 King Street, London W6 0QU; tel/fax 020-8741 4867. Notary public and licentiate with over 35 years' experience in Spanish law.

John Howell & Co Solicitors & International Lawyers, The Old Glass Works, 22 Endell Street, Covent Garden, London WC2H 9AD; ☎020-7420 0400; fax 020-7836 3626; e-mail info@europelaw.com; www.europelaw.com. They have independent associates in Alicante, Barcelona, Benidorm, Madrid, Menorca, Tenerife and many other locations. They will answer any queries on starting a business in Spain.

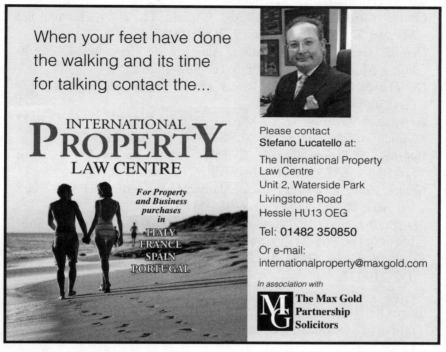
Mr Stefano Lucatello, The Max Gold Partnership Solicitors (incorporating The International Property Law Centre), Unit 2, Waterside Park, Livingstone Road, Hessle, HU13 0EG; ☎01482 350-850; fax 01482 642799; e-mail internationalproperty@maxgold.com. Gibraltar qualified solicitor and expert in the purchase and sale of French, Italian, Portuguese and Spanish Property and businesses, and the formation of offshore tax and trusts.

Spain

Adarve Corporacion Juridica, C/ Presidente Alvear 5, 1º, Las Palmas de Gran Canaria; ☎928-361072; fax 928-231476; e-mail info@adarve.com.

Becker-Cid Abogados, Chantal Becker-Cid, Madrid office: C/ Ayala, 4-3º izda., 28001 Madrid; ☎915-750544; fax 915-759 006; Marbella office: Travesía Carlos Mackintosh s/n, Edif. Puerta del Mar,

Portal A 7°4, 29600 Marbella; ☎ 952-861850; fax 952-861852; e-mail chantal@becker.jazztel.es.

Consult Card Law Office, C/ del Capitan 12, 29640 Fuengirola, Málaga; ☎ 952-463081; fax 952-588031.

Delgado Canovas, Juan Bautista, Alameda de Cervantes 1, 30800 Lorca, Murcia; ☎ 968-467996; fax 968-442865.

Dr. Fruhbeck, Marqués de Riscal 11, 5, 28010 Madrid; ☎ 917-004350; fax 913-102882.

Ferrer and Niederleytner, La Marina 7, 9, Edificio Hamilton, 38002 Santa Cruz de Tenerife; ☎ 922-246490; fax 922-243214.

Gabernet & Blanco Abogados, Benalmádena-Costa; ☎ 952-446456; fax 952-446473; e-mail gabernetblanco@teleline.es.

Gomez, Acebo y Pombo, Ignacio Alamar, G.V. Germanias 49, 46005 Valencia; ☎ 963-513835; fax 963-516074.

Martin Bruckhaus, C/ Castanos 22, 5B, 03001 Alicante; ☎ 965-161606; fax 965-217111; e-mail abogados@abogados.de.

Represa de Castor, Felipe, Alameda Principal 13, 8, 29001 Málaga; ☎ 952-219932.

Scornik Gerstein, Fernando, Gines de Castro 12, Planta 3, A y B, 35500 Arrecife, Lanzarote; ☎ 928-815258; fax 928-802200. Also has offices in Madrid, Tenerife and Gran Canaria.

Chambers of Commerce

The network of Chambers of Commerce in Spain offers a variety of information-based services to the potential entrepreneur. However, bear in mind that these can vary wildly in terms of the services offered, the quality of those services and the ability to speak English not only between Autonomous Communities but also between individual chambers.

> **All of the Chambers of Commerce offer an information service** (*Servicio de Creacion de Empresa*) **for those who are think-ing of starting a business.** They will be able to advise you on all aspects of business creation, from the types of legal entity that can be formed to the different incentives available locally for business creation. The Chambers will also be able to help you to research

the market prior to making your business plan (see below). Usually these services are completely free, although occasionally you may be charged a small administration cost.

Whilst all Chambers of Commerce will be able to offer advice and orientation to potential entrepreneurs, those Chambers which include a *Ventanilla Unica Empresarial* will also guide them through the processes involved in incorporating and registering a business. Further information on the network of VUEs is provided below.

Finally, the Chambers of Commerce offer another service for the creation and development of business in the area, known as the *Instituto Cameral de Creación y Desarollo de la Empresa (INCYDE)*. The INCYDE foundation is financed by the European Social Fund and offers free advice and personalised assistance to people wanting to set up a company and also to those who wish to set up as self-employed. Included in this service is support with complex procedures such as making a business plan. The foundation also offers special programmes for certain groups including women, the long term unemployed and the disabled.

The INCYDE provides ongoing support for entrepreneurs once they have established their business enterprise. There are around a hundred consultants attached to the foundation who travel around the country visiting businesses and offering free advice regarding their development and consolidation.

General advice about the network of Chambers and the services that they offer can be obtained from the High Council of the Chambers of Commerce (Consejo Superior de Cámaras de Comercio, C/ Velazquez 157, 1ª planta, 28002 Madrid; ☎ 915-906900/906974; fax 915-906908; e-mail info@cscamaras.es). However, in order to locate your nearest Chamber of Commerce visit the website www.camaras.org, click on *buscador de cámaras* and select your region.

Ventanillas Unicas Empresariales (One-Stop Shops for Businesses)

For years the process of establishing a business presence in Spain for both Spaniards and foreigners alike was characterised by the need to invest a great deal of time and patience into visiting a vast array of different offices, all with inexplicable opening hours and lingering queues. However, in 1999, the first ray of hope appeared for a rationalisation of this process, when the first *Ventanilla Unica* was opened in Valladolid.

Developed by the chambers of commerce and industry, and launched by the Ministry of Public Administrations (www.map.es), the network of *Ventanillas Unicas Empresariales* has created an integrated system providing future entrepreneurs with information and advice on the formalities required to start up a business. However, what makes this service so innovative is that all the facilities for setting up a business are provided in a single location, precluding the need to travel great distances and produce an inordinate number of duplicated documents. It should also reduce set-up costs as the service is government-sponsored and therefore free.

Pilar Solana Elorza – Coordinator of the VUE in Madrid.

The VUE is the product of a great deal of collaboration, combining representatives from the Chamber of Commerce, the Treasury and the Ministry of Labour and Social Affairs. We can provide, in one physical space, co-ordinated advice relating to starting any kind of business and most of the necessary administrative procedures in order to create a small to medium-sized business. All the customer has to do is change seats. In the case of establishing an autónomo (sole trader), *it is possible to do everything here in the VUE and in only one day. In the case of an S.L., it will be necessary to also see a notary public, and to go to the Companies' Register, but everything else will be done here and if all goes well, the company will be ready to start operations within a fortnight. All of this service is completely free.*

Last year, in the Madrid office alone, we were able to start around 400 businesses and the number of people we advised was at least triple that.

Visitors to a *Ventanilla Unica* go through three separate phases:

Information and guidance. This area acts as a 'first filter'. Entrepreneurs are pointed in the right direction, based on their requirements and provided with basic information on starting businesses.

Advice. A personal advisor then studies the business plan and following a personal interview, gives an assessment of the project and a range of alternatives. Advisors provide entrepreneurs with information regarding the suitable legal form for their business, labour obligations, private financing and government aid and subsidies.

Formalities. Suitable projects are then forwarded to the procedure management centre, where the officer-in-charge, in close co-operation with representatives of the tax and social security authorities and the regional and local authorities, will co-ordinate all of the procedures needed to set up the business.

The VUE can help with the following procedures:

o   Obtaining municipal licences: Opening licence, licence for minor work on the premises, licences for tables, chairs and umbrellas for bars and restaurants, etc.
o   Fiscal obligations: Obtaining the CIF (company tax identification number), registering for IAE (tax on business activities), registration at the *Agencia Tributaria* for tax purposes etc.
o   Labour and social security obligations: Registration of workers for social security, making sure that you are covered under the prevention of occupational risks regulations.

There are now twenty-six such offices in Spain, and between them they have facilitated the creation of more than 9,300 businesses and have dealt with over 44,000 enquiries. There is also a virtual online VUE, which provides detailed information and help for those wishing to set up a business and a 'virtual advisor'. However, the site is only available in Spanish (www.vue.es).

The system is not yet perfect as the offices are targeted at helping only those businesses which fall within the local area. So far only twelve of the seventeen autonomous communities are included in the scheme, leaving important areas such as Catalonia and Galicia without a similar service. It is also unclear as to whether the network of VUEs will continue to grow in the future. Furthermore, the service makes no language concessions to foreign entrepreneurs. The language of Spanish administration is Spanish, and if your language skills are not up to it, you will have no choice but to employ the services of a translator. The 26 current offices are listed below but the main website has further information on which areas and organisations are covered by the scheme (www.ventanillaempresarial.org). There is also a central number which you can call for general advice: ☎902-100096.

Valladolid: VUE, Avda. Ramón Pradera s/n, 47008, Valladolid; ☎ 983-381434 / 902-100096; fax 983-378492; e-mail valladolid@ve ntanillaempresarial.org.

Palma (Mallorca): VUE, C/ Estudi General 7, 07001, Palma de Mallorca; ☎ 971-721234; fax 971-719148; e-mail mallorca@ventanill aempresarial.org.

Santa Cruz (Tenerife): VUE, Pza. de la Candelaria 1, (Edificio Olympo) 4 planta de oficinas, 38003 Santa Cruz de Tenerife; ☎ 922-533784; fax 922-533766; e-mail tenerife@ventanillaempresa rial.org.

Las Palmas (Gran Canaria): VUE, C/ León y Castillo 24, 35003 Las Palmas de Gran Canaria; ☎ 928-432220; fax 928-432222; e-mail laspalmas@ventanillaempresarial.org.

Madrid: VUE, Pza. de la Independencia 1, 28001 Madrid; ☎ 902-181191; fax 915-383776.

Getafe: VUE, C/ Diesel s/n, Polígono Industrial EL LOMO, 28906 Getafe (Madrid); ☎ 916-843053; fax 916-016924; e-mail getafe@ ventanillaempresarial.org.

Burgos: VUE, C/ San Carlos 1, 1º, 09003 Burgos; ☎ 947-256750; fax 947-276520; e-mail burgos@ventanillaempresarial.org.

Murcia: VUE, Plaza de San Bartolomé 1, 30004 Murcia; ☎ 968-229434; fax 968-229435; murcia@ventanillaempresarial.org.

Oviedo: VUE, C/ Santa Susana 6, 33009 Oviedo; ☎ 985-207792; fax 985-207467; e-mail oviedo@ventanillaempresarial.org.

Zamora: VUE, C/ Pelayo 6, 49014 Zamora; tel/fax 980-535896; e-mail zamora@ventanillaempresarial.org.

Navarra: VUE, C/ General Chinchilla 4, 31002 Pamplona; ☎ 948-077077; fax 948-077081; e-mail navarra@ventanillaempresarial.org.

Segovia: VUE, Casa del Sello de Paños, C/ San Francisco 32, 40001 Segovia; ☎ 921-440123; fax 921-440294; e-mail Segovia@ventani llaempresarial.org.

Toledo/Castilla – La Mancha: VUE, Avda. Reyes Católicos s/n, 45002 Toledo; ☎ 925-283070; fax 925-256201; e-mail toledo@ve ntanillaempresarial.org.

Sevilla: VUE, Plaza de la Contratación 8, 41004 Sevilla; ☎ 954-502530; fax 954-561857; e-mail sevilla@ventanillaempresarial.org.

Valencia: VUE, C/ Poeta Querol 15, 46002 Valencia; ☎ 963-103929; fax 963-516349; e-mail Valencia@ventanillaempresarial.org.

Avila: VUE, C/ Eduardo Marquina 6, 05001 Avila, ☎ 920-353580; e-mail avila@ventanillaempresarial.org.

Zaragoza: VUE, Paseo Isabel la Católica 2, 50009 Zaragoza; ☎ 976-791160; fax 976-791274; e-mail zaragoza@ventanillaempresarial.org.

Cartagena: VUE, Muelle de Alfonso XII s/n, 30201 Cartagena, Murcia; ☎ 968-321335; fax 968-321353; cartagena@ventanillae mpresarial.org.

Salamanca: VUE, Plaza de Sexmeros 4, 37001 Salamanca; ☎ 923-280075; fax 923-280076; salamanca@ventanillaempresarial.org.

Ciudad Real / Castilla – La Mancha: VUE, C/ Lanza 2, 13004 Ciudad Real; ☎ 926-271768; fax 926-227011; e-mail ciudadreal@ventanillaempresarial.org.

Albacete / Castilla – La Mancha: VUE, C/Tesifonte Gallego 22, 02002 Albacete; ☎ 967-550790; fax 967-511474; albacete@vent anillaempresarial.org.

Mirando de Ebro: VUE, Ronda del Ferrocarril 31, 09200 Miranda de Ebro (Burgos); ☎ 947-335200; 947-313593; e-mail Miranda@ven tanillaempresarial.org.

Cuenca: VUE, C/ Calderón de la Barca 12, 16001 Cuenca; ☎ 969-241710; fax 969-227391; e-mail cuenca@ventanillaempresarial.org.

León: VUE C/ Fajeros 1, 24002 León; ☎ 987-276440; fax 987-276441; e-mail leon@ventanillaempresarial.org.

Santander: VUE, Plaza de Velarde 5, 39001 Santander; ☎ 942-365000; 942-365010; e-mail santander@ventanillaempresarial.org.

Guadalajara: VUE, C/ Mayor 28, 19001 Guadalajara; ☎ 949-234491; 949-226453; e-mail Guadalajara@ventanillaempresarial.org.

The New Business Project (Sociedad Limitada Nueva Empresa S.L.N.E.)

Small and medium-sized enterprises generate around 78% of Spain's total employment and are vital for the country's economy as a whole. In recognition of this fact, the government has a number of plans afoot to speed up and simplify the procedures involved in their incorporation and try to encourage people away from operating as sole traders. One of these plans, the *Proyecto de Nueva Empresa*, has created a new speciality of the Sociedad Limitada (S.L. – the most common form of limited liability companies for new businesses), known as the S.L.N.E. The project was introduced in the summer of 2003 and is still in its initial stages. So far there are only around a thousand of these new entities and only around 5%-10% of these made use of the new fully-automated business creation system designed specifically for the S.L.N.E. However, there are plans to expand the project throughout Spain and introduce new measures to increase its popularity. Details of how the S.L.N.E. differs from an ordinary S.L. can be found in *Which Business Structure?*

The object of the new business project is to bring Spain into line with the European Union in terms of ease of business creation. This entails providing entrepreneurs with the means to set up a company much more rapidly and at far less cost by improving the legislation regarding the creation of businesses and developing better relations between business and public administration.

According to Alberto Salmerón of the High Council of the Chamber of Commerce in Spain, it is possible to incorporate an S.L.N.E. in around seven days via conventional methods and in only two days using the new automated system, which involves only one visit to the Ventanilla Unica Empresarial and one visit to the notary public. However, the necessary technology for automated business incorporation so far only exists in the VUEs in Madrid, Valencia, Murcia and Cartagena and for everybody else it will still take at least a week to incorporate a company.

If you do choose to incorporate an S.L.N.E. via conventional methods, these are outlined below (*Necessary Steps to Establish and Incorporate a New Company*). However, there is one difference.

Clearance for use of the name of the new company, which is usually issued by the Companies' Registry, can only be obtained online at the website www.circe.es. Having completed the necessary procedures online, the certificate can either be collected from the Registry or sent by post.

Those who are able to make use of the new automated technology will be directed to a *Punto de Asesoramiento e Inicio de Tramitación (PAIT)*, where the entire incorporation process, minus the execution of the deed of incorporation before a notary, can be done online. This should only be attempted if your Spanish is really up to it. The new software used at these PAITs is able to connect many of the agencies and public organisations involved in business incorporation, such as central and local tax agencies, central and local business registers, social security administration and so on. Once the electronic document (DUE) is filled in, it is then sent to each of these agencies who add their required data immediately and send it back. At the end of the process, the client receives a copy of all of the necessary documents and needs only to visit the notary to complete the incorporation.

The technology involved is really quite advanced, but the project is still in its infancy and has not yet enjoyed too much success. This is due to the fact that people are not keen to have the name of their company dictated to them (it must be made up of the Christian name and surname of one of the company's directors, plus a number). Secondly, by operating as a business entity rather than a sole trader, it is necessary to deal with the complexities of corporation tax, which often involves employing an accountant at extra cost. There are plans to simplify the fiscal obligations of small businesses, but these have been in the pipeline for months and have yet to materialise.

Further information on developments regarding this project can be found, in Spanish only, at www.circe.es.

RESEARCHING THE MARKET

Whatever the size of the business, making a comprehensive study of the proposed market is the best way to avoid failure and disappointment. Often people fail to study the market properly because they know deep down that the business is not viable and they are caught up in the emotion of starting a new venture. Your research may not tell you what you want to hear, but it is always a good idea to be prepared for every eventuality.

Good market research is necessary for the entrepreneur to ascertain who are the potential consumers for his product or service, both their quantity and their qualities. This will include information on the target population's location, needs and tastes, buying power, age, sex etc. This information is also very useful when deciding how to target your marketing strategy.

However, clients and consumers only make up around half of the market research. It is also necessary to make a thorough study of the competition. The type of questions that need answering include:

- Who are the market leaders and what are the reasons for their success?
- Which businesses in the sector are having difficulties and what are the causes?
- How can we offer our products in a form that is perceived as more attractive than the competition?
- Which products perform similar functions to ours or satisfy the same need?
- Which businesses offer products or services that are complementary to ours and is collaboration possible?

Finally a good study of the market should include information on possible suppliers of materials or stock for your business. Often suppliers can be an important source of information regarding the characteristics of the market.

If there is a deficient market, then it really is necessary to abandon the project before you've even started, or at least modify it dramatically. Therefore it is sensible to put as much time and effort as possible into identifying your potential customers, suppliers and competition.

There are a number of specialised market research companies who will do the work for you, but they are expensive and for a smaller business, usually unnecessary given the amount of information publicly available and on the internet. The type of research that you do and the questions that you ask will vary enormously depending on the business. If, for example, you are starting a country hotel then you need to consider the variables affecting the number of visitors you are likely to have such as the traffic throughput, the weather conditions, local attractions and so on. If your business is fairly small scale, then all of this information will be available simply by asking local businessmen and observing trade in the area.

If your business is on a larger scale, you may need to do some more in depth investigation. A good place to start for general information is the local Chamber of Commerce (see above). Some of the better equipped chambers, such as those in Madrid and Zaragoza will be able to carry out a full study of the geographical area and the level of competition within it, although they may well charge you for a full market study (*estudio de mercado*). Smaller chambers may only be able to give you a general guide and offer advice on further sources of information.

Sector and market reports are often available on-line. For example in Britain, the international arm of the Department of Trade and Industry, now known as UK Trade and Investment offers a variety of country-specific reports on various sectors of the economy online (www.uktradeinvest.gov.uk). Many online market reports and databases such as Euromonitor, Business Monitor International and Datamonitor are subscription only and very expensive. However, this expense can be avoided by a visit to the UK Trade and Investment Information Centre, which subscribes to all of the main databases and allows free access to entrepreneurs (Kingsgate House, 66-74 Victoria Street, London SW1E 6SW; ☎ 020-7215 8000; fax 020-7215 4231).

Consumer associations, trade publications and trade fairs and exhibitions are all good ways of investigating the market, and your local Chamber of Commerce or the British Embassy in Spain will supply details of these. If you are setting up in Spain as a professional, then the professional college (*colegio*) which you join will be able to tell you exactly what other similar businesses are operating and where.

Fools rush in. Peter Lytton Cobbold, Masia Rentals, near Barcelona
It is far better to spend time seeing what you are going to do before rushing into setting up a company. Otherwise, you could get caught

up in all the bureaucracy before you fully understand the market. You have to remember that it is a different country and that you are an immigrant. It takes time to do even the basic things and you cannot use previous experience at home as a basis for what you think other people will spend their money on in a completely different market.

Spain was a poor country up until the last twenty-five years. The salaries are still much lower and people have less to spend. It is also a beautiful country full of most of the things that any sane person could wish for at reasonable prices, so trying to compete with that is difficult. It is hard to come up with a new idea and, if it is a good one, making sure that it cannot be copied too easily.

Spain has some of the best business schools in the world, so there is no shortage of skilled, young entrepreneurs. Don't see it as a market ripe for the taking. Live here for a while and try to understand the way the markets work before starting a business.

Making a Business Plan

Producing a business plan is not obligatory for new businesses as in France, nor will it guarantee your business success. However, what it will do is to force you to examine the viability of the business proposal in a realistic way. According to John Howell & Co. Solicitors and International Lawyers, one of the main reasons for people going bust is that they do not have a realistic business plan. It will also provide you with a useful document to present to third parties when, for example, asking for the opinion of a business advisor, looking for private investment or applying for public subsidies, and also when looking for collaborators for the business. Even if you are planning to take over a business which is already up and running, the business plan will help you to consider the logical and viable steps for development in the future.

The business plan should be well presented and state clearly and concisely your two main objectives:

- To identify, describe and analyse the business opportunity.
- To analyse the technical, commercial and financial viability of the business proposal.

The business plan should not be taken lightly.
It will involve a great deal of work, speaking to potential clients, gathering information regarding the competition, making a projection of all the possible costs that the business will have to confront, and of the capital needed to start up. Maximising the depth of your investigation should mean minimising the risks involved later on.

A mistake which people often make, even if subconsciously, is that they fool themselves. They are very optimistic about their income and tend to minimise their projected outgoings. It may well be worth seeking the help of a qualified accountant (*contable* or *asesor fiscal*) or even a *gestor* to help you to avoid these pitfalls and to make sure that your plan follows an accepted format and is realistic.

The information included in a business plan for a hairdressing salon will obviously be vastly different from that of an estate agents, however the structure of the plan will be more or less the same. An outline of the form which a business plan in Spain should take can be found in the chapter *Financing Your Business*.

SELF EMPLOYMENT AND PROFESSIONAL MOBILITY

If you want to work for yourself in Spain, as a doctor, surveyor, lawyer, plumber, carpenter, journalist, language teacher etc., or if you run a business in your own name as a sole trader (*empresario individual*) you will come under the category of *cuenta propia* or 'working on your own account'. This is also known as *autónomo* for the purposes of the Spanish Social Security system. EU nationals and permanent residents with a *residencia* can be self-employed in a profession or trade in Spain, although they must meet the legal requirements and register with the appropriate organisation. For example, professionals must register with their professional *colegio* (see below). The main disadvantage of operating as self-employed is that you do not have the protection of limited liability should your company fall into debt. This is discussed further in *Which Business Entity?*

Professional Bodies in Spain

Architects: *Consejo Superior de los Colegios de Arquitectos de España*, Paseo de la Castellana 12, 28046 Madrid; ☎ 914-352200; fax 915-753839; e-mail cscae@arquinex.es; www.cscae.com.

Commercial Agents: *Consejo General de Colegios de Agentes Comerciales de España*, C/ Goya 55, 28001 Madrid; ☎ 914-363650; fax 915-770084; e-mail consejo@cgac.es; www.cgac.es.

Doctors and Dentists: *Consejo General de Colegios Oficiales de Médicos*, C/ Villanueva 11, 28001 Madrid; ☎ 914-317780; fax 915-764388; e-mail administrador@cgcom.org; www.cgcom.org.

Estate Agents: *Consejo General de los Colegios Oficiales de Agentes de la Propiedad Inmobiliaria de España*, Gran Via 66, 2a planta, 28013 Madrid; ☎ 915-470741; fax 915-593255; cgcoap@consejocoapis.org; www.consejocoapis.org.

Lawyers: *Consejo General de la Abogacía Española*, C/ Paseo de Recoletos 13, 28004 Madrid; ☎ 915-232593; fax 915-327836; www.cgae.es.

Nurses and Midwives: *Consejo General de Colegios Oficiales de Enfermería de España*; www.ocenf.org.

Pharmacists: *Consejo General de Colegios Oficiales de Farmacéuticos*, C/ Villanueva 11, Madrid 28001; ☎ 914-312560; fax 914-328100; e-mail congral@redfarma.org; www.portalfarma.com.

Veterinarians: *Consejo General de Colegios Veterinarios de España*, C/ Villanueva 11, 28001 Madrid; ☎ 914-353535; fax 915-783468; e-mail consejo@colvet.es; www.colvet.es.

Mutual Recognition of Qualifications

In recent years, the recognition of foreign qualifications for EU citizens has been rationalised. The General System for Mutual Recognition of Professional Qualifications was introduced to enable fully qualified professionals from one EU country to join the equivalent profession in Spain without having to re-qualify. If you hold a qualification entitling you to practice a regulated profession in your Member State of origin, this is sufficient to establish that you are eligible for consideration under the general system.

There are two EU directives regarding this. To be eligible for assessment under EU directive 89/48/EEC you must have successfully completed a degree level course of at least three years' duration and also successfully completed any professional training required to enable you to practice the profession concerned. The second directive is 92/51/EEC which covers those educated below degree level (i.e. qualifications gained through any post-secondary course of more than one year, such as NVQs or SVQs, or work experience).

A comparison between foreign qualifications and those recognised in Spain can be obtained from any Spanish employment office (INEM) where there is a representative of NARIC, the National Academic Recognition Information Centre, or from the head of NARIC in Spain, Federico Curto, *NARIC España*, Subdirección General de Títulos, Convalidaciones y Homologaciones, Paseo del Prado, 28, E-28014 Madrid (☎ 915 0655593; fax 915 065706; e-mail federico.curto@educ.mec.es). It is better to contact your UK or Spanish Employment Agency rather than contact NARIC directly as you should not be charged for the service. Further information, in English, can be found at the NARIC website, www.naric.org.uk. You should not contact NARIC in the UK if you are going to work in Spain.

British crafts or trades people such as hairdressers or construction workers who wish to work in Spain can apply to have their experience certified under the UK Certificate of Experience scheme administered by the Department for Education and Skills. Their role is to implement Directive 99/42/EEC (the so called Third Directive) concerning the mutual recognition of experience gained in a profession in EU member countries. A certificate costs £105 and takes fifteen days to process. Contact DfES, Certificates of Experience Team, Qualifications for Work Division, Room E3B, Moorfoot, Sheffield S1 4PQ; ☎ 0114-259 4237; www.defs.gov.uk/europeopen. A great deal of information on professional bodies and EC directives can be found on the EU website http://citizens.eu.int.

Transferring my qualifications was a nightmare – Liz Arthur – Registered Midwife, Costa del Sol

There is a big problem with registration out here. It took me twelve months and a good deal of expense, what with the cost of the verification certificate, the cost of the solicitor, the postage and the telephone calls. It really was a nightmare. I followed the guidelines given by the Spanish government to the UK Nursing and Midwifery Council. I had all of my qualifications translated, filled in the forms, paid the money and sent it all off to Madrid. I then took everything to the Ministry of Sport, Education and Culture in Malaga who stamped it and sent it back to Madrid. It took seven months before I got any response and when I did, I took everything to the nursing council here, who told me my documents were out of date! So I had to spend even more money on getting another certificate, having it translated and stamped. It was then sent to England to be verified and then to the Foreign Office, just to make sure it was official. Finally it all came back to me, I took it to the nursing council and I think they agreed just because they felt sorry for me. I was then able to start practicing. I am now a member of the College of Midwives here, the Colegio de Enfermería.

The problem is that we are very accustomed to having Spanish doctors and nurses in England, but they have very little experience of having English medical practitioners in Spain.

Foreigners who wish to become self-employed will go through exactly the same procedure as a Spaniard. All self-employed people must register for income tax, social security and VAT. In order to register at the local Tax Office as self-employed, you will usually need a copy of your NIE and passport and completed forms 037 (tax registration) and 845 (business tax – *IAE* – registration).

Autonomous workers are required by law to pay into the Spanish Social Security System under the *autónomo* scheme and as a result they are entitled to medical benefits through the Spanish National Health scheme. They may also receive sickness pay when ill, at the rate of 75% of the minimum wage, on receipt of a doctor's certificate testifying that he/she is unable to carry out their profession. Self-employed workers also qualify for a pension but they cannot qualify for unemployment benefit. Further information on these issues can be found in *Tax, Social Security and Other Matters.*

In order to register as self employed with the Social Security Office, you will need the original and copies of your NIE and passport, a copy of Tax Office form 845 and the completed form TA.0521.

OPERATING OUT OF YOUR OWN HOME

Recent estimates suggest that as many as 60% of new businesses operate out of their own homes. Unlike in France where there are strict regulations about operating a business out of residential premises, in Spain it is perfectly acceptable to register a business at your own residence or at rented accommodation as long as the landlord agrees to it. Obviously many landlords would object to a point of sale business within a residential property due to the wear and tear caused by people tramping through the building. Offices however (*oficinas y despachos),* are usually perfectly acceptable.

One advantage of operating out of your own home, other than the fact that you will not have to pay any extra rent, is that it is not usually necessary to apply for the opening licence, *licencia de apertura* from the town hall, which can take up to six months. This is the case if you are running a small office in your home.

Operating a point of sale business from your home

Should you decide that you wish to operate a business from your principal residence that involves receiving customers or having goods delivered then you will need permission from the local council. For example, if you chose to operate a small shop or restaurant out of part of the building, then it would be considered a change of use and there is much more paperwork involved. Firstly it would be necessary to approach the *ayuntamiento* (town hall) with your proposition to see whether in theory they would approve such a change. It is then necessary to employ an architect, who would approach the High Council of Colleges of Architects (*Consejo Superior de los Colegios de Arquitectos de España*; www.cscae.com) or the local *colegio* in order to ascertain the current planning regulations for such a business. The architect would then submit a project, and the suggested work, such as installing the correct amount of toilets and following fire regulations, would have to be carried out to the letter. Only then could you apply to the local council for a *licencia de apertura*, allowing you to operate the business from those premises. It is by no means guaranteed that the *ayuntamiento* will grant the licence, but they will not even consider it before the necessary work has been done.

Company directors have the right to work from home under the same conditions as self-employed people. The company must have a registered headquarters, but there are no restrictions as to where this is. Unless there is a clause in your lease preventing you from doing so, then you can continue to work from home indefinitely and have your company registered at your home.

From the point of view of taxation, the law allows you to deduct a proportion of your joint home and business expenses from your taxable income. It will be necessary to declare the percentage of space which is taken up by business activities in your home and that percentage of the rent is then deductible. The same is true with utility bills, you can deduct a percentage of the total from your taxable income, your accountant will be able to advise you as to how much you can get away with.

Your principal residence is protected against creditors in the event of bankruptcy as long as it has not been purchased in the company's name.

NECESSARY STEPS TO ESTABLISH AND INCORPORATE A NEW COMPANY

In order to create a new business entity from scratch, perhaps the most important prerequisite is an enormous amount of time and patience. It is often necessary to visit a vast range of offices and officials, such as the lawyer, the national tax agency or *Hacienda*, the social security office and so on. David Searl, author and broadcaster on Spanish law, suggests that the procedures associated with starting a business may include as many as fifty-seven different steps. For this reason, he estimates that around 40% of businesses remain unlicensed.

However, the whole frustrating process will be far more palatable if you make use of an experienced professional. There are a great number of qualified and English-speaking lawyers and *gestores* who will guide you through the apparently impenetrable web of bureaucracy.

It is important to remember that Spain's decentralised system of government means that some of the legal steps will vary between the autonomous communities, so it is vital that you seek advice which is specific to your particular area. The procedures may also differ depending on the type of legal entity that you choose to form, although there are few differences in the legal steps for incorporating an S.A. or an S.L.

Costs involved in setting up an ordinary S.L. or S.A.	
Stamp Duty	1% of capital contributions.
Share Capital (minimum)	€3005 (S.L.) / 25% of €60,101 (S.A.).
Certificate of company name	€12.
Company registration	Approx. €150 – fees are assessed on the capital investment and may not exceed €2,181.
Legal fees	Min. €1000.
Opening Licence	Price depends on a number of factors such as the location and size of the business premises.

Step 1 – Pre-registration of the company name. The first step on the path to obtaining the deed of incorporation is to register the name of the company at the commercial register (*Registro Mercantil Centro*). Having decided upon a name, it is necessary to ensure that no other company has the same, or a similar name and to obtain a certificate documenting this (*Certificacion Negativa del Nombre; CNN*). The cost of this certificate currently stands at around €12. This process may seem fairly minor, and indeed should only take about forty-eight hours, due to a new simplified procedure. However, without the certificate it is impossible to proceed.

The *Registro Mercantil Central* can also be checked online and in English at the following site: http://www.rmc.es/default_ing.htm. The site allows you to consult existing names and submit new ones. It is also possible to find the nearest office.

Step 2 – Application for the taxpayer's ID number (*CIF*). Before you can open a bank account in the company's name, it is necessary to register with the central tax agency, known as the *Hacienda* or more correctly as the *Agencia Tributaria*. Here you will receive the *Código de Identificación Fiscal*, which identifies the new company for tax purposes. It is possible to apply for the CIF online via the internet at www.aeat.es. Otherwise, the owners of the company or their legal representatives should contact the Tax Authorities' Office corresponding to the address where the company intends to be incorporated. It is possible to find full contact details for your local *Hacienda* at www.aeat.es/agencia/direc/.

You will be provided at this time with a provisional tax number. Once the company has been fully registered in the Mercantile Registry, it must obtain the definitive CIF within a maximum period of six months from the issuance of the provisional number.

Step 3 – Deposit. In order to incorporate a company it is necessary to decide on the amount of capital with which the company will be formed. There are established minimum capital amounts depending on the type of legal entity chosen (see *Which Business Structure?*). For an S.L. all of the minimum capital of around €3005 must be paid in and for an S.A. 25% of the €60,000 minimum must be paid in. This capital must be deposited in a bank account made out in the name of the company and for this you will receive a certificate – the *Certificado del Desembolso Efectuado*. It is mandatory to obtain this certificate before a company can be incorporated.

Step 4 – Execution of the public deed of incorporation. The deed of incorporation must be signed before a Notary Public. The following fundamental documents must be submitted in order to establish the company within the eyes of Spanish law:

- A certificate registering the name of your company.
- A certificate from the bank showing that the necessary share capital has been deposited in an account in the name of the company.
- The company statutes containing all of the agreements reached by the shareholders.

The Notary Public will also require the persons who appear before him to demonstrate evidence of their identity and, where applicable, power of attorney to represent a third party. It is also necessary to provide the notary with the bylaws of the company.

The deed of constitution will present the following crucial points:

- **Name, nationality and residence of all share holders.**
- **Company name:** This should also indicate the legal form of the business, such as S.L. or S.A.
- **Company aim:** Setting out all of the proposed activities of the new business.
- **Start of business activity:** Indicating the official date that the business will start to operate.
- **Duration of the company:** An estimate of the period of time that you intend to operate.
- **Company headquarters:** Detailing the address of where the majority of business activities will occur and a point of contact for the shareholders.
- **Share capital:** You must indicate the exact amount of capital invested at the moment of incorporation.
- **Board of directors:** Indicating the person or persons who will be responsible for the administration of the business.

If the company is being incorporated as an S.L. it will need to present additional information such as:

- The capital contribution of each shareholder as well as the nominal value attributed to it.
- Method of establishing and summoning the general meeting of shareholders and the form which the decision making process will take.

If the company is being incorporated as an S.A., the deed of incorporation should also clarify elements such as:

- Personal details of all shareholders and a declaration of their desire to form an S.A.
- The contribution of money, assets or rights of each shareholder.

○   The cost of incorporation.

Step 5 – Payment of the transfer tax. This duty must be paid within thirty business days of the execution of the public deed of incorporation. A special form must be filled in and presented along with a copy of the deed of incorporation at the tax office corresponding to the company's address for tax purposes (www.aeat.es). The tax is levied at 1% of the current value of the capital contributions made.

Step 6 – Registration at the Companies' Registry. Once the above-mentioned steps have been completed, and within thirty days of the execution of the deed, the new company must be formally registered with the *Registro Mercantil Central* (www.rmc.es). The following documents must be presented in order to register the company:

○   The public deed of incorporation.
○   The *Certificacion Negativa del Nombre* obtained from the companies' registry.
○   Evidence of having paid the stamp duty.

Registration fees are assessed on a sliding scale of officially approved charges according to the amount of capital contributed (the larger the capital, the lower the rate). The total amount of the fee may not exceed €2,181.

Step 7 – Obtaining the permanent tax identity number. One final trip to the tax office is required before the company is considered to be a fully incorporated legal entity. For the purposes of exchanging the temporary CIF for a permanent one, the tax office will need to see:

○   The certificate of the temporary CIF number.
○   A copy of the deed of incorporation.
○   A photocopy of the registration entry in the companies register.

NECESSARY FORMALITIES BEFORE BEGINNING OPERATIONS

Having followed the above steps, the business is now fully incorporated and registered. However, before the company can start operating there are a number of legal and fiscal obligations which must be fulfilled. Again these obligations can vary depending on the type of business and where it is based. There are also a number of specially regulated activities which may require additional administrative authorisation such as restaurants, travel agencies, security, toxic substances storage etc. However a good *gestor* or lawyer will advise you as to the specific details of such operations.

Municipal Licences

Opening licence. Any business that operates from business premises must obtain a *Licencia Municipal de Apertura*, a municipal opening licence. This licence certifies that the planned facilities and the business activity are in accordance with the applicable municipal regulations. It must be obtained from the Municipal or District Council (*Ayuntamiento*) where the offices are to be located. For a new *local* (premises) it is necessary to employ the services of a *gestor* and an architect, to submit a project to the town council. Usually the council will visit the business premises and make sure that they fulfil all legal and sanitary conditions. The cost of the opening licence depends on the location of the premises and its size in square metres, but it can be as little as €100 for a small shop, or €200 for a bar or restaurant.

Unfortunately, when applying for an opening licence, you are completely at the mercy of your ayuntamiento. It is not unusual for a town council to take six months or more examining the project before issuing a licence. Additionally, there is no guarantee that they will approve the project, even if all of the refurbishment has already been done.

However, if you are taking over existing business premises, then there is a possibility that the licence can simply be transferred as the licence is for the premises rather than the business itself. This is not possible if the two business activities are very different, but there is usually a standard licence for any kind of office.

Finally, because obtaining an opening licence relies on the local council who are often fairly lax in making inspections and granting licences, many people operate merely on the basis of a stamped application for a *licencia de apertura*. If you take this route you should be aware that it is not altogether legal. However, it is usually tolerated by the authorities (as it is their fault that you do not have a licence) and if you exercise a little discretion there should not be any problems.

Works licence: Any construction work which needs to be done on the premises requires the appropriate works licence. Again it must be obtained from the Local Council office and the granting of this licence implies that the Local Council accepts that the planned works are in accordance with the existing town planning regulations.

Fiscal Obligations

Registration of the company for the purposes of business activities tax. The *Impuesto sobre Actividades Económicas (IAE)* is levied annually on any business activity conducted within the territory of the municipality. It is likely that the company, if it is a fairly small enterprise will not have to pay any IAE contributions as in 2003, in a move to stimulate small business, the government abolished this tax for anyone with a turnover of less than €1 million per year. At the time of writing however, there were plans to overturn this move or replace the IAE with an alternative tax in order to compensate local councils for a vast loss of revenue. The administration of this tax has also been removed from the municipalities and returned to the central Tax Agency, so it is now necessary to apply to register at the *Agencia Tributaria*.

Despite the fact that you probably will not have to pay the IAE, it is still necessary to register as you must have a tax category assigned for your business. A special form must be filed at least ten days before the company starts its business. If payable, the tax is levied at the moment of inception and annually thereafter.

Registration of the company at the census of taxpayers. The company must be registered or listed for control of its subsequent tax obligations at the *Agencia Tibutaria*. A special form must be filled in at the Tax Office documenting various data on the company's future activities.

Legalisation of official books. Every company must keep a number of tax and accounting 'books' such as the Journal (*Libro Diario*) and the Inventories and Annual Accounts Book (*Libro de Inventarios y Cuentas Anuales*). These must be physically taken to the nearest Companies' Registry for stamping, before business activities commence.

As well as the accounts journals, companies should have a Minutes Book (*Libro de Actas*) recording all of the agreements taken at general meetings. S.L.s also need a *Libro de Registros de Socios* recording the quantity of participation units held by each company owner. A *Libro de Matricula* logs personnel registration as well as the visits that the Labour Inspectors (*Inspección de Trabajo*) pay to the work centre. These books and any others which your accountant or *gestor* advises to be necessary must be presented at the Companies' Registry.

Labour Obligations

Registration of the company for social security purposes. It is obligatory for all businesses to register with the Social Security Treasury prior to starting their activities so that the company will later be able to employ workers. You will need:

○ The original and copies of the business owner's N.I.E. and passport.
○ A copy of the insurance policy for accident and health cover (paid for out of social security contributions).
○ A copy of the deed of incorporation (*escritura*).
○ A copy of the form from the tax office (845) showing that you have registered for business tax.
○ Completed form TA.6

The company will be issued with a social security identification number and advised as to their social security obligations. If you already have a labour supply, then you must file first-time registration of the workers who do not have a social security number (*afiliación*), or a renewal of those who are already registered (*alta*).

For each new employee, you must supply the Social Security office with the original and copies of the employee's NIE and passport and a completed form (TA.2/S).

Further information on social security, in Spanish only, can be found at the *Seguridad Social* website, www.seg-social.es/inicio.

Registration at the provincial office of the Ministry of Labour and Social Affairs. The labour authorities must be made aware of the start of operations in a work place within thirty days. The relevant form must therefore be completed and delivered to the above office (*Ministerio de Trabajo y Asuntos Sociales*). The address of your nearest provincial office can be found at the following web address: www.mtas.es/infgral/provin/espana.htm.

Which Business Structure?

CHAPTER SUMMARY

- 99% of businesses in Spain are small or medium-sized enterprises (PYMEs). 200,000 new small businesses are created every year and this is due to the relative ease of establishing them.
  - The required level of share capital is low.
  - The government offers a number of incentives and subsidies for such enterprises.
- The entrepreneur must decide which structure his business will adopt. This is an important decision affecting the individual liability of share-holders, the form of taxation payable and the amount of capital invested.
- 68% of new businesses opt to operate as sole traders. This is the most efficient form for small businesses and involves less red tape.
  - The sole trader assumes both the risks and the profits of his labour.
- Those who choose to incorporate a company usually opt for the S.L. (*Sociedad de Responsibilidad Limitada*). This has been the traditional investment vehicle for small and family-run businesses in Spain. Larger companies usually choose to form an S.A. (*Sociedad Anónima*).
- Both an S.A. and an S.L can be formed with a single owner-occupier (*unipersonal*).
- **Partnerships:** allow two or more people to set up in business together sharing profits, management burdens and risks.
  - There are two main types of partnership, the Sociedad Colectiva and the Sociedad Comanditaria.
- There are a number of ways of establishing a business presence in Spain without actually forming a separate legal entity. These include branches, joint ventures, distribution agreements and franchising.

SMALL AND MEDIUM-SIZED ENTERPRISES IN SPAIN (PYMES)

It is a well-known characteristic of Spanish enterprises that they are generally small in size. Recent statistics registered more than 2.7 million businesses in Spain, of which 99% are Pequeña y Mediana Empresas (PYMEs) or small and medium-sized enterprises. In fact there are only around 3,450 businesses in Spain with more than 250 employees. Of these PYMEs, 94% are considered *micro-empresas* as they employ less than ten salaried workers, although it is important to remember that the proportion of freelancers is higher in Spain than the European average.

The fact that there are so many small and usually family-run businesses in Spain is due at least in part to the relative ease of establishing them. According to the Spanish National Institute of Statistics, more than 200,000 new small businesses are created every year in Spain. This is because the required level of share capital is low (see below), the government offers any number of subsidies for the creation of such businesses (see *Financing Your Business*) and as a result, all that is needed is an enterprising nature and some business acumen. Further information and advice on PYMEs can be found at the website of the *Dirección General de Política de la PYME* administered by the Ministry of the Economy – www.ipyme.org.

However, the very nature of an economy dominated by small business leads to a number of problems for the entrepreneur. One major concern is competition. With so many small businesses operating, unless you have a completely new product or service to offer, it is likely that the market will be saturated. This is a particular drawback in resort areas where there is an abundance of bars, cafés, restaurants and shops catering to the tourist trade. Not only do small businesses have to compete against each other, but also the larger corporations. Here they have traditionally faced a number of disadvantages. For example, smaller companies have reduced financial flexibility and as a result a reduced capacity to invest in research and development, marketing and human resources. As a result they can often get left behind in terms of innovation, and their position in the market place.

There are however, a number of advantages to forming a small company and these advantages have allowed PYMEs to be so competitive within the Spanish economy. Firstly, PYMEs are very flexible. They are very aware of their customers and can adapt quickly to changes in the market place. They are also able to take vital decisions very quickly under pressure. The boss of a small company is able to increase and decrease production capacity, or hire and fire staff at any given moment depending on the fluctuations of the market. PYMEs also have very quick reaction times, allowing them to respond very efficiently to changes in fashion and the level of competition in any given market. Finally, PYMEs have the enormous advantage over larger companies, that they are able to have far greater personal contact with the client. Spain is a country where personal relationships within business are vital. The Spanish will not do business with you unless they feel that they know you and can trust you and this is perhaps an important reason why there is such a business culture of PYMEs in Spain. From the point of view of your clients, they will appreciate the fact that within a smaller business it is very easy to identify the correct person to talk to, and more often than not they will be able to make a business decision very quickly and without recourse to endless meetings.

CHOOSING THE CORRECT LEGAL ENTITY FOR YOUR BUSINESS

One of the first decisions that the entrepreneur should make, having analysed the viability of his business, is which form of business enterprise he should adopt. There are a number of legal entities that a Spanish business may assume and choosing the right structure for your business should be the subject of extensive study. Taking legal advice on this subject is a must and a good lawyer will direct you to the most appropriate format for your particular business. However, it is important to know what your options are.

One of the main considerations is finding a good balance between keeping the administration simple and protecting your personal assets. It is impossible to establish general criteria to determine the legal form that your business should take, as each particular project will have its own characteristics and requirements. Remember that the decision which you do make will determine aspects such as the individual liability of the shareholders, the form of taxation payable and the amount of capital invested.

A COMPARISON OF THE DIFFERENT TYPES OF SPANISH COMPANY

Entity	Type	Number of Partners	Working Capital	Liability	Taxation
individual	Empresario Individual (sole trader)	1	no legal minimum	unlimited	Individual income tax
individual	Comunidad de Bienes (group of owners)	min. 2	no legal minimum	unlimited	individual income tax
corporate	Sociedad Colectiva (co-partnership)	min. 2	no legal minimum	unlimited	corporate taxation
corporate	Sociedad de Responsibilidad Limitada S.L. (limited-liability)	min. 1	min. €3,005.06	limited to the capital contributed	corporate taxation
corporate	Sociedad Anónima S.A. (Corporation)	min. 1	min. €60,101.21	limited to the capital contributed	corporate taxation
corporate	Sociedad Comanditaria por Acciones (limited partnership)	min. 2	min. €60,101.21	unlimited for some partners, limited for others	corporate taxation
corporate	Sociedad Comanditaria Simple (limited partnership)	min. 2	no legal minimum	unlimited for some partners limited for others	corporate taxation

Many small businessmen operate as sole traders or *empresarios individuales*. Indeed this format accounts for around 68% of the new businesses that are created each year. The main disadvantage of operating as a sole trader is that the owner of the business is personally liable for any debts which the business may accrue. In order to limit personal liability it is necessary to operate as a corporate entity. The most significant forms of larger business enterprise are the Corporation (*Sociedad Anónima* or *S.A.*), the Limited Liability Company (*Sociedad de Responsabilidad Limitada* or S.L.), the General Partnership (*Sociedad Colectiva* or S.C.) and the Limited Partnership (*Sociedad Comanditaria*). Traditionally the S.A. was by far the most commonly used form. However, in recent years the S.L. has gained popularity as a result of its lower minimum capital requirement and it is certainly the most convenient legal form for a small or medium sized business. Indeed, Chantal Becker-Cid, a Spanish lawyer who specialises in business creation for foreign clients, claims that of the new companies which are being formed in Spain at the moment, approximately 80% are S.L.s, 12% are S.A.s and the rest are a mixture of the other types of entity – '*I would always advise a new business to form an S.L. It really makes little sense to go for anything else these days, unless there is a specific problem with the type of business that you want to form*'.

Some of the most important features of the different corporate forms are summarised below. However, the *Instituto Español de Comercio Exterior* stresses that the law only provides general rules for business and that the founders of a company have a great deal of flexibility in tailoring the structure of the company to their specific needs.

INDIVIDUAL FORMS OF ENTERPRISE

Sole Trader (Empresario Individual)

The *Empresario Individual* is a sole trader, offering goods or services without being bound by any labour contracts or to any other business and assuming both the risks and the profits of his labour. Most very small business concerns will be better with sole trader status as it is the most efficient form for small businesses, and can be more economical. It is also the form with the least bureaucratic procedures involved in setting up given that no legal entity must be established that is distinct from the entrepreneur himself. Despite the name, a sole trader does not have to operate on his own, it is possible to take on employees.

The main advantage of this type of operation is that sole traders make their own business decisions and do not have to answer to anybody else. The fiscal obligations for a sole trader are also much simpler as the taxes which you have to pay are reduced only to the individual income tax, known as IRPF and VAT, known in Spain as *IVA*. There is no minimum amount of working capital required and no initial registration tax. Furthermore, there is much less red tape involved in setting up the business and this is a distinct advantage when compared to the complex bureaucracy associated with forming a limited company. You merely need to register for social security under the *autónomo* scheme and register for the IAE (tax on business activities). It is likely that you will not need to pay the IAE, which was abolished for smaller businesses in 2003, but it is still necessary to register. Finally in certain cases, the sole trader may have to obtain municipal licences, for example if you operate out of business premises you will need a *licencia de apertura*, an opening licence which certifies that the business premises are suitable for your business activity. *Empresarios Individuales* are not obliged to register at the *Registro Mercantil* as other businesses are, but your lawyer may advise you that it is opportune to register anyway.

The major disadvantage of working as a self-employed person or a sole trader, is that you do not have the protection of a limited company should your business fail. You are personally responsible for any business transactions, which in effect means that your personal income from whatever source, your house, your car and even your estate after your death can be used to pay off the debts of the business. You are also not entitled to unemployment benefit should the business fail, so it is important to consider worse case scenarios and seek professional advice before deciding on sole trader status over limited company status.

Comunidad de Bienes (Co-ownership)

A *Comunidad de Bienes* is a business which is not an independent legal entity and belongs to two or several proprietors who assume unlimited responsibility. The advantages of such a business are that there is no minimum capital contribution needed to set up and that the business association is at all times voluntary and can be dissolved at any point should one co-owner wish it. Also, the constitution of such a company is quick and simple, usually requiring only a verbal or written contract between the co-owners. Indeed, a public deed is only necessary where real estate is involved.

However, as with sole trader status, the members of a Comunidad de Bienes have unlimited liability for any debts which the business may accrue, should they be more than the value of the assets owned by the business itself.

In order to form a Comunidad the following steps are necessary (for further information on these steps see *Procedures for Starting a New Business*):

○   There must be a contract (verbal or written) defining the constitution of the Comunidad.
○   The business must obtain a CIF, the tax identification number, from the *Agencia Tributaria* (Tax Office).
○   Registration of the company at the census of taxpayers.
○   Registration for the tax on Business Activities (IAE). The Comunidad acts as a single unit and therefore it is the business that must be registered rather than the individual members.
○   Registration for social security purposes, bearing in mind that if you employ staff, they must be registered under the general regime, whereas the directors of the business must register as *autónomos*.

From a tax point of view, the Comunidad is not a legal entity so it is not liable for corporation tax. However, the VAT, known as *IVA* in Spain, will be declared for the whole company and the individual members of the business will have to pay income tax on their individual earnings.

LIMITED LIABILITY COMPANIES

Sociedad Anónima (S.A.)

The Spanish *Sociedad Anónima* is the equivalent of a British public limited company (plc) or an American corporation (Inc.). This is a widely used form of business entity in Spain and is used for investments in major projects. This option is only really advisable for experienced businessmen making a large investment. The minimum amount of share capital required is €60,101, as opposed to the €3005 needed to establish an S.L. The capital must be fully subscribed and at least 25% of it must be paid in at the time of incorporation. Participation is represented by shares that qualify as negotiable securities. Furthermore, shares of an S.A. may be quoted on the stock exchange (*Bolsas de Valores*). Shareholders can be individuals or companies of any nationality and residence. There is no minimum number of shareholders required by Spanish law, although sole shareholder companies are subject to a special system (see box below). Contributions may be made in the form of money, goods or intellectual property, which can be valued.

Shareholders are not personally liable for the company's debts other than to the extent of their capital contribution.

The shareholders or their representatives are obliged to appear before a notary public in order to execute the public deed of incorporation. This deed is subsequently registered in the Mercantile Register giving the company legal status and capacity. Further details of how to incorporate your company can be found in *Procedures for Starting a New Business*.

The corporation must have a Board of Directors (*Consejo de Administración*), joint directors or a sole director, and a Shareholder's General Assembly (*Junta General de Accionistas*). The company bylaws set out at the time of incorporation will identify the people initially entrusted with the management and representation of the company. Any amendment to the bylaws must be approved at a Shareholders' General Meeting. The shareholders' meeting appoints the S.A.'s directors, who cannot serve for more than five years.

For two years after incorporation, the company's shareholders' meeting must grant prior of approval for any acquisitions of assets involving amounts in excess of the 10% capital stock. In such cases there should be an independent valuation by an expert appointed by the Mercantile Register and the directors must issue a report for shareholders.

The obvious disadvantage of the S.A. is that the business is held accountable to its shareholders. The shareholders have certain basic rights which must be observed under Spanish corporation law. Obviously these include the right to a share in corporate earnings and also in the assets in the event of liquidation, as well as preferential rights to subscribe new shares. However, they also have the right to obtain information about the company's affairs and to attend and vote at shareholders' meetings, held every year, and to challenge corporate resolutions.

Sociedad de Responsabilidad Limitada (S.L.)

The S.L. is a far simpler form of incorporation with a reduced capital and often a reduced number of shareholders. As a result, it is the ideal way to enter the entrepreneurial world without running huge risks and this is the form which the majority of smaller and medium sized companies in Spain will assume. It is also worthwhile noting that an S.L. can always be upgraded to an S.A. after a few years, if the business is very successful.

In 1995, a new law was passed which overhauled the legal framework of the S.L. One of the main objectives of this law was to create greater flexibility in terms of setting up and the rules concerning the internal governance of the company. As a result, the S.L. has become far more popular than it was previously and around 80% of newly incorporated companies are S.L.s.

Technically, the capital of an S.A. is divided into shares whereas the capital of an S.L. is divided into participation units. These units may not be represented by means of certificates, nor considered securities. The participation units need not all be equal and consequently they carry different voting weight. The liability of the share-holders is limited to the individual portion of capital invested. Whereas shares in an S.A. are usually freely transferable, this is not the case with the participation units of an S.L., which may only be transferred to other unit holders. Only shares of an S.A. can be listed on a stock exchange. Participation units of an S.L. cannot.

As mentioned above, the minimum capital required for incorporation of an S.L. is €3005.06. There is no maximum capital and some larger companies choose this business structure as a result. Again, the share capital must be fully subscribed but in contrast to the S.A. the capital must be fully paid up at the moment of incorporation. Only one shareholder is required but there is no limit on the number of shareholders.

Shareholders have the right to participate in company decisions and the right to be elected as company administrators. They also have the right to company information at regular intervals which are established in the deeds of incorporation.

A further advantage is that the S.L. is subject to less reporting and auditing requirements than the S.A.

S.L.s are incorporated in much the same way as an S.A. and full details of the necessary steps to setting up can be found in the chapter, *Procedures for Starting a New Business.*

SOLE SHAREHOLDER COMPANIES

Both S.A.s and S.L.s may be set up as, or can consequently become, a company having a sole shareholder or a sole participation unit holder. However, it is important to get specific legal advice. Unless you follow the correct procedures, the company may lose its limited liability status and you may find yourself personally liable for the company's debts. It must be written into the company's articles that the business is *unipersonal* in order to give some defence against creditors.

Sole shareholder companies are subject to a specific regime involving special reporting requirements and registration requirements. These include the obligation to acknowledge single owner status on all company correspondence and commercial documents. Furthermore, contracts between the company and its sole owner must be recorded in a special company register.

Sociedad Limitada Nueva Empresa (S.L.N.E.)

The S.L.N.E. is a specialised version of the S.L. designed to be set up quickly and at a lower cost (see *Procedures for Starting a New Business*). The legislation surrounding this legal entity is still quite new and as yet there are very few S.L.N.E.s in operation. However there are plans for expansion of the project in the future and for simplifying the every day accounting requirements for such businesses, so it is likely that this form of business entity will become more popular.

The S.L.N.E. is very similar to an ordinary *Sociedad Limitada*. One of the major differences is that the name of the company is restricted. The company name must be made up of the name of one of the company's founders plus a numerical code which is issued. The capital is divided into participation units, which cannot be traded publicly, and the liability of each shareholder is limited to his capital contribution. However, in order to keep the S.L.N.E.s quite small in size, the maximum number of share-holders is restricted to five at the moment of incorporation. The minimum capital required to incorporate an S.L.N.E. is €3,012, similar to an S.L. However there is a maximum total capital of €120,202 and all capital must be made up of monetary contributions (not goods or intellectual property).

The main advantage of the S.L.N.E. is that theoretically it is quicker and easier to establish. Currently though, this is only the case if your Spanish is very good and if your business entity is within one of the three regions where the *Ventanilla Unica Empresarial* has the necessary technology for on-line incorporation. A further advantage is that the structure of an S.L.N.E. is fairly flexible and allows for substantial change and development of the business activity without having to revise the company statutes. There are also a number of fiscal advantages to the S.L.N.E. However, despite plans to simplify the tax obligations for smaller businesses, such entities are still subject to complex corporation tax.

PARTNERSHIPS

Setting up a partnership allows two or more people to set up in business together sharing profits, management burdens and risks. The partnership must be based on ties of personal trust between the associates and for this reason it is the ideal legal entity for a family business, or a business run by friends with high aspirations but little capital. A partnership should not be undertaken lightly. It is necessary for partners to have complete confidence in one another as partners remain liable for all the debts of the business, not just for the half or third relating to their partnership share. Spain has two main types of partnership.

Sociedad Colectiva (General Partnership)

The *Sociedad Colectiva* is the simplest of the commercial entities. It is essentially an independent legal entity owned by two or more general partners, all assuming unlimited responsibility for the company. All partners are duty bound to participate in the management of the company, contribute that which was agreed at the moment of formation, refrain from competing against the partnership and accept joint liability for the company's debts. In return, partners take a share of the profits.

The partnership must be formalised by public deed and registered in the Companies' Registry. The steps necessary to form a partnership are almost identical to those for forming a company and are detailed in *Procedures for Starting a New Business*. The name of a partnership is made up of the names of all the partners or some of them with the expression '*y compañia*' added. The names of non-partners may not be included.

Partnerships pay corporation tax, which is currently 35%, or 30% for smaller entities.

Sociedad Comanditaria (Limited Partnership)

The *Sociedad Comanditaria* is very similar to the General Partnership described above, in that it is an independent legal entity owned by more than one partner. However, in this case, ownership is divided between one or more general partners who assume unlimited responsibility and one or more limited partners whose liability is limited to the amount of capital contributed but who play no part in managing the company.

There are two types of limited partnership. The first is called a *Sociedad Comanditaria Simple*, and the second a *Sociedad Comanditaria por Accione*s. In the latter, the contribution of the silent partners is divided into public shares. The minimum capital necessary to form this kind of partnership is €60,101, which must be fully subscribed and at least 25% of it paid in at the time of incorporation (as with an S.A.).

In a Sociedad Comanditaria, the general partners are subject to exactly the same rights and obligations as partners in a Sociedad Colectiva. Again the name of the partnership is made up of the names of the general partners. The names of the silent partners cannot feature.

The limited partnership must be formally constituted by public deed of incorporation and registered in the Companies' Registry. As such, these partnerships are subject to pay corporation tax at either 35% or the reduced rate of 30%.

ALTERNATIVE METHODS OF DOING BUSINESS IN SPAIN

There are a number of ways of establishing a business presence in Spain without actually forming a separate legal entity. For example, a foreign businessman might form an association with other entrepreneurs already established in Spain, known as a joint venture, or a foreign parent company might choose to set up a branch of the company in Spain. Indeed, an investor wishing to operate or distribute goods in Spain need not even physically establish a centre of operations there. There are various alternatives including signing a distribution agreement, operating through an agent and operating as a franchisor. Each of these forms of doing business in Spain offers distinct advantages and problems from both a legal and fiscal perspective.

For British investors, the best way to gather information on such enterprises is by contacting UK Trade and Investment, either at the British Embassy in Spain (C/ Fernando el Santo 16, 28010 Madrid; ☎ 917-008200; fax 917-008272; www.ukinspain.com), or before you leave in London (Kingsgate House, 66-74 Victoria Street, London,

SW1E 6SW; ☎ 020-7215 8000; www.uktradeinvest.gov.uk). They have staff working throughout Spain whose aim is to help British exporters of goods or services win business in the Spanish market. They will be able to advise you on appropriate strategies to enter the market and put you in touch with key contacts in Spain such as local representatives, agents and distributors. They will also advise you on setting up a branch in Spain.

Branch Offices (Sucursal)

As well as the numerous forms of business enterprise created under Spanish law, foreign investors may operate in Spain through a branch. Unlike a company, this organisation is not a legal entity of its own, but depends on a head office. It is therefore subject to the legislation of its country of origin. The branch must have a legal representative, empowered to administer the affairs of the branch,

Generally speaking, the requirements, procedural formalities, accounting and initial costs for a branch are very similar to those for a corporation, and a branch operates much like a corporation in its dealings with third parties.

The choice between forming a branch or a legal entity in Spain may be affected by commercial reasons. For example, some may see a company as providing a more solid presence than a branch. The main legal differences between a branch and a separate company are set out below:

Legal Status: a branch is not a legal entity and has the same legal identity as its parent company.

Minimum Capital: whereas an S.A. requires a minimum capital of €60,101 and an S.L. requires €3,005, a branch does not require any minimum assigned capital.

Liability: whereas the liability of the shareholders of a subsidiary incorporated as an S.A. or an S.L. is limited to the amount of capital contributions they make, in the case of a branch, there is no limit to the parent company's liability.

Tax: both a branch and a company are generally taxed under Spanish corporate income tax at 35% on their net income. However, there are some other aspects of taxation which require special mention. If the parent company is non EU-resident, it is possible that remittance of branch profits may be taxed at 15%, though many non EU countries have tax treaties with Spain, in which case remittance is not taxable in Spain. Also, in general it is easier for the parent company's overheads to qualify as deductible in the case of a branch.

Registration of a Branch

The requirements for the constitution of a branch are the same as for setting up any other business in Spain (see *Procedures for Starting a New Business*). As with a new Spanish company, a branch must be set up through a public deed, executed before a public notary and registered at the Companies' Registry. As well as the documents required at the incorporation of a new company (i.e. evidence of the identity of the person appearing before the notary, their power of attorney, the method of contribution), the following documents will also be required for the registration of a branch:

- A copy of the deed of incorporation and articles of association of the foreign partner.
- A copy of the minute of the foreign company's Board of Directors' meeting establishing the decision to open a branch in Spain, including the capital assigned to it, the name of the general manager and his powers.
- A certificate from a Spanish bank showing that the transfer of capital assigned to the branch has been deposited in a bank account.

The incorporation deed and the foreign company's bylaws must be translated into Spanish.

As with the formation of a new company, the following procedures must be followed before beginning operations:

- The branch must be assigned with a tax identification number.
- Transfer tax must be paid.
- The branch must be registered at the Companies' Registry.
- The branch must be registered for the tax on economic activities

(IAE).

o The branch must be registered for VAT purposes.

o Payment of opening licence tax.

o Registration for social security purposes.

o Compliance with labour formalities.

Joint Venture

Foreign investors often find that a joint venture with a Spanish company allows the parties to share risks and combine resources and expertise. Many choose to use a Spanish corporation or limited liability company as the vehicle for joint ventures. However there are a number of different options available, according to Spanish legislation, when it comes to cooperation between companies:

Temporary Business Associations (UTEs): Such projects are very common for engineering and construction projects, although they can be used in other sectors as well. UTEs are defined under Spanish law as temporary business cooperation vehicles set up for a specified or unspecified period of time in order to carry out a specific project or service. They allow several companies to work together in one common project, although each company will keep its legal status. They are not corporations and they have no legal personality, but they are formed by deed in the presence of a notary public and are registered in a special UTE register held by the Spanish Ministry of Finance. They may also be registered at the Companies' Registry.

UTEs must comply with all of the accounting and bookkeeping requirements that a company complies with.

Economic Interest Groupings (EIGs): These differ from UTEs because they are separate legal entities. However, they are not-for-profit companies and may only be created in order to help the members achieve their objectives. The EIG is most commonly used to provide a centralised service within the context of a wider group of companies, for example centralised purchasing, sales, information management or administrative services. Like a UTE, they must be formed by a deed of incorporation witnessed by the notary and entered in the Companies'

Registry. The members of an EIG are personally and severally liable for the entity's debts.

There is also a European EIG (EEIG), with its own legal personality, which was established by the European Commission as a means of encouraging cross border cooperation between businesses in different parts of the EU. It differs from the EIG because it is governed by EU regulations rather than Spanish company law. The EEIG is totally free to move around the EU member states.

Silent Partnership (Participation Account Agreement). Many foreign entrepreneurs choose this route, which involves providing monetary or 'in kind' contributions to another entrepreneur in order to share an interest in the activities carried out. This interest may be either positive or negative, depending on whether there is a profit or loss on the business activity. These contributions are not the same as capital contributions and investing as a silent partner does not therefore make you a shareholder. In fact this type of agreement does not require any legal formality such as incorporation or registration. However, in practice, it is fairly common for both parties to reflect the agreement in a public deed.

Other Methods of Investing in Spain

Distribution Agreements. Under a distribution agreement a company operating in Spain will undertake to achieve wide distribution of a product or service belonging to the foreign investor. This method offers foreign investors an attractive means of entering into commercial cooperation with previously existing entrepreneurs for carrying out their operations in Spain, as the initial investment required is very low. There are several broad categories of distribution agreements:

- *Exclusive distribution agreements.* The supplier provides his product to only one distributor within a specified territory.
- *Sole distribution agreements.* As above, but the supplier reserves the right to supply the products himself to the specified territory.
- *Selective distribution.* This applies only to certain products which

require special handling and distributors are carefully selected in order to preserve an image or brand name.

Generally distribution agreements are fairly unregulated and allow the parties discretion to decide on the contents of the contract. However, the provisions which may be included in a distribution agreement are as follows:

- Details of supplier and distributor.
- Payment terms in an agreed currency.
- A minimum volume of sales.
- Supplier's liability for defective products.
- Duration of the agreement.
- Law and jurisdiction applicable in the case of a dispute.
- The geographical area covered by the agreement.

Note that it is important to protect your intellectual property when signing a Spanish distribution contract as your home country protection may not be valid. Local legal assistance on this issue is a must.

The income for the non-resident supplier of goods is usually not taxable in Spain.

Agency Agreements. These are agreements where an agent negotiates commercial operations on behalf of another, without assuming the risk of those operations. This is therefore another useful method of expanding your business operation into Spain without the complications of establishing a legal entity there. An agent is duty bound to safeguard the interest of your company and not act for companies offering similar goods or services without agreement. They can be paid a fixed sum, a commission or a combination of the two.

Agency contracts can be indefinite or they can last for a specified period of time. Indefinite contracts may be terminated at any time by either party as long as there is prior written notice. Under some circumstances it is possible for the agency agreement to include a non-competition provision to restrict the professional activities of the agent for up to two years after a contract has ended.

Generally a non-resident of Spain using a Spanish agent will record business income in Spain on the sale of goods and this tax income will usually not be taxable in Spain. The law and jurisdiction applicable in the case of a dispute is usually that of the company's home country, rather than Spain.

Franchising. Another possible way of marketing goods and services in Spain is to franchise. As a franchisor, it is possible to sell the concept of your business to those wishing to set up in Spain. The Spanish business will be legally and financially independent from you, but there will be close co-operation between the two enterprises. Franchisees pay to use your brand name or trademark and business procedures in return for ongoing provision of commercial and technical assistance. The individual franchisees are obliged to do business under your rules and guidelines.

The 1998 Royal Decree on franchises in Spain set out the following stipulations:

O That the franchisee has access to a common business name or sign and standardised presentation of the premises or transport.
O That the franchisor transfer his or her business know-how.
O That the franchisor gives continued provision of commercial or technical assistance during the term of the agreement.

The franchisor must have written information which franchisees are sent before deciding whether or not to sign a contract. As a franchisor you will receive:

O The initial registration fee, a one-off payment for joining the franchise network.
O Royalty fees which continue as long as the franchise lasts and range from four to twenty per cent of the revenue.
O Advertising fees are often paid annually to the franchisor. These rarely exceed three per cent of gross sales.

Anybody operating a franchise in Spain must be registered with the Franchisor's Register run by the Directorate-General of Internal Trade of the Ministry of the Economy, who will issue you with a certificate and supply public information to the Autonomous Communities and to interested parties. This must take place a maximum of twenty days prior to the signing of the franchise contract, otherwise the franchisor is liable for serious fines for non-registration.

The tax status for the franchisor however is fairly complex and should be analysed by an accountant as the amount paid by the franchisee could be considered royalties rather than business income and therefore taxed in Spain at 25% or the reduced tax treaty rate.

Acquiring a Business or Business Premises

CHAPTER SUMMARY

○ The number and variety of existing businesses for sale in Spain is quite staggering. The majority are undoubtedly bars, cafés and restaurants but there are literally hundreds of specialist business agencies with all kinds of enterprises on their books.

○ **Buying an existing business:** brings a number of advantages, such as reduced risk, immediate cashflow, an established customer base and existing licences and permits.

○ Anyone planning to buy a business should obtain an independent valuation. Never take actual or projected figures at face value. Many people in Spain fail to keep accurate tax records.

○ **Commercial estate agents:** offer a full pre and after sales service to the potential entrepreneur.

○ Location can make the difference between success and failure in the early years of a business, so entrepreneurs should research the area and its potential.

○ There are leasehold, freehold and rental businesses available on the market. By far the most common is the lease, largely because it is cheaper and is easy both to buy and to sell on later if required.

○ **Franchises:** are growing rapidly in Spain with around 5000 new franchise establishments set up every year. There are a huge number of franchise opportunities available.

○ The Spanish make a strict distinction between the business and the premises. Those who buy an existing business tend to pay a lump sum for the fixtures, fittings and 'goodwill' and then rent the building which houses it.

○ For new companies, it is far more common to rent business premises than to buy due to the initial expense.

○ **Contracts:** for the purchase of a freehold are often short, containing the details of the vendor and purchaser, the

> purchase price, a legal description of the property, the date set for completion and the type of payment.
>
> O The cost of renting office space, retail outlets and other commercial premises in Spain compares very favourably with other European countries.
>
>   O All rental contracts are for a fixed term, which is agreed between the two parties.

Many people choose to take over an existing business, which is one of the simplest and quickest ways of setting up although it has certain disadvantages (see *Possible Types of Business)*. The Spanish make a strict distinction between the business and the premises. Those who buy existing businesses tend to pay a lump sum for the 'goodwill' or reputation and customer base of the business and then rent the building which houses it. However, it is possible to buy both the business and the premises, or to buy or rent just the premises for your own business venture.

The relative cheapness of property is a compelling reason to start a business in Spain. For those in the commercial sector, the location and cost of the property that they choose will play a crucial role in whether or not their business succeeds. In the early years of a business, weak cash flow is the main killer and keeping your fixed overheads low is therefore crucial.

FINDING A BUSINESS OR BUSINESS PREMISES

There are a huge number of specialist business agencies throughout Spain, and many real estate agents also sell businesses. The best place to start looking is the publication *Dalton's Weekly*, sold in newsagents, which comes out every Thursday and costs £1. The 'Business Abroad' section is made up mostly of companies and individuals selling businesses in Spain and its islands. Other UK national publications also list a few businesses for sale such as *Exchange and Mart* and *The Daily Telegraph*.

The English-language press in Spain is a useful source of classified advertisements offering leasehold and sometimes freehold businesses and often empty *locales* (business premises). For a full list of the

English language press in Spain see *Marketing Your Business*. If you are researching from outside Spain, some of the newspapers' websites include classified advertisements. For example, it is possible to access the business opportunities advertised in both the *Costa Blanca News* and the *Costa del Sol News* at www.costablanca-news.com/property-business.htm. More specifically aimed at the Costa del Sol, *Sur in English*, is Málaga's daily English language newspaper and its website, www.surinenglish.com, has a classifieds section including businesses for sale. For the Canary Islands, try *Island Connections* (www.newscanarias.com).

Major Spanish newspapers such as *El Pais* (Miguel Juste 40, E28037 Madrid; www.elpais.es) and *ABC* (Serrano 61, E28006 Madrid; www.abc.es) also include some advertisements for businesses for sale.

Although some preliminary research and investigation can be done from outside Spain, it is essential to visit the country on at least one inspection trip before making a shortlist. For those considering the purchase of any business connected with tourism or leisure, as many expatriate businesses tend to be, it is particularly important to see how the business varies seasonally. Remember that you will still have to pay the rent, rates and salaries for any employees even in periods when there are far fewer customers.

Commercial Estate Agents

There are literally hundreds of specialist business agencies selling businesses of all kinds and empty *locales* (premises). For those looking simply for commercial property, rather than an existing business, the list is much longer as most of the residential real estate agents also deal in commercial premises. What follows is merely a selection.

A2Z Properties: Avda. Europe, Benissa 03720; Alicante; ☎965-733492; fax 965-732890; e-mail a2zproperties@wanadoo.es; www. a2zpropertiesspain.com.

Bizbalears: Avenida Rei Jaime I, 100, Santa Ponsa, Calvia, Mallorca; ☎971-699881; fax 971-699882; e-mail office@bizbalears.com; www.bizbalears.com. Business sales and support in Mallorca, Menorca and Ibiza.

Business Finder Mallorca: Gran Via 24, Port Adriano Village, 07182 El Toro, Mallorca; ☎971-234543; freephone from UK 0800-1982082; fax 971-237207; e-mail info@businessfindermallorca.com ; www.businessfindermallorca.com. Commercial transfer agents and valuers for bar and catering businesses, clubs, discos, shops, hotels, yachting, industry, investments, with over eighteen years experience in the Baleares. Leasehold prices range from laundrettes at £7,000 to yacht brokerages at £220,000.

Costa Blanca Business Consultants: Avda. Alfonso Puchades 27, Ed. Coblanca 26, Local 7, 03503 Benidorm; ☎966-812190; fax 966-804386; www.costablancabusinessconsultants.com. One of Spain's foremost commercial property brokers, dealing with the sale, lease and rental of bars, cafes, restaurants, hotels and all other types of business.

Diamond Commercial Specialists S.L.: C/ Poeta Salvador Rueda 53 Bajo, Los Boliches, Fuengirola, 29640 Malaga; tel/fax 952-665574; freephone from UK 0800-6528817; e-mail info@diamondcommerc ials.com; www.diamondcommercials.com. Commercial estate agent selling businesses on the Costa del Sol.

Global Property Services S.L., Calle Casablanca Bajo 307, Edificio la Nogalera 29620, Torremolinos, Malaga; ☎952-382208; fax 952-058355; e-mail info@global-properties-spain.com; www.global-properties-spain.com. A family-run company specialising in the sale of commercial and residential properties on the Costa del Sol and inland.

Jaime and Sheldon S.L., C/ Palmira 6, Local 1, Paguera, 07160 Calvia, Mallorca; ☎ 971-686210; freephone from UK 0800-9175148; fax 971-686192; www.jaimeandsheldon.com; info@jaimeandsheldon.com. Professional, ethical and friendly, English owned and run, legally registered Spanish company, with a first class after-sales service.

Javeamar Properties: Avda. de la Fontana, 6-bajo 1, Javea; ☎ 965-793521; fax 965-793195; e-mail info@javeamarproperties.com; www.javeamarproperties.com.

Lanzarote Bar and Restaurant Agency: Calle Panama, Las Gaviotas D32, Costa Teguise, 35509, Lanzarote; ☎ 928-827291; e-mail info@lanzabar-agency.com; www.lanzabar-agency.com. Commercial property brokers in Lanzarote.

Marbella Now Property Consultants: Local 24, Marbella Real, crta-N-340-km178, Marbella 29600; ☎ 952-903290; fax 952-902090; www.marbellanow.co.uk.

Property Network Spain S.L.: Calle Mercurio, Edificio Pueblo Sol Fase 2, Local 77, 29631, Arroyo de la Miel, Benalmádena, Malaga; ☎952-447722; fax 952-446101; e-mail benalmadena@propertynet workspain.com; www.propertynetworkspain.com. The website links over 75 agents across Spain and the Balearic Islands selling both businesses and residential property.

Medbars: MPS Properties, Avda. Los Boliches, Nº 48, Los Boliches – Fuengirola; ☎952-663534; fax 952-566912; e-mail info@mpsproperties.com; www.medbars.com. Business sales on the Costa del Sol.

Portico Properties S.L.: 33-35 CC Trebol, Avda Alfonso Tavio, Costa del Silencio, Arona, Tenerife; tel/fax 0871-717 4224; www.porticoproperties. com. Business transfer and residential property agent in Tenerife.

Property Scene S.L.: Ctra. Cabo La Nao Nº64-2b, 03738 Javea, Alicante; ☎966-470770; fax 965-771779; e-mail enquiry@property-scene.com; www.property-scene.com.

Salvador Perez Gestion Inmobiliaria: C/ Marqués de Campo 15, Apartado de correos 73, 03700 Denia, Alicante; ☎966-4211656; fax 966-422002; e-mail sperez@salvadorperez.com; www.salvadorperez.com.

Spain Business Network: Shaftesbury Centre, Percy Street, Swindon, SN2 2AZ; ☎01793-554762; Spain: Nº228, Ctra Denia-Ondara KM1, L-19, 03700 Denia, Alicante; e-mail ajb@spainbusinessnetwo rk.com; www.spainbusinessnetwork.com.

BUYING, LEASING OR RENTING A BUSINESS

The number and variety of existing businesses for sale in Spain is quite staggering. Whilst the majority are undoubtedly bars, cafés and restaurants, even the most cursory of glances in the window of a commercial estate agency will expose the enormous diversity of businesses available to foreign buyers. For lease there are fully stocked supermarkets at around €50,000 and video rental shops for around €100,000. For sale, there are charter boats for €200,000 and car parks for nearly six million euros. There are nightclubs, tea shops, boutiques, gift shops,

hairdressing salons, laundrettes, gymnasiums, internet cafés, estate agencies, car rental companies and hotels. Almost every imaginable business comes up for sale at some point if you know where to look.

Buying an established business can be less risky and much easier than setting up a new one. The obvious advantage is that you are buying a business that is already producing an immediate cash flow and has an established customer base. Most entrepreneurs would agree that the hardest thing about starting a new business is that it can take years to establish a reputation and clientele. During those years many have to survive on virtually no profit and work exceedingly long hours just to make ends meet. Buying an established business helps to avoid those lean years. The risk is also reduced because studying the accounts of a business will allow you to analyse the past performance of a business before buying.

As well as reduced risk, an immediate cash flow and an established clientele, there are numerous other advantages. These include an established location, existing licences and permits, existing suppliers and equipment and sometimes even trained employees.

The advantages of buying an existing business. Tim Stonebridge, Diamond Commercial Specialists S.L., Fuengirola

Normally people come to us looking for an up and running business because they are already established and have an existing client base. In terms of paperwork, it is also much less hassle. All you have to do is to transfer the licence to the name of the new owner.

Obviously if they are looking for an empty local (premises) *then we can find one, but to obtain a new opening licence it is necessary for an architect to submit a project to the town hall and it can take up to six months to receive an answer. You will require sanitary and health inspections and even after all the waiting they may still turn you down.*

If you take over a business with a current licence, then everything will be up and running much quicker.

In spite of all of these apparent advantages, buying a business that is a going concern is not by any means easy and the need for comprehensive research cannot be over-emphasised. Small Spanish businesses are usually passed from generation to generation and are rarely sold to foreigners, although the leasehold may be. The other problem is that thriving Spanish businesses are not usually sold without a very good reason. It is imperative that the buyer finds out what this is before signing anything. More often than not the reason will be that the business is failing, or there may be a hidden motive such as imminent construction works, which would adversely affect the performance of the business. You should always check local planning permissions for roads, housing developments, rival businesses, factories and anything else that may affect your business.

Anyone planning to buy a business should certainly obtain an independent valuation. Never take actual or projected turnover or profit figures at face value, especially if they are provided by either the current owner or the estate agent. Theoretically the company's books will show the past performance of a business before you buy it. Unfortunately this benefit is almost entirely negated by the fact that in certain businesses, very few people keep accurate tax records. The declared turnover for tax purposes is often lower than the actual turnover. According to John Howell & Co. Solicitors and International Lawyers (The Old Glass Works, 22 Endell Street, Covent Garden, London WC2H 9AD; ☎ 020-7420 0400; fax 020-7836 3626; www.europelaw.com), the tendency to under-declare income in order to pay less tax is so rife that it is very difficult to obtain an accurate idea of the value of the business. The business owner will usually tell you what they consider to be the actual turnover, but whether they are telling the truth is an entirely different matter.

There are many factors affecting the value of a business. It is fairly easy for example to put a value on the tangible assets such as equipment, fixtures, inventory and so on. However, intangible assets such as the reputation of the business, its customer base and its strength within its own competitive market, are the most valuable. It is these assets which will produce your cash-flow and are the best indicator as to whether the business will sink or swim. Other factors, which a buyer should take into consideration, include location, lease terms or possible ownership of premises, competition, reputation, years in business, the industry's outlook for the future, special permits and terms of sale.

In order to ensure that you are paying the correct price for a business, it is better to take professional advice about the viability of a business from an accountant, gestor or lawyer.

Choosing a Commercial Estate Agent

It may seem very tempting to buy privately, especially with so many businesses on the market, but unless you speak the language very well and have a great deal of experience in business, it is advisable to use an agent. A reputable agent will ensure that your business has all the relevant paperwork and will make you less vulnerable to some of the con merchants that operate, especially on the Costas where businesses change hands very rapidly.

Agents take a commission from the vendor rather than the potential buyer, so you should not hand over any money to them. Potential buyers should thoroughly check the credentials of the estate agent that they intend to use before employing them. Some agents will sell businesses that they are fully aware are not viable, safe in the knowledge that the buyer has little or no protection against things going wrong. There are even a large number of illegal agents. For example around 44% of the commercial estate agents selling businesses to foreigners in Mallorca operate illegally out of small apartments, so be sure to check them out carefully.

Many agents however, do offer a full pre and after sales service and some even offer domestic support packages, helping you with non-business related matters such as finding somewhere to live, healthcare and schooling etc.

The range of pre and after sales services that commercial estate agents offer varies enormously and should be considered when choosing an agent to help find your ideal business (see below).

If you do decide to buy a business without the help of an agent, then it is certainly essential that you employ a *gestor*, to help you establish that the business is free of debts and holds the appropriate licences which can be simply transferred. One of the most common errors that people make when buying a business without using an agent, is that they hand over the 10% deposit to the vendor, thereby running the risk of losing that money if the vendor decides to sell to someone else. Most agents will ensure, and you can personally ensure, that the deposit is lodged at the *gestoría* until the day of completion, when the money is transferred to the vendor.

SOME OF THE SERVICES OFFERED BY COMMERCIAL ESTATE AGENTS

Pre-Sales Service	After Sales Service
Advice and assistance.	Application for Opening Licence transfer.
Discounted inspection trips.	Application for residence permits.
A personal meeting to discuss your business requirements and budget.	Registration with the Social Security Office and Tax Office.
Personal tour of a range of suitable businesses.	Help to arrange advertising, publicity and printing.
Advice on good local legal services either from a lawyer or *gestor*.	Help to arrange any necessary alterations to the premises.
Thorough check of exactly what is for sale – leasehold, freehold or rental contract, fixtures and fittings, stock, 'goodwill' etc.	Help to arrange the transfer of electricity, water and telephone contracts where appropriate.
Thorough check that the business has no current debts (these would be transferred to the new owner).	Introductions to suppliers and help to negotiate introductory offers and discounts.
Planning check – that the business has a current Opening Licence, which can be transferred to the new owners. If not, they should help you to apply for a new licence.	Help with extras including: quarterly tax and VAT returns to be submitted; food handlers certificate (where necessary); guidance on matters not related to the business.

It may also be worth while taking advice from an English speaking business consultant. Whilst *gestores* are usually very reliable when it comes to performing tasks that you have specifically asked them to do, often they will fail to point out potential problems or suggest more efficient and cost effective ways to proceed. This is where business consultancies such as Start With Us (Avda. de Mijas 5a, 29630 Benalmádena, Malaga; ☎ 952-575306; www.startwithus.es2000.com) come into their own, with local knowledge and a background in business and management.

Choosing a Business

The first question you need to ask when analysing any business is 'why is it for sale?' Around 40% of new businesses fail so it is not unlikely that the answer will be that the business is losing money, whether or not that is what the accounts show. Obviously there are numerous other reasons why a business could be on the market, but it is in your interests to ask searching questions of the owners. Clearly you do not want to find yourself lumbered with a poorly located business that has changed hands several times in a short space of time.

Because of the intangible nature of the 'goodwill' involved in a business transfer and the unreliability of Spanish accounts, it is not an easy task to assess an existing business. Unlike in the UK or France, there are no hard and fast rules for valuing a business. In most cases the vendor of a business will dictate the price based not on the intrinsic value of the business's tangible and intangible assets but based on recovering what he paid for it with a little extra to cover the transfer fee to the freeholder and the agent's fee. This leads to the fairly ludicrous situation where the price of businesses snowballs by 5% or so each time it changes hands, regardless of whether or not the business has been successful. Many entrepreneurs will sell a business on at the same price, or even higher even if the business has been failing. Unfortunately the demand for businesses is so great that they can usually get away with this. It is essential that the potential buyer has his wits about him as paying more than a business is worth is one of the principal reasons for businesses failing at an early stage. The majority of the businesses sold to foreigners are bars and restaurants in the resort areas and these are notorious for changing hands every six months or so. Agents have very little influence over the price of a business but the good ones will inform you if a business has been on the market for a long time, or if they consider it to be over-priced.

Due diligence. To accurately evaluate whether you are getting a good price you will have to take into account the following factors:

- Cost of 'goodwill' for a freehold and a leasehold business.
- Cost of rent (for a leasehold or rental business).

- Previous three years accounts (and their accuracy).
- Running costs (based on previous years books and your own estimates).
- Insurance.
- Employee's contracts.
- Stock/inventory.
- Credit to customers.
- Working capital requirements.

The 'goodwill' includes the customer base and the reputation of a business, but there are other intangible assets included in a business transfer such as the name of the business, the location, the right to continue a lease and so on. The contract should state exactly what these intangible assets are. Even something as simple as a promise from the existing owner that he will not set up a similar business around the corner has value and should be negotiated into a contract. There are numerous horror stories of former leaseholders taking all of their clients with them and decimating the clientele of the new business. The equipment needed to run the business and the stock are tangible assets and are simpler to value.

Assessing the value of 'goodwill' is so hit and miss that Glen Reader of Property Network, Málaga advises his clients not to factor it into their decision: *'You should look upon the business as an empty shell. Ignore the goodwill and focus purely on what you think you can do with the business. Then any benefits of the goodwill are a bonus'.*

Location. The most important of the intangible assets is almost certainly location. A greengrocer's has little future if it is next door to a supermarket and bars and cafés rely on passing trade. Admittedly businesses that have built up a reputation rely more and more on people seeking them out, so location is not so important. In the early years of a business though, it makes the difference between success and failure and potential entrepreneurs should research the area and its potential, both during and outside of the tourist season. If not, you could end up losing everything.

> **Location, location..... Rita Hillen, Hostal Los Geranios, Torremolinos.**
>
> *When you are buying a new business you have to put the location first. This is difficult because you are new to the country and you don't know the nuances of different areas. You have to wait. You have to stick around. You cannot buy a business within three weeks or a month. You have to look, talk to people, do some investigation for yourself. People come here in a great rush – they want to start making money straight away. No. It's better to take a couple of months to take in the different areas and the amount of trade for a particular business. People come and look at bars in the summer when the sun is shining and the sky is blue. You have to wait until it's raining to get a true picture.*

Turnover. As mentioned previously, the Spanish often do not keep accurate records of the business turnover. Many businesses will not even allow you to see the books and even if they do there is no guarantee as to their accuracy. According to Jerry Whitehouse of Jaime and Sheldon, commercial estate agents (see above), there are ways around this. For example, many bars will have a 'day book' in which they record the takings for every single day. Such books are only for the business owner's personal use, not for the tax-man and are therefore likely to give a more accurate reflection of takings. Ask also to look at purchase invoices, see how much stock the business regularly needs to buy and the value of assets which have been invested in. Another handy tip is to look at the takings on any games machines or jukeboxes etc. in a bar or restaurant. Although you cannot investigate this personally, your agent can contact the companies that distribute and manage these machines and such information will give a rough approximation of the business's client base.

WHAT TYPE OF CONTRACT?

As in the UK, it is possible to buy the business and then either lease the premises or buy the freehold for the premises. Rental businesses also occasionally appear on the market. By far the most common situation is the leasehold, largely because it is considerably cheaper and is easy both to buy and to sell on later if required. Even if it is within your budget to consider buying a freehold, it might be worthwhile to opt first for a lease and then trade up later, especially if this is your first Spanish venture. Some contracts offer a leasehold with a view to purchase, which allows the buyer to agree a price with the vendor at the start of, for example, a five year lease. When the lease expires the buyer can then trade up at the original agreed freehold price.

Unless you are buying a freehold, you will not need to employ the services of a Notary Public because the contract you sign will be a 'private contract'. Nevertheless, it is advisable to employ the services of a solicitor or *gestor* to check the contents of the contract and ensure that the business is free from debt.

Leasehold

The Spanish lease is known to most as a *traspaso* (transfer), although it is now officially called a *cesión* (cession). If you buy a cesión, then the landlord still owns the shell of the building, for which you will pay him a monthly rent but you own everything else. The lease can be anything from five to twenty-five years and sometimes it is for an indefinite period. However, five or ten years is the normal lease period these days and leases can usually be renewed for another term without payment of a further premium. Note that the operator of the business who sells you the leasehold in many cases is not the actual owner of the premises. If you lease directly from the owner, then you usually have the automatic right to renewal when the term is up.

> **Terms of the lease.**
> The term 'traspaso' sometimes causes confusion to foreign entrepreneurs and Spaniards alike. Many seem unaware that the law has changed and that in fact the word traspaso itself no longer has any legal significance. All lease agreements are called cesións and have no set formula. The exact terms of the lease must therefore be specified to the letter in the contract.
>
> There are still traspaso contracts around which people may try to sell you, but unless the contract specifies the exact terms of the lease, it is worthless.

When taking on a lease it is a good idea to negotiate as long a contract as possible. Although the landlord will usually renew the lease for another term, often the contract in fact says that this is only 'con mutuo acuerdo' – by mutual agreement and therefore the landlord can refuse to renew the lease if he is not happy. Also, when a lease does run out, the landlord can raise the rent considerably, whereas during the term of a lease he can only raise it with inflation.

During the agreed period of your lease, the rent can only increase by the annual 'cost of living index' as published by the Spanish government, currently around 2% to 3%. During your term as the leaseholder, you will be responsible for the service charges of the business, which may include gas, electricity, water, council taxes, your own taxes and social security payments. The landlord will usually be responsible for real estate taxes, but study the contracts to make sure of this.

One important difference between the *traspaso* and a UK lease is your position if the lease is broken. In the UK you can be held responsible for the full term, regardless of what happens but in Spain you normally need only give two months notice and you are then able to pass the property back to the landlord. As the leaseholder, it is possible to sell the lease to someone else as long as it is written into the original contract. However you must first offer it to the landlord at the same price as your prospective purchaser has offered. The landlord always has first refusal. If you do sell the lease, you normally have to pay a commission to the landlord of between five and twenty per cent of the sale value. The landlord will normally agree a new lease term to the buyer as per your original contract, for example ten years, rather than the balance of the years remaining.

As the leaseholder you must abide by certain laws. Firstly, you are responsible for the licensing of the business. You should ensure that all necessary licences have been obtained before signing a contract, or at least make the contract provisional on the necessary licences being granted. You cannot structurally alter the building without the owner's permission, nor can you sublet the business. The landlord cannot terminate the lease for any reason other than non-payment of the rent. If you miss three payments then the freeholder is entitled to take you to court and have you removed from the premises.

Costs. A 10% deposit will be required to secure the purchase of the lease and the balance is usually payable in 30-60 days. Should you change your mind once the deposit has been paid, then you will lose that money, although if you do not complete because there is a problem with the contract, then you should not lose your deposit. Upon comletion, the landlord must be paid a security deposit of two month's rent and your rent will be paid monthly in advance.

For a normal business transfer you should allow approximately €1,220-€1,400 (£750-£850) for legal fees, which will include the preparation of the new lease contract on the premises, licence transfers, *residencias* and NIE, social security and census registrations, plus any other necessary documents.

For many businesses such as bars and restaurants, sufficient working stock is normally included in the sale price. If not, you will have to calculate the initial price of stock.

On the agreed date, the outgoing tenant will sign a release document relinquishing the rights of the lease and the purchaser will sign a new lease agreement with the landlord. Payment in full should be made at this stage and the lease, business and fixtures pass to the new owner.

Freeholds

Freeholds are far more difficult to obtain as quite often the Spanish consider rental income from leasing a business as their pension or inheritance for their children.

The freehold is more expensive than a lease but has the obvious advantage that there is no monthly rent to pay. Another benefit is that the freeholder always has the option of selling the leasehold of his business, for which he will receive a one-off payment for the lease and a monthly rental income. Freeholders also often write a sell-on fee into the contract, so that they profit every time the business lease changes hands. The value of this fee varies, but it can be as high as 20%.

A further advantage of owning a property is that whilst the real estate boom continues even if the business is not a success you are likely to make money on the property, which may be rising in value by as much as 20% each year. Those who lease a business also have the disadvantage that they may not get back any money that they spend on improving the premises. With a freehold this is not the case.

Estate agents tend to advise that if you have the money and you are sure about the property, then take the freehold when it is offered. Freeholds are so rare that many businesses still find themselves leasing after twenty years or so.

Costs. You should allow an extra eight to ten per cent of the purchase price for transfer taxes, legal and notary fees. The purchase of a business is almost identical to that of buying commercial property detailed below. The only real difference is that when purchasing an existing business the cost will be much higher than if you were simply buying a property because you are paying for tangible assets such as existing licences and also the intangible assets such as the reputation and existing client base of the business.

On the agreed completion date both parties will attend the office of the notary public in order to sign the *escritura de compraventa* (the title deed). Note that the notary public will not check the details of the purchase but will confirm that both parties have agreed to them. Payment is made in full at this stage, usually via a bankers draft or guaranteed bank cheque and possession passes immediately to the purchaser.

Rental Businesses

These occasionally appear on the market and the contracts are usually renewable on an annual basis. Some contracts have a 'try before you buy' option to purchase the freehold, built into them. Often landlords will ask for a year's rent in advance and the deposits required are often substantial, although refundable upon return of the business to the owner. This is because with a traspaso, you have effectively bought all of the fixtures and fittings within the building. With a rental however, the landlord needs some guarantee against any potential damage done to the premises, fixtures and fittings. A fair amount of initial capital is therefore required to rent a business.

Tim Stonebridge of Diamond Commercial Specialists S.L., does not recommend renting a business: *'Rentals come onto the market fairly infrequently and when they do, they are often in poor locations. I would not usually advise someone to rent a business, mainly because there is less security. You could spend a lot of money building up a thriving business and then the owner could decide not to renew the contract. All of your hard work would have been for nothing'.*

UNDER-DECLARATION OF TAXES – A WORD OF WARNING

Any potential buyer of either a commercial property or a going concern should be aware of the heavy cash culture that exists in Spain. The reality is that often Spanish accountants do not see their job as to present accurate accounts for their clients, but to minimise their clients' tax obligations. As a result, when buying you may well be advised to only declare around 70% of the price, so that the vendor receives a reduced capital gains tax and *plus valia* bill and you, the buyer, pays less VAT at 7%. Buyers of a leasehold may even find that they are advised by the vendor, the agent or their accountant to pay the entire amount in cash and avoid paying tax altogether.

The short-term advantages of this method are clear, but the procedure is highly inadvisable. Apart from being illegal, you are also running the risk of shooting yourself in the foot later on when you come to sell. Capital gains tax is calculated by subtracting the purchase price from the sale price. If you have under-declared at purchase then clearly you will have to pay capital gains on a far higher amount.

BUYING A FRANCHISE

An alternative to buying an existing business or starting a new business is to buy a franchise. 'Business format franchising' is the granting of a licence by the franchisor to the franchisee allowing them to trade under a specific trade mark or trade name. This licence usually includes an entire package comprising all of the necessary elements to establish a previously untrained person in the business and to run it for a predetermined period. Each business outlet is owned and operated by the franchisee but the franchisor retains control over the way in which the products and services are marketed and sold.

The franchise is one of the most rapidly growing business concepts in Spain though it only really started to take off in the 1980s. There are currently over a thousand franchise chains operating out of 48,388 locations in Spain, but it is still a growth area and around 5,000 new franchise establishments are set up every year. In the last six years alone, the number of franchises has doubled. A huge number of franchise opportunities are available in Spain, in the following sectors: travel agents, estate agents, food, beauty and cosmetics, training and education centres, health centres, fashion, construction, furniture and textiles, sports, pharmacies, photography, hostelry and restaurants, printing, jewellery and accessories, cleaning, office supplies, bakeries, theme parks, services, specialist shops, dry cleaning.

Pros and Cons of Buying a Franchise

The major advantage in setting up a business as a franchisee is that there is less risk involved and the failure rate is considerably lower. One of the major stumbling blocks for totally new enterprises is the difficulty in building up a reputation and client base in the early stages. However, as a franchisee you will be supplying a product or service that has already proven to be popular, using a system that has already proven to be successful, and trading under an established and possibly well-recognised brand name. Of course, all of this comes at a cost, but the initial franchise fee also covers your training, help to obtain, equip and stock the premises and on-going support.

The high success rate of franchises also means that it will be easier to raise the money to start your business. Banks are fully aware that they face less risk in lending to franchisees and as a result offer far better lending terms. *Franchise World* magazine states that they will often lend on a ratio of 2:1 and sometimes better, rather than the normal start-up rate of 1:1. The backing of a franchisor will also help you to gain suitable premises for your business. Landlords are sometimes hesitant to lease to people starting out on their own for the first time.

Whilst the franchise may well be a safe option for those with little business experience or limited capital, there are a number of drawbacks. The more experienced businessman may find it incredibly frustrating to lack free rein over the decision making process and how the business is run. A franchisee has very little option but to stick rigidly to the system as set out in the franchise manual and to accept sporadic changes. The franchisor will have access to your figures and may run regular security and quality checks to ensure that you are not under-declaring your royalties, or failing to meet operating standards.

There is also the issue of royalties to the franchisor, sometimes as high as 10% of the turnover, which may eat drastically into your profit margin.

It is not then, an issue to be taken lightly. Franchise terms can vary greatly amongst companies and some may not be favourable.

ADVANTAGES AND DISADVANTAGES OF BECOMING A FRANCHISEE

Advantages	Disadvantages
One of the simplest ways of running your own business if you have limited knowledge of the business world. Good franchisors will offer comprehensive training programmes.	Although it is your own business, you will be constrained by the franchisor's system.
You can talk to existing franchisees before you buy and investigate the pros and cons of a particular chain.	Your business is part of a chain and the image and reputation of that chain as a whole is in somebody else's hands.
The business already has a proven position in the market and a recognisable brand, making it easier to obtain start up capital and premises.	The franchisor has access to your figures and may run regular security and quality checks.
There is less risk because your business will benefit from the brand name and you will be following a path that has proved to be successful in the past.	You must commit to a certain number of years on the franchise contract. If you decide to quit, to re-sell or lease the franchise, you will be subject to any penalties agreed in the contract.
You will benefit from the financial backing of a large organisation. Small businesses cannot usually afford to buy in bulk or spend large amounts on research and development or marketing.	You must pay a franchise fee to join the network and then continue paying royalties throughout the contract period.
You will receive ongoing technical support.	You may be required to make publicity contributions.

Finding a Franchise

There are a number of sources of information and advice for potential franchisees in Spain. A good place to start, if your Spanish is not up to much, is by contacting the British Franchise Association (Thames View, Newtown Road, Henley-on-Thames, Oxon RG9 1HG; ☎01491-578050; fax 01491-573517; e-mail mailroom@british-franchise.org.uk; www.british-franchise.org.uk). Although their main role is to provide information on franchises in Britain, they have some useful general advice available in English. Information in English is also available from the European Franchise Federation (Bd. de L'Humantie 116/2, 1070 Brussels, Belgium; ☎+32 2523-9707; e-mail eff-franchise@euronet.be). The EFF is an international non-profit association, whose role it is to promote franchising in Europe and to exchange information between the European national federations and associations.

   A list of all of the franchise chains currently operating in Spain can be obtained from the Spanish Franchise Association, *AEF* (Avda. de la Ferias s/n, PO Box 476, Apdo 476, ES – 46035 Valencia; ☎963-861123; fax 963-636111; e-mail aef@feriavalencia.com; www.franqui ciadores.com). The website has listings for every Spanish franchise. To access this information, visit the above website and select '*Franquicias 2004*'. Each listing includes the following information:

- Company information – company nationality, location of the head office, name of the director of franchises, how long the business has been going, countries covered by the franchise.
- Requirements of the business premises – minimum area in square metres, minimum population in the surrounding area, acceptable locations.
- Financial data – franchise fee, royalties, marketing royalties, minimum necessary investment.
- Other facts of interest – number of establishments under this franchise, duration of the franchise contract, annual turnover.

There are a number of other useful websites with information in Spanish only, including: www.tormo.com; www.quefranquicia.com;

www.franquiciadirecta.com; www.franquicias.net.

For any further professional advice regarding franchises, contact a group of specialist franchise consultants such as *Tormo & Asociados*, Consultores en Franquicia (Cardenal Marcelo Spinola 42, Madrid; ☎ 913-834140; e-mail mcuadrupani@tormo-asociados.es; www.tormo-asociados.es).

Choosing a Franchise

Choosing a franchise is a fairly personal decision and depends on factors such as personal interests and location. However, once you have made a short-list of potential companies, you then have to make a judgement on the quality of the companies and their products and services. You should also consider whether they cater to a market which is likely to grow in the long term. Ask the franchisor to disclose to you his financial record, the records of the Directors and the basis of the financial projections they make on your particular franchise.

The simplest way to assess the business and also the franchisor's ability to run it is to talk to other franchisees. One of the major advantages of the franchise is that you have this opportunity to get a good idea of exactly what running the business will entail, so speak to as many people as possible in order to reduce the risk of being hit by any nasty surprises. Try to find out how many franchisees have left in the last twelve months, whether the sales projections have been realistic and whether the franchisor delivers on his promises.

Another huge factor is of course the costs involved. In order to help analyse the viability of your franchise agreement, the likely franchise costs are set out below:

O **Canón de Entrada.** The franchise fee is paid at the outset and can vary tremendously. Sometimes it can even vary within a franchise, depending on the characteristics of the business premises. Some of the smaller Spanish franchises will not charge a franchise fee and will simply skim off royalties. Nevertheless, the majority of franchisors will charge a fee somewhere between €3000 and €60,000.

O **Royalty de Explotación.** Franchisors also take ongoing management service fees. Most franchises charge a monthly percentage of the turnover, which is usually around 5% (although it can be as much as 10%). Some franchises though will make a fixed monthly charge regardless of income.

○ **_Royalty de Publicidad._** One of the advantages of having the commercial backing of a larger company is that they will take care of the marketing and advertising costs, on a local, regional or even national scale. Nevertheless, many of the larger franchises will charge from 0.5% to around 5% of turnover. Others make a fixed, annual publicity charge.

○ **_Inversion Inicial._** Finally, all franchises will require a minimum amount of investment capital to help get the business started. This is not a payment, but your money which you are investing into your business. However, it will often cover furnishings, installations and decoration, all of which are dictated by the franchisor. The initial investment will vary depending on the size and reputation of the franchisor. Some demand an investment of as little as €25,000 and others could require as much as €500,000.

These are just the costs of the franchise. Remember that you may have to pay more money in legal fees should you decide to run the business as a legal entity rather than run it on your own. Also remember that the business premises will be a huge expense. Although the franchisor gives guidelines as to the minimum size of the premises (_local_) and the characteristics of its location (_ubicación_) and may help you to find the most appropriate _local_, ultimately the premises are your responsibility.

Having found a suitable franchise agreement, it is always a good idea to have it checked over by a specialist lawyer.

Master Franchises

Those with more ambitious business plans might like to consider running a master franchise. This entails importing a foreign franchise concept into Spain and establishing a new network of outlets. In the UK many of the most successful franchise operations such as Domino's Pizza and Kall Kwik have been imported from abroad by British master franchisees.

As the master franchisee, you would act as the franchisor in Spain, recruiting and training your franchisees in the development of their business with the help of your parent franchisor. Whilst admittedly the costs and responsibilities of such an enterprise would be far greater, so also would the potential for growth of the business. However, such a manoeuvre would require a great deal of financial planning and market research and certainly should not be undertaken by someone with little business experience.

If you are looking for a master franchise, a good place to start is the British Franchise Association (Thames View, Newtown Road, Henley-on-Thames, Oxon RG9 1HG; ☎ 01491-578050; fax 01491-573517; e-mail mailroom@british-franchise.org.uk; www.british-franchise.org.uk). The BFA has a large number of international contacts and also a list of BFA members who are seeking international franchisees for their businesses.

BUYING BUSINESS PREMISES

For new companies, it is far more common to rent business premises than to buy due to the initial expense. However, this decision depends very much on the type of business that you intend to run and in the current economic climate, buying any property can be a good investment. Buying commercial property follows identical regulations and procedures to buying residential property, so if you already have a house in Spain, you will know what needs to be done (see Dan Boothby's *Buying a House in Spain*; Vacation Work Publications; 2003). Spanish law stipulates that if any income is derived from receiving customers at the premises, then it is a commercial property and this will be stated on the deeds. For example, businesses with accommodation such as a hotel or a shop with a flat above are classed as commercial properties.

Costs of Buying

Total inclusive costs (lawyers, land registry, *notario*, taxes, bank charges, associates fees etc.) bring the overall costs of conveyancing to around 10% of the cost price of a resale property in mainland Spain, and between 7 and 9% on such properties in the Canary Islands. The cheaper the property, the greater the likelihood of that percentage rising due to the minimum charges imposed by lawyers and others involved in the conveyancing.

The typical costs involved in conveyancing are as follows:

- **Notary Fee:** for preparation of the title deed (usually around €500-€900).
- **Land Registry Fee:** dependent on the value of property (around €400-€800).
- *Plus Valia* **Tax:** paid to the municipality on the transfer of property. It is dependent on the value of the land on which the property sits. The vendor should pay this, but contracts of sale often try to impose the fee on the buyer. It can come to several thousand pounds and is usually around 0.5% on a property that last changed hands ten years previously.
- **VAT/Transfer Tax/Stamp Duty:** depends on the value of the property, the type of property and where the property is situated. There is no stamp duty threshold as in the UK. If you buy a new property from a developer, *IVA* is charged at the rate of 7% of the declared price. In addition, you will have to pay a further 1% for the Legal Documented Deeds Tax. If you buy a resale property, the transfer tax payable is usually 7%.
- **Sundry Expenses:** Registration with the Spanish Tax Authorities and obtaining a foreigners' identification number (NIE): This can be done by your solicitor for a fee. You should also allow another €300 to cover miscellaneous items such as fees for carrying out searches against the property at the Land Registry and Town Hall, bank charges etc.
- **Power of Attorney:** Granting your solicitor power of attorney, if you are not able to appear before the notary in person, will costs somewhere in the region of €200 to €250.

EXAMPLE OF COSTS ON THE PURCHASE OF A €125,000 PROPERTY

Notary Fees	Preparation of *escritura*, registering of ownership, stamp duty	€1,950
Legal Fees	Making searches on registries, preparation of *escritura*, translation of contracts, etc.	€1,250
Plus Valia	Capital Gains Tax levied by the Town Hall on increased value of land since last sold	€120
VAT (IVA) 7%	Payable on the declared value of the property	€8,750
Connection Charges	Water, electricity, gas, drainage, telephone	€425
TOTAL		€12,495
Fees exclusive of VAT		

Lawyers

It is very important to employ an *abogado* to look after your personal interests when purchasing business premises. A solicitor should check that the vendor of the property is the legal (and sole) owner of the property and whether there are any outstanding charges or bills on it. They should be able to check that the property has proper planning permission and all the necessary licences. They should check that the terms of the contract are fair and reasonable and prepare a report of their findings for the potential buyer's information. Given the go ahead, the solicitor can then arrange for currency to be transferred to Spain, the title deeds (*escritura*) to be transferred into the buyer's name and registered with the Land Registry and for fees and taxes to be paid.

A list of lawyers specialising in commercial law can be found in chapter three, *Procedures for Starting a New Business*. Be wary of using the services of a lawyer recommended by the vendor or their estate agent, as their impartiality may be, though probably isn't, questionable. Most abogados are found through recommendation. If your grasp of Spanish is shaky then you should definitely find a lawyer who speaks English. The lawyer will be able to:

- advise a client as to whose name should be registered as the owner of a property (the individual or the company) as ownership will have knock-on effects with regards to taxation.
- advise on how to pay for the property – whether through a mortgage, re-mortgaging, forming a company, cash, etc., and how to minimise costs.
- arrange for Power of Attorney should it be necessary.
- arrange for the signing of the *escritura* and making purchase payments, and may also be able to organise currency exchange and the transferral of funds from a buyer's home bank account into Spain.
- check that there are no cases pending against the property with regards to planning permission not having been obtained when the property was originally built.
- draw up the contract for the sale of the property.
- guide a client through the legal processes involved in buying property in Spain.
- look after the conveyancing procedures.

If you are hoping to buy property with land attached in a rural part of Spain then your lawyer will be useful in finding out about what the planning restrictions are in the area and if there are local bylaws in force with regards to water, grazing or hunting and access rights on the land. You will also want your lawyer to check out where property boundaries end and begin as these may differ from what has been written in the *escritura*, what the owners of the property believe, and what is registered in the Land Registry.

You should get your lawyer to check everything that is put on the table by the agents before signing anything. Don't rely on a notary to do the work that a lawyer would normally do. Another good reason for getting a lawyer is that they may well be able to advise you on the most financially beneficial way to deal with the conveyancing process, saving you money by guiding you through the taxation systems of Spain and the UK.

Lawyers fees

The fees charged by a lawyer for their work buying a commercial property are likely to be about 1% of the price of the property, although there may be a minimum charge (around £1,000). You will need to be aware that apart from the basic fee, should additional negotiations need to be undertaken on your behalf you will be charged. For example there may need to be further clauses added to a contract, or negotiations over the price of a property; if there are irregularities in the *escritura* these will need to be corrected before change of title can take place. There will also be correspondence generated between the solicitors and a mortgage company if you are taking out a mortgage and all these matters will incur further fees.

Consulates and embassies in Spain will hold lists of English-speaking lawyers in your locality. In the UK the Law Society (see useful addresses below) also holds lists of registered English-speaking lawyers in Spain. The *Consejo General de la Abogacia Española* (see below) regulates the legal profession in Spain and also holds lists of lawyers.

Useful Addresses

The Law Society: 113 Chancery Lane, London WC2A 1PL; ☎020-7242 1222; www.lawsoc.org.uk.

Consejo General de la Abogacia Española: C/Paseo de Recoletos 13, Madrid 28004; ☎915 232 593; fax 915 327 836; www.cgae.es.

Mr Stefano Lucatello, The International Property Law Centre, Unit 2 Waterside Park, Livingstone Road, Hessle HU13 0EG; ☎01482-350850; fax 01482-642799; e-mail internationalproperty@maxgold.com.

John Howell & Co Solicitors & International Lawyers, The Old Glass Works, 22 Endell Street, Covent Garden, London WC2H 9AD; ☎020-7420 0400; fax 020-7836 3626; www.europelaw.com.

Florez Valcarcel, Lawyer and Notario: 130 King Street, London W6 0QU; tel/fax 020-8741 4867.

CONVEYANCING

Contracts

Once you have found the right property, you will probably have to act swiftly to ensure that you get it, as at present there is a sellers market in Spain – the property market is booming and the larger cities are characterised by a lack of available office space and strong demand. However, never sign anything without having first sought independent legal advice. If there is for some reason such a pressing time limit that you may lose a property that you are interested in unless you sign NOW, then at least try to fax over a copy of the contract to your legal representatives. Contracts are often short, containing the details of the vendor and purchaser, the purchase price, a legal description of the property, the date set for completion and possession of the property and the type of payment involved in the sale.

There are three differing types of contract that you may be asked to sign at this stage:

- **Offer to Buy:** A formal offer to buy the property at a fixed price – the contract being valid for a set period of time. Should the vendor accept your offer then a non-returnable, negotiable deposit will be payable and the contract will become binding between the two parties.

- **Reservation Contract:** An agreement between the potential buyer of a property and the vendor or estate agent. This type of contract dictates that the property is taken off the market for a set period of time. A reservation fee is paid by the potential buyer, which, if a full contract to buy is signed within the set period, will count toward the full price of the property to be paid. If problems concerning the property are unearthed during the reservation period (such as the vendor not being the named owner on the *escritura*) and the potential buyer decides to pull out, then the reservation fee will be lost. The clauses in this type of contract, therefore, need to be carefully checked.

- **Private Purchase Contract:** A full and binding contract to buy. You will pay a negotiable deposit of around 10% of the purchase price, the balance to be paid on the signing of the *escritura*. Obviously, before signing such a contract you will want to get your lawyer to check it.

The contract will be prepared by either an estate agent or if you decide to buy privately from an individual, by the vendor's lawyer. Whichever contract is offered to you, have it presented to you in your mother tongue as well as in Spanish, and make sure that you have your lawyer check it before you sign. There may well be clauses that either you or the vendor will not accept and these will need to be negotiated, as will the purchase price and the amount of deposit payable.

There are strict conditions relating to the repayment of deposits. Make sure that you are informed of these by your lawyer. When paying a deposit ensure that the money is kept by the estate agent or legal representative of the vendor in a bonded account until the sale has gone through. This will guard against a crooked vendor, or estate agent, taking your deposit and then deciding to sell the property to someone else. Though they will be acting illegally, getting your money back through the courts may take quite a time and will certainly leave a nasty taste in your mouth.

If the vendor has a mortgage on the property then it is possible to transfer the mortgage and for you to take on exactly the same terms or to renegotiate with the lender better conditions. This is known as a *novación*. Alternatively you could choose the subrogation (*subrogación*), which entitles you to change to a different mortgage lender and obtain a new mortgage on the property, with better interest rates.

Registries. The Land Registry (*Catastro*) contains details of the physical and topographical details of a property as well as a valuation, while the Property Registry (*Registro de la Propiedad*) only holds the details of ownership and title. These two registries may have differing details of the same property and a potential buyer should check that the description of a property in the contract tallies with that in both the Property and Land Registries. It may take a month or so for the Land Registry to provide a *certificado catastral* outlining the boundaries and measurements of a property so you should ask for it as soon as you have found the property of your choice.

The Notary. The Spanish Notary Public, the *notario*, although a lawyer, does not give legal advice to either the vendor or the purchaser of a property. The job of the notario is to witness the signing of the title deeds (*escritura*) in his or her office located in the area where the property is being purchased and to deal with other administrative matters. Once the escritura has been signed, the purchase price of the property is then handed over to the vendor, or the vendor confirms that payment has already been received. Proof of payment is then noted down in the escritura which is then registered in the local Property Register. Before preparing the escritura, a notario will ensure that the purchaser has received the property as stated on the contract and that the vendor has received the correct purchase price. The notario will also advise on taxes that are due on the property.

Notaries collect their fees from the vendor and the purchaser and these fees are charged in accordance with a sliding scale of charges set by the Spanish government. These will vary depending on the price of a property and the amount of work the *notario* has done on behalf of the two parties in preparing documents. Note that not all notaries will speak English and you may need to be accompanied to meetings by a Spanish speaker.

Power of Attorney. The person buying or selling a property does not necessarily have to be present when the title deeds are signed in front of the notario and, for a fee, a Power of Attorney can be granted which will allow another person to attend on the vendors behalf instead. If a Power of Attorney has been arranged outside Spain, it will need to be witnessed and stamped by a notario in Spain.

The signing of the *escritura*. The date of the signing of the escritura will have been fixed in the contract to buy, though in reality the date may slip a little depending on the status of the checks on the property made by your lawyer. It should normally take place two to three months after signing the contract to buy a resale or new property but will take longer if you are buying off-plan. If there are problems such as sorting out ownership of the property or outstanding taxes on the property then this can obviously hold matters up.

When the notario has received all the documentation he or she needs to complete the escritura you should receive a draft copy, which it is advisable to have scrutinised by your lawyer to check that all is as should be. Though a notary is a trained lawyer who has taken further exams to qualify for the post of notary, it is not a requirement of the job to do the work of a lawyer. Make a last check on the property to see that everything is in order, that what was agreed as included in the purchase price in the contract of sale remains in or with the property (e.g. fixtures and fittings).

Once everything has been settled the vendor and the purchaser (or someone acting on their behalf who has been granted Power of Attorney) meet at the notario's office. The notary will read through the escritura after which the two parties will sign the document.

For properties that are ready for immediate occupation, full payment is made before signing the escritura and taking possession of the property. It may be that the money paid for a property is to be transferred to wherever in the world the vendor wishes to receive it. However, if the purchase price is paid into a Spanish account, then the importation of currency will need to be registered with the Spanish authorities and your solicitor should deal with this for you. Many people hand over a banker's draft at this point as it can be witnessed by the notario there and then, but other methods of payment are available. At the same time the notary will collect his fee and inform the purchaser of any taxes payable on the transfer of property. Remember that if the vendor is a non-resident there will be 5% withheld from the purchase price, which will be paid to the Spanish Tax Agency on the vendor's behalf due to Capital Gains Tax liabilities.

After the signing of the escritura, the payment of the purchase price and all fees, the notary will pass the purchaser a copy (*copia simple*) of the escritura and the keys to the property. The original (*primera copia*) will be sent to the Property Register and the new owner's name registered. It can take several months for the process of registering the change of title deeds as all taxes and fees must be paid before a property can be registered in the new owner's name. Once a certificate has been issued stating that the name of the owner of the property has been registered, the purchaser's lawyer should collect it and forward it on to the new owner.

RENTING BUSINESS PREMISES

When buying an existing business, leasehold contracts are very common and rentals are very rare. The reverse is true with premises for a new business. One bad practice that still exists in Spain is that estate agents and individuals will occasionally try to sell you a lease for empty business premises and offices. In most cases if you buy a lease for an empty *local* all you are purchasing is the rental contract. The lease is often worthless, so if you do pay an initial lump sum for the premises, make sure that the contract specifies exactly what you are paying for.

Costs

The cost of renting office space, retail outlets and other commercial premises in Spain, compares very favourably with other European countries. Clearly the cost of renting premises in the centre of Madrid is far higher than it would be in a small town, but even in the capital rent is far lower than many other European capitals and indeed has been coming down over recent years due to new commercial developments.

At the end of 2003, office space in Madrid cost around €324 per square metre, per annum. This compares favourably with €965 in London's West End and €686 in Paris. The cost of a high street retail outlet was also far cheaper, standing at €1,596 per square metre, per annum, compared to €3,108 in Oxford Street, London and €4,731 in Paris.

SUMMARY OF RENTAL LEVELS IN SPAIN (2003)			
City	Office / retail space	Average rent(euros/ sq. metre per annum)	Typical lease length (years)
Barcelona	Office space	280	3 to 5
	Retail (high street) premises	1,350	3/5/10
Bilbao	Office space	156	3 to 5
	Retail (high street) premises	1150	5 to 10
Madrid	Office space	312	3 to 5
	Retail (high street) premises	1,660	3 to 5
Malaga	Office space	180	3 to 5
	Retail (high street) premises	720	5 to 10
Palma de Mallorca	Office space	125	3 to 5
	Retail (high street) premises	700	3 to 5

Sevilla	Office space	144	3 to 5
	Retail (high street) premises	*1200*	*3 to 5*
Valencia	Office space	150	5 to 10
	Retail (high street) premises	*1200*	*5 to 10*
Zaragoza	Office space	120	3 to 5
	Retail (high street) premises	750	3 to 5

In some areas of Spain, the concept of business centres and serviced offices is beginning to take off. These offer office space to rent for a temporary period, either during the early stages of a business while more permanent premises are being sourced, or for the duration of a specific project. The amount of space and the fittings can usually be adapted to the needs of just about any small to medium-sized business. Spaces are offered fully equipped with computers, phones and fax machines, copying and printing services, full internet and ADSL connections. The centres also employ multi-lingual staff with practical local information who are experienced in international business.

Such centres can be found in all of the major cities and also in resort areas such as Marbella. They can be found on the internet simply by entering 'business centres' followed by the location.

Start small and build up. Richard Spellman, Ambient Media and Communications S.L., Madrid

For me, the main advantage to working in Spain is that my fixed costs are very low. There is no way that I could work in the centre of London, in a suite of offices for the same price as I do here in Madrid. Away from the capital prices are even lower!

It is a general rule of business here in Spain that you never re-dimension yourself more than you need to. Spain, although it is a growing economy, is still quite volatile and it is very difficult to make sales projections, so keep your fixed costs low. There is no compunction here about operating out of small premises, even an apartment, and you don't need pot-plants and girls in mini-skirts to make the business work. Start small, sign short-term rental contracts (you can always renew them) and build up slowly.

The Rental Contract

Renting business premises is very similar to renting a residential property. The main difference is that there is no such thing as short-term and long-term lets when it comes to commercial premises. All contracts are for a fixed term, which is agreed between the two parties. A further difference is the VAT situation. Spanish VAT (*IVA*) is not applicable to a domestic property, but it is applicable to commercial property. The law states that 1% of VAT must be paid to the landlord as part of the rent and the remaining 15% must be paid quarterly to the VAT office. The VAT returns of the landlord and tenant are then compared to make sure that they correspond. This method was established to try and prevent landlords from avoiding VAT by claiming that the premises were unoccupied.

The legal provisions on renting and letting business premises in Spain are contained in the Law of Urban Lettings (*Ley de Arrendamientos*) of 1994 and applies to all rental contracts made after 1 January, 1995. What follows is merely a summary and a lawyer should always be consulted before any contracts are signed. The landlord and tenant may make oral agreements about both parties' rights and obligations but it is always advisable to state the rental conditions in a written contract, drawn up by a lawyer or *gestor*. The contract should include the following information:

O   Details of the landlord and tenant.

O   Description of the property.

O   **The contract term**. Both parties should agree the term for which the property will be rented. However, if this is not stated then the contract will run for one year. If at the end of the period stated in the contract neither party has given notice of their intention to terminate the contract, then it will be renewed annually until either party decides to terminate it.

O   **Amount of rent and payment terms**. This should be agreed and detailed within the rental contract. If not, rent will be paid seven days before the end of each month. The landlord may not ask for more than one month's rent to be paid in advance. The landlord must give a receipt for each payment and these must be kept as proof of payment. Unless otherwise stated, the rent will increase only according to the consumer price index (inflation) for the first five years, and then according to what both parties have agreed thereafter.

o   Sometimes landlords will slip in a clause declaring that the tenant should pay any property taxes applicable to the premises. These should be paid for by the freeholder, so make sure that you understand exactly what extra costs you may be forced to undertake.

o   Any other legal provisions that the parties agree.

All rental contracts should be made before a lawyer or gestor and recorded at the Spanish Property Registry (*Registro de la Propriedad*). The landlord is within his rights to demand a security deposit, known as a *fianza*, which will be equal to two months rent. This will be returned when the tenant moves out, assuming that the property is in good condition.

Repairs. Generally the landlord must make all necessary repairs to keep the property in a suitable condition. However, if damage is caused by the tenant, then it is not the landlord's responsibility. The tenant is responsible for any small day-to-day repairs. The landlord should be notified of any urgent maintenance repairs that are undertaken to avoid any further damage to the property and should reimburse the tenant for these costs.

If the landlord decides to undertake any major repairs which may affect health and hygiene or the ability to use part of the property, then he must give three months' notice. The tenant may renounce the rental contract within a month of the notice, or may stay on at a reduced rent. These repairs entitle the landlord to increase the rent after the initial five years of the contract.

Subletting and transferring the rental contract. Unless specifically prohibited in the contract, the tenant may sublet the premises or transfer the rental contract to a third party without the landlord's previous consent as long as the landlord is given one month's notice. In these circumstances the landlord may raise the rent by 10% if the property is partly sublet and by 20% when subletting all of the premises or transferring the rental contract. When a rental contract is transferred to a third party, so then are all of the rights and obligations within the contract.

Sale of the premises. Should the landlord decide that he wishes to sell the property during the life of the rental contract, then the tenant has the right of first refusal, *derecho de tanteo*. In order to sell, the landlord must make an offer to his tenant, who then has thirty days to reply. If this offer is not made, then the tenant could have the sale annulled within one month of completion.

Tentant's right to indemnity upon termination of the contract. If your landlord decides not to renew the contract after the initial five year period, then he must pay an indemnity of an amount agreed in the original contract However, many rental contracts include a clause renouncing the tenant's right to this indemnity.

Revoking the contract. The contract may only be revoked by the landlord if the tenant fails to pay the rent or the deposit, rents the premises to a third party without the landlord's consent if required, deliberately causes damage to the property, undertakes repairs without the landlord's consent, or performs dangerous activities.

The tenant may only revoke the contract if the landlord fails to make the necessary repairs to keep the property in good condition, or disturbs the tenant's use of the premises.

Financing your Business

BUYING FOREIGN CURRENCY FOR YOUR BUSINESS ABROAD

If you're starting a business abroad for the first time, you've probably got enough to do without worrying about exchange rates. You've found your ideal location and secured the price of your property, and now all you have to do is look forward to making a successful start. Right? Well, partly. Somewhere along the line you will have to change your pounds into euros, and that's where even the best business plan can fall apart if you don't plan ahead. Whether you're importing and exporting goods, buying a property outright or buying from plan in installments, protecting yourself against exchange rate fluctuations can save you hundreds, if not thousands of pounds.

As you are no doubt aware, foreign exchange markets are by nature extremely volatile and can be subject to dramatic movements over a very short space of time. In some ways it's all too easy to leave your currency exchange to the last minute and hope that the exchange rates fall in your favour. But it makes good business sense to protect your capital and save yourself paying a lot more than you bargained for.

As a matter of course, many people will approach their banks to sort out their currency, without realising that there are more cost-effective alternatives in the marketplace. There are a number of independent commercial foreign exchange brokers who can offer better rates and a more personal, tailored service. Their dealers will explain the various options open to you and keep you informed of any significant changes in the market. They will also guide you through every step of the transaction so that you are ultimately in control and able to make the most of your money.

If you're still not convinced of how planning ahead can help you, take a look at the following example.

In recent history the euro stood at 1.54 and within six months had fallen to 1.38. Therefore, in just 6 months the cost of a €200,000 office location would have increased by over £15,000!

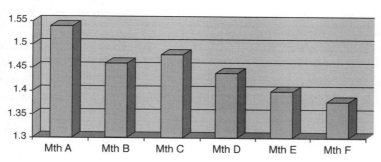

Although changes in the economic climate may be beyond your control, protecting your capital against the effect of these changes isn't.

There are a number of options available to you:

- **Spot Transactions – Buy now, pay now.** These are ideal for anyone who needs their currency straight away as the currency is purchased today at the current rate. However, if you have time to spare before your payments are due, it may be wiser to consider a Forward Transaction.
- **Forward Transactions – Buy now, pay later.** These allow you to secure a rate for up to 18 months in advance to protect yourself against any movements in the market. A small deposit holds the rate until the balance becomes due when the currency contract matures. This option not only protects against possible drops in the exchange rate but also gives you the security of the currency you need at a guaranteed cost, regardless of fluctuations in the market.
- **Limit Orders** allow you to place an order in the market for a desired exchange rate. This has the advantage of protecting you against negative exchange movements whilst still allowing you to gain from a positive movement. Your request is entered into the system and an automatic currency purchase is triggered once the market hits your specified rate.

With the stress of organising your business abroad you may find that you simply don't have the time to shop around for the best exchange rate, but that's where a reputable currency company can really come into its own. With specialists in the field ready to explain all the pitfalls and possibilities to you in layman's terms and guide you through each stage of the transaction, you can be sure that your currency solutions will be perfectly tailored to your needs.

Currencies Direct has been helping people to understand the overseas property markets since 1996. Specialising in providing foreign exchange solutions tailored to clients' individual financial situations, they offer a cost-effective and user-friendly alternative to the high-street banks.

With offices in the UK, Australia and Spain, *Currencies Direct* is always on hand to help you. For more information on how you can benefit from their commercial rates of exchange and friendly, professional service, call the *Currencies Direct* office in London on 020-7813 0332 or visit their website at www.currenciesdirect.com.

CHAPTER SUMMARY

- The majority of people starting new enterprises sell up at home and put everything into their news lives abroad. There are however, a number of other ways to finance your venture that may allow you a greater comfort zone.

- Spain is one of the most favoured nations in the EU when it comes to economic incentives and foreign firms are entitled to the same treatment as their Spanish counterparts.

- Numerous incentives and grants are aimed specifically at small and medium-sized enterprises (PYMEs).

- Large amounts of money will need to be imported into Spain to cover the costs involved in starting a business. Specialised currency exchange houses can help by offering a better rate than banks, without commission and giving you the possibility of 'forward buying'.

- **Banks:** It is still fairly difficult for a foreigner to get a bank loan for a business start-up unless they are prepared to put up a personal asset as security. A clearly-presented business plan will maximise your chances of obtaining financing.

  - Foreign businesses are more likely to obtain a loan from a savings bank. These offer a more personalised and friendly service than the clearing banks and are recommended for local businesses.

  - Opening a business account in the name of the company is done at the time of incorporation. The deed of incorporation requires a certificate from the bank proving that the start-up capital has been deposited.

  - Banking in Spain is sophisticated and modern, but bank charges cover just about every imaginable transaction and are notoriously high.

- The introduction of the euro and the lifting of nearly all exchange controls has allowed residents to obtain mortgages against their property in Spain from any bank in the world.

The scourge of new businesses throughout Europe is poor financial planning and a lack of cash flow. It is easy to get caught up in the excitement of a new venture and as a result fail to foresee every eventuality. The process of starting up a new business will always cost far more than you budget for and unless you are very lucky, the first few years will be a struggle. Indeed, many foreign businesses report that it can take years to even start making a profit. It is therefore vital to make a realistic and well-researched financial plan for the first three years. Although projecting how long it will take for the business to become profitable is easier said than done, if you are realistic and consider all of the worst-case scenarios then you will have a much greater chance of success.

The majority of people starting new enterprises sell up at home and put everything into their new lives abroad. There are, however, a number of other ways to finance your new venture that may allow you a greater comfort zone. This chapter discusses your financial options in some detail.

Whilst loans, mortgages and incentives are all available, no matter what the EU regulations say, as a foreigner any prospective financiers will regard you with much greater suspicion. Even the Spanish rely predominantly on personal and family financing. It is therefore advisable that you take local advice on your business finance options and use a *gestor* or accountant to guide you through the procedures.

OFFICIAL BUSINESS INCENTIVES, GRANTS AND SUBSIDIES

Spain is certainly one of the most favoured nations in the European Union when it comes to economic incentives and foreign firms are entitled to the same treatment as their Spanish counterparts. However, the decentralised nature of Spain's government creates a tangled web of grants offered by the European Union, the federal government, the autonomous regions and even municipal regions. Add to these a confusing array of region-specific subsidies, industry-specific grants, employment and training subsidies and tax credits, and it all appears just a little too mind-boggling to cope with.

The good news is that in theory there is plenty of aid available for new initiatives and there are a number of sources of advice and information to turn to. In practice however, actually obtaining the money seems to be far more difficult and even when a grant has been promised, it may be withdrawn at the last minute. Often, receipt of the subsidy is dependent on work having already started, or the money having already been paid. Should you manage to get the grant, it may well arrive up to two years after the investment has been made. It is therefore advisable not to factor official subsidies and grants into your plans when studying the viability of a business. The project should always be viable without the grant or subsidy and if one arrives it should be treated as a bonus.

How to Find Official Grants and Subsidies

There are numerous possibilities that exist for official financial aid, and the grants, subsidies and fiscal incentives that a business is eligible for vary greatly, depending on the individual circumstances of the business. They may also come from any number of different institutions and official organs. Look out for the occasional seminars which the Spanish government organises. These include advice from banks and lectures from established business people.

A good source of free information on official funding for businesses is your local Chamber of Commerce office, or the *Ventanilla Unica Empresarial*, part of the Chamber of Commerce in certain locations in Spain. These will be able to guide you through the types of funding available to your specific business and they will be happy to help, although they will not necessarily be able to do so in English. In order to find your nearest Chamber of Commerce, visit the website www.camaras.org and click on *Buscador de Cámaras*. A list of V.U.E.s can be found in Chapter 3, *Procedures for Starting a New Business*.

European Union grants. To search for European grants and incentives visit the website of the Dirección General de Política de la PYME (www.ipyme.org) and click on '*Inform. Europea*'. This allows you to search for European aid programmes relevant to your business. Alternatively visit the European Union on-line (www.europa.eu.int), select 'enterprise' and then 'grants and loans'.

At State level. There are a number of websites, available only in Spanish, which will help you to locate state grants and subsidies and allow you to tailor the search to a particular business or area. These include the virtual *Ventanilla Unica Empresarial* site (www.vue.es. Click on *ayudas y subvenciones*).

State business creation grants are administrated by ENISA, *Empresa Nacional de Innovación S.A.* (Paseo de la Castellana 141, 1º C, 28046 Madrid; ☎ 915-708200; fax 915-704199; e-mail enisa@enisa.es; www.enisa.es).

Grants dealing specifically with the creation of small businesses (PYMEs) are co-ordinated by the *Dirección General de Política de la PYME* (☎ 915-450937; www.ipyme.org).

Finally, any subsidies or grants based on job creation are controlled by the INEM, *Instituto Nacional de Empleo* (www.inem.es).

At Autonomous Community level. Most of the Spanish local investment promotion agencies are listed below, complete with websites. They will provide you with up-to-date information on local incentives:

Andalucía: *Instituto de Fomento de Andalucía (IFA)*, C/ Torneo 26, 41002 Sevilla; ☎955-030700; fax 955-030775; www.ifa.es.

Aragón: *Instituto Aragonés de Fomento (IAF)*, C/ Teniente Coronel Valenzuela 9, 50004 Zaragoza; ☎976-70 21 01; fax 976-702103; www.iaf.es.

Asturias: Instituto de Desarrollo Económico del Principado de Asturias (IDEPA), Parque Tecnológico de Asturias, 33420 Llanera (Asturias); ☎985-980020; fax 985-264455; www.ifrasturias.com.

Balearic Islands: *Oficina de Promoción Industrial*, C/ Reina Constanza s/n, 07006 Palma de Mallorca; ☎971-176507; fax 971-176154; www.idi.es.

Basque Country: *Sociedad para la Promoción y Reconversión Industrial, S.A. (SPRI)*, C/ Gran Vía 35-3º, 48009 Bilbao; ☎944-037000; fax 944-037022; www.spri.es.

Canary Islands: *Sociedad Canaria de Fomento Económico, S.A. (SOFESA)*, Consejería de Economía, Hacienda y Comercio, C/

Nicolás Estévanez nº 30-2º, 35008 Las Palmas de Gran Canaria; ☎928-307456; fax 928-307467; www.invertirencanarias.com.

ZEC Tenerife, Avenida José Antonio, 3 - 5º, Edificio Mapfre, 38003 – Santa Cruz de Tenerife; ☎922-298010; fax 922-278063; www.zec.org.

Cantabria: *Sociedad para el Desarrollo Regional de Cantabria, S.A. (SODERCAN)*, C/ Eduardo Benot 5-1º-C, 39003 Santander ☎ 942-312100; fax 942-217011/273240; www.sodercan.com.

Castilla La Mancha: *D.G. Promoción y Desarrollo Empresarial*, Avd. Río Estenilla s/n, 45071 Toledo; ☎925-269800; fax 942-267872; www.jccm.es.

Castilla – León: *Consejería de Industria, Agencia de Desarrollo Económico (ADE)*, C/ Duque de la Victoria 16-2º, 47001 Valladolid; ☎983-361233; fax 983-361244; www.jcyl.es/ade.

Cataluña: *Centro de Innovación y Desarrollo Empresarial (CIDEM)*, C/ Provenza 339-5º, 08037 Barcelona; ☎934-767284; fax 934-767303; www.cidem.com.

Consorcio de Promoción Comercial de Cataluña (COPCA), Paseo de Gracia 94, 08008 Barcelona; ☎934-849627; fax 934-849666; e-mail info@copca.com; www.copca.com/infoexport.

Extremadura: *Sociedad de Fomento Industrial (SOFIEX)*; Avda. José Fernández López nº 4, 06800 Mérida (Badajoz); ☎924-319159; fax 924-319212; www.sofiex.es.

Galicia: *Instituto Gallego de Promoción Económica (IGAPE)*, Complejo Administrativo San Lázaro s/n; 15703 Santiago de Compostela (La Coruña); ☎981-541180; fax 981-551190; e-mail dg@igape.es; www.igape.es.

La Rioja: *Consejería de Hacienda y Promoción Económica*, Agencia de Desarrollo Económico de la Rioja, C/ Muro de la Mata 13-14, 26001 Logroño; ☎941-291500; fax 941-291544; e-mail ader@ader.es; www.ader.es.

Madrid: *Instituto Madrileño de Desarrollo Económico (IMADE)*, José Abascal 57-2º, 28003 Madrid; ☎913-997400; fax 913-997459; www.investinmadrid.com.

Murcia: *Instituto de Fomento de la Región de Murcia*, Avda. de la Fama 3, 30003 Murcia; ☎968-362207; fax 968-366163; www.murcia-inversiones.com.

Navarra: *Sociedad de Desarrollo de Navarra (SODENA)*, Avda. Carlos III 36, 1º Dcha, 31003 Pamplona; ☎948-421942; fax 948-421943; www.sodena.com.

Valencia: *Instituto Valenciano de Exportación (IVEX)*, Plaza América 2, 7º, 46004 Valencia; ☎961-971500; fax 961-971540; www.ivex.es.

Incentives Aimed Specifically at Small and Medium-Sized Enterprises (PYMEs)

Recent years have seen a distinct increase in the interest shown both by the Spanish government and the Autonomous Community governments in promoting and developing PYMEs. A plan for 'the consolidation and competitiveness of the small and medium-sized enterprise' was launched for the years 2000-2006 and promotes the granting of certain incentives and aid schemes designed especially for the PYME. Small businesses may be the direct beneficiaries of funds for projects relating to innovation in business techniques.

It is the responsibility of the Autonomous Community governments to establish the rules governing these subsidies. Each community will accept applications in the first quarter of each year, process the applications and decide who is to benefit and finally distribute the funds. They also control and monitor the approved projects.

A further aid instrument for PYMEs sponsored by the public sector is the 'Linea PYME, allowing preferential access to official credit. PYMEs can finance up to 70% of their net investment projects with money borrowed from the Official Credit Institute (ICO, Paseo del Prado 4, 28014 Madrid; ☎ 915-921600; www.ico.es). A total of €3 billion is made available to PYMEs every year via this credit line. In 2003 the rates of interest were 0.4% for businesses with between one and nine workers and 0.5% for businesses with between ten and two hundred and fifty workers, to be paid back in a period of three, five or seven years.

The European Commission also runs programmes to help finance small and medium-sized enterprises, one such scheme is run by the European Investment Bank (EIB). The EIB grants loans to intermediary banks which in turn provide funding for small-scale business initiatives. Specifically in Spain these loans are routed through the ICO (see above), BSCH and BBVA (Spain's two largest banks. See *Banking* below) and Banco Popular. There are many types of loans and credits with varying maturities, amounts and interest rates, but generally they will cover up to 50% of the overall investment costs. Amounts awarded range from €20,000 to €12.5 million and must be repaid over a period of between four and twenty years. These loans are free of fees and other charges, except for minor administrative expenses.

State Incentives

There are a number of industry specific incentives granted by the central government, but the majority of these are aimed mainly at much larger businesses and industry, and cover sectors such as energy, mining, research and development, the audiovisual industry and tourism. However smaller businesses may be able to take advantage of the following aids:

Employment incentives. It is possible to make significant savings in labour costs through state initiatives. For example, the Spanish Central Government offers a wide range of employment incentives consisting mainly of reductions in employer social security contributions aimed at promoting the stable hiring of workers. Further information on this can be found in Chapter 8, *Employing Staff.*

Initiatives to promote activities of rural interest. There are a number of government incentives aimed at fostering the diversification of rural life consisting of incentives for investments and employment. The investment aid consists of interest relief on loans obtained to finance investments, of up to €72,121 for each full time job created. These benefits are granted by the Ministry of Agriculture, Fisheries and Food (www.mapa.es).

The employment aid is made up of up to 50% of the labour cost of jobs created in the first year, with a ceiling of €3,606. These subsidies are approved and paid by the relevant Autonomous Community governments.

Regional incentives. The economic disparity in Spain is very apparent. Whilst certain areas such as the Basque region, Catalonia and Madrid are the powerhouses of the country, three-quarters of Spain lags far behind in terms of economic development. A government run programme of special assistance for 2000-2006 has therefore been made available to these under-developed regions. The Economic Promotion Areas (ZPEs) are eligible for cash subsidies for a percentage of investment expenditure, usually between 40% and 50%. However, these incentives are really only aimed at larger investments (over €600,000) and therefore the majority of smaller businesses will not be eligible.

Autonomous Community and Local Initiatives

The Spanish Autonomous Community governments provide similar incentives on a much smaller scale for investments made in their region. These are usually granted on an annual basis. Each community has very distinct incentives and information on these can be obtained from local Chambers of Commerce and the above local investment promotion agencies. Job creation is almost always a vital prerequisite for such benefits. The main types of incentive are non-refundable subsidies, special loan and credit terms and conditions, technical counselling and training courses and tax incentives.

Local employment initiatives. There are numerous projects sponsored by autonomous communities and municipal governments aimed at generating economic activity and new jobs in local areas. Applications for these incentives must be filed with the National Employment Institute (www.inem.es), who select eligible projects. These projects must provide for the incorporation of a new company, for the hiring of new workers, for the production of products or services which either relate to emerging economic activities, or which cover unsatisfied needs of the area in the case of traditional activities. If the INEM agrees that a project meets all of these requirements, then it is possible to receive reduced interest rates on loans granted to the company relating to its incorporation, a subsidy for the support of management activities, subsidies for the hiring of highly-qualified technical experts and a one-time subsidy for each indefinite term employment contract amounting to €4,808 for each worker hired on a full-time basis. All of these incentives can be increased by 10% if the project is related to certain activities, among which are those connected with the protection of natural areas, waste management, collective transport, the development of local culture and the care of children, the handicapped and the aged.

Canary Islands Special Zone. The Canary Islands Autonomous Community enjoys a regime of commercial freedom involving tax exemption for retail activities and less indirect tax pressure. As a result the tax system in the Canary Islands Special Zone (ZEC) is distinct from the rest of Spain. For further details see *Tax, Social Security and Other Matters*.

The government is very flexible in granting regional incentives to the Canary Islands and investments in the peripheral islands require a much lower level of investment than the rest of Spain in order to receive subsidies. There are also special incentives aimed at upgrading the banana and tomato growing and fishing-related industries.

IMPORTING CURRENCY

Large amounts of money will need to be imported into Spain to cover the costs involved in starting or buying a business, and buying or leasing commercial property. When you find a business or property in Spain to buy, you will of course know the price in euros. However, until you have bought all of the euros you will need to pay for it you won't know the total costs involved. Depending on the exchange rate fluctuations between your home currency and the euro during the conveyancing procedures, the property could eventually cost you more or less than you had originally thought. Importing money into Spain can take time and there are various ways of going about transferring funds. Some solicitors can transfer money between accounts held at home and in Spain, and for many potential buyers this may be the quickest and easiest way of doing things.

Another method of transferring funds is to obtain a banker's draft from your home bank. This is a cheque guaranteed by the bank, which can be deposited into your bank account in Spain or anywhere in the world. When making the final payment on the purchase of a property at the notary's office it is advisable to hand over a banker's draft made payable to the vendor. Note that a banker's draft works along the lines of a cheque, and once it is paid into an account there will be a short period of waiting before it is cleared and you are able to access the money. You can also transfer money by SWIFT electronic bank transfer. This procedure can take several days and rates of exchange will vary. Unless you are conversant with Spanish banking procedures transferring money electronically may also lead to problems.

Because of currency fluctuations converting currency, for example sterling to euros, will always be something of a gamble. If the pound falls against the euro you will end up paying more than you budgeted for. If, as soon as you sign the contract to begin the process of buying, you convert the total cost of the property into euros you may be happy with the conversion rate but you will lose the use of the money while further negotiations take place over the settlement of the property or business.

To avoid this, a specialised company such as *Currencies Direct* (Hanover House, 73-74 High Holborn, London WC1V 6LR; ☎ 020-7813 0332; fax 020-7419 7753; www.currenciesdirect.com) can help in a number of ways, by offering better exchange rates than banks, without charging commission, and giving you the possibility of 'forward buying', i.e. agreeing on the rate that you will pay at a fixed date in the future, or with a 'limit order', i.e. waiting until the rate you want is reached before making the transaction. For those who prefer to know exactly how much money they will need for their purchase, forward buying is the best solution, since you no longer have to worry about the movement of the pound against the euro working against you. Payments can be made in one lump sum or on a regular basis.

There is a further possibility, which is to use the services of a law firm in the UK to transfer the money. They can hold the money for you until the exact time that you need it. However, remember that law firms will also use the services of a currency dealer themselves, so you may be better off going to a company like *Currencies Direct* yourself to avoid any excess legal fees.

Also remember that if the vendors of the property or business are

non-resident in Spain they are likely to want the purchase price paid
in the currency of their home country.

Exchange Control. Spain abolished all its laws on exchange control
in 1992 and at present there is no limit on the amount of foreign currency or euros which can be brought into Spain and no limit on the
amount of currency and euros which anyone is allowed to take out of
the country. However, any amounts over €6,010.12 are required to be
declared to customs within 30 days.

BANKING

All banking activity in Spain is controlled by the *Banco de España*
(Alcalá 50, 28014 Madrid; ☎ 915-385000; www.bde.es), which has
branches in all provincial capitals. Banks in Spain are divided into
clearing banks and savings banks (*cajas de ahorros*) and there are also a
number of foreign banks operating throughout the country.

The two banking giants in Spain at present are the BSCH (*Banco
de Santander Central Hispano*), which resulted from the merger of the
Santander, Central and Hispano banks, and the BBVA (*Banco Bilbao
Vizcaya Argentaria*). Other banks in Spain include the *Banco Atlántico*
and *Banco de Andalucía*. *Barclays*, Britain's third largest bank, also has
a very large presence in Spain, having bought out *Banco Zaragozano* in
2003. Most large towns will have at least one branch of these banks and
in the cities there will often be several branches, offering all the usual
banking facilities, including mortgages and internet and telephone
banking facilities. Standard bank opening times are from 9am to 2pm
on weekdays and from 9am to 1pm on Saturdays, although these may
vary from bank to bank.

Banks in resort areas and cities usually have at least one member
of staff who speaks English, however, those in rural areas generally
don't. Service in small local branches is often more personalised than
in larger branches and the staff less harried but smaller branches may
not offer such a choice of banking services.

There are now ATMs (automated teller machines) all over Spain
and you can usually even find them in the larger villages. Three
ATM networks operate in Spain – *4B* (the most common), *ServiRed*

and *6000* and you can generally use any ATM to draw money from your account, although there may be a fee charged. As well as cash withdrawals, paying cash into your account and consulting your balance, some ATMs now allow you to carry out other transactions such as renewing your mobile phone card or making theatre seat reservations. Spanish ATMs offer you a choice of language.

Bank Accounts

Those who are resident in Spain for tax purposes may open the type of current account (cuenta corriente) and savings account available to all Spanish citizens. Non-residents may only open the current and savings accounts available to foreigners (cuenta extranjera), which will still allow you to set up direct debits to pay utility bills while you are away and keep a steady amount of money in the country. However at a company level, both resident companies and branches with parent companies abroad are able to open similar accounts. Note that current accounts pay very little interest on the balance. Sometimes it is as low as 0.1%. It is therefore sensible to keep as little as possible to tide the business over in a current account and deposit the rest in a savings account.

The *Cajas de Ahorro,* are similar to British building societies and American savings and loans organisations. They usually offer a more personalised and friendly service than the clearing banks and are recommended for local businesses. The cajas have branches throughout Spain which, apart from the *Catalan La Caixa* and *Caja Madrid,* tend to be regional. Many of the savings banks actually started out as agricultural co-operatives and many still act as charitable institutions – investing part of their profits each year in social and cultural causes. They are therefore far more open to providing credit and overdrafts for individuals and businesses than the retail banks. The savings banks all issue a bank card enabling the holder to withdraw money from the ATMs that they operate.

For a short-term savings account you can open a deposit account (*libreta de ahorro*), from which withdrawals can be made at any time. Interest will also be added twice yearly to the average credit balance, but this is likely to be negligible unless the account balance is £1,000 or more. For larger amounts of money, long-term savings accounts (*cuentas de plazo*) and investment accounts are also available and will earn more interest, as the money has to be left in the account for an agreed period of time – probably at least six months. Obviously, the longer the money remains untouched the better the interest earned. Interest rates vary and the best rates are obtained from accounts linked to stocks and shares although, of course, there are associated risks of losing some or all of your investment.

INTERNET BANKING

Over recent years the use of internet banking in Spain has flourished. Spanish banks offer some of the most sophisticated home banking software in the world. This is largely because Spain was a fairly late developer in this area, so when they finally decided to establish internet banking facilities, they were able to do so with the most up-to-date technology on the market. Almost all banks offer internet banking and once you have set up an account with a username and password, it is possible to carry out most banking transactions online.

There are also a number of internet/telephone only banks operating in Spain such as *ING Direct* (☎ 901-020901; www.ingdirect.es), part of the Nationale Nederlande group; *Patagon* (☎ 902-365366; www.patagon.es), owned by BSCH; *Evolvebank* (☎ 902-157213; www.evolvebank.com), part of the Lloyds TSB group; and *Uno-e* (☎ 901-111113; www.uno-e.es), owned by BBVA and Telefónica. Internet banks often offer relatively high-interest current accounts.

Internet banking is obviously very useful for checking on your account and carrying out banking transactions while abroad.

Opening an account

Individual Accounts. To open an individual account in Spain you will be required to present your passport or some other proof of identification, proof of address, resident's permit and an NIE number. It is advisable to open an account in person rather than rely on a *gestor* to do it for you. It is also advisable to open an account with one of the major banks as they are likely to have far more branches.

Opening a Spanish bank account from the UK. Although some people may be more confident opening an account with a Spanish branch of a UK bank, they will find that the Spanish branches of British banks function in just the same way as the Spanish national banks. HSBC and Barclays are the most widely represented of the British banks in Spain with branches throughout the country. Those who wish to open an account with one of the branches in Spain should contact their local branch in the UK, which will provide the relevant forms to complete. Alternatively, the London offices of the largest Spanish banks are also able to provide the forms necessary to open an account with their Spanish branches. The banks which will provide such a service include *Banco De Santander Central Hispano; BSCH* (Santander House, 100 Ludgate Hill, London EC4M 7NJ; ☎020-7332 7451; www.bsch.es); *Banco Bilbao Vizcaya Argentaria; BBVA* (100 Cannon Street, London EC4N 6EH; ☎020-7623 3060).

Business Accounts. Opening an account in the name of a company rather than an individual is done as part of the incorporation procedure. It is necessary to deposit the company start-up capital in a bank account in order to receive the *certificado del desembolso efectuado*, which is required by the notary public in order to incorporate the company. In these circumstances you may well need the certificate of the company name from the *Registro Mercantil* and you will certainly need to provide the company tax number (*CIF*), acquired from the *Agencia Tributaria* (see *Procedures for Starting a New Business*). The banks will also require a copy of the passport of all signatories and the bank's application form.

Opening a second account in the company's name, for example a current account, will require a different set of documents. Again you will need to provide the bank with the appropriate application forms and copies of the signatories' passports. However, you will also need to provide the notarised deed of incorporation, which will include the CIF and you may also require an additional notarised deed empowering the signatories to operate the account. Your bank will advise you on this.

Opening an account for a branch, where the parent company operates abroad, requires all of the above documents plus a copy of the board resolution to form a branch and empowering the signatories to operate the business. This must usually be notarised in the country where the parent company operates and then translated into Spanish.

Banking Procedures

Bank statements are usually sent out to all customers every month and are available on request at any time. All of the usual services that you would expect in other countries are available such as standing orders, direct debits, credit facilities and overdrafts.

Overdrafts, known as *giros en descubierto,* have a peculiar non-legal status in Spain as officially all debts must be documented so that a bank can take legal action against a customer who defaults on payments. However, overdrafts are readily available and the interest on them is limited to 2.5 times the current rate. Note that it is illegal to overdraw your Spanish bank account without prior agreement.

One useful tool for businesses, which they should negotiate with their *caja* is the *Linea de Descuenta,* or a 'Discount Line', which allows the businessman to get an advance on any money owed, similar to 'factoring' in the UK. This is particularly useful because payment terms are often very bad in Spain and lack of cash flow is the largest problem for new businesses. If you have negotiated a Discount Line you can present the bank with an invoice for goods or services delivered that is not due to be paid for ninety days, for example, and they will give you an advance on that amount minus a small fee. For this service there is usually a handling charge of around 0.04%, a transaction charge of around 0.02% and a 3% per annum charge on the total amount.

Finally, all tax residents in Spain should remember that 15% of any interest earned on their account will be retained and paid to the Spanish tax office on their behalf. However, this tax can be deducted from tax payable on the next year's income tax return.

Banking for your company – Richard Spellman, Ambient Media and Communications S.L., Madrid
Banking here in Spain is very sophisticated and modern. Even in very

> *rural areas, the two main banks and the Caja de Ahorros will have a presence. A company should always have two accounts, one with a retail high street bank and the other with a savings and loans based bank, a caja. The Caja de Madrid was happy to give me a credit line and also a discount line for when I need early payment. The cajas are more likely to give you a discount line and it is well worth having. The cajas are non profit making organisations and are obliged to put some money towards social reforms, so they are generally more generous minded towards an individual and you can get a better rate – they'll trust you more. For this service they usually charge a small commission but if it's a fairly sizable amount of money, you don't mind giving a few percent away as long as you can have the cash today, so that for example, you can pay a VAT bill and not have to pay a 10% fine for late payment.*

Bank Charges

Do not expect to get anything free from the bank. Spanish bank charges cover just about every banking transaction imaginable and are notoriously high. Unlike in the UK, charges are levied on day-to-day banking procedures in Spain, including on all credit card and cheque transactions.

Particularly high are charges made for the payment of cheques into your account and for transferring money between accounts and/or banks. Before opening an account be sure to ask for a breakdown of any charges that may be forthcoming, including annual fees. If you plan to make a lot of transfers between banks and accounts you may be able to negotiate more favourable terms.

Offshore Banking

Offshore banking is a favourite topic of conversation all over the world among expats looking for high returns on their savings. Offshore banks offer tax-free interest on deposit accounts and investment portfolios through banking centres in tax havens such as Gibraltar, the Cayman Islands, the Isle of Man and the Channel Islands. More and more high street banks and building societies along with the merchant banks are setting up offshore banking facilities. Deposit account inter-est rates work on the basis that the more inaccessible one's money is, the higher the rate of interest paid.

Banks and financial institutions in Spain also offer offshore banking services. In return for tax-free interest, clients are generally expected to maintain minimum deposit levels, which can be very high, and restrictive terms and conditions often apply. The minimum deposit required by each bank will vary, the norm being between £1,000 and £5,000. Usually, a minimum of £10,000 is needed for year-long deposit accounts, while the lower end of the minimum deposit range applies to 90-day deposits. Instant access accounts are also available.

For the expat living along the southern coast of Spain, the banks in Gibraltar offer a convenient place to stash cash in a tax-free account. However, sound financial advice should be sought regarding one's financial and tax position before placing one's life savings in an offshore account. Buying property through an 'offshore' company is sometimes practiced in Spain, although you should be aware that the Spanish Tax Office charges such companies even higher taxes than usual.

BANK LOANS

Despite the fact that Spanish banking has come on in leaps and bounds in the last two decades, it is still very difficult for a foreigner to get a bank loan (*préstamo*) for a business start-up. The banks are very wary of anyone who has no credit history with them and often they will only offer loans against some kind of personal guarantee such as a house or some other asset (see below).

This is not to say that it is impossible to get a loan however, and those who are able to demonstrate some business ability, who have a well thought out business idea and a cash flow forecast do stand a chance obtaining a loan. Theoretically, both residents and non-residents should be eligible for loans in any EU country, in any currency. However, this will usually be no more than the amount which the business itself injects in cash. Such a loan would normally need to be repaid over a period of between five and seven years.

The chances of obtaining a loan are far higher at one of the savings banks (*cajas de ahorro*). It is worth doing a little research before approaching the bank, you will definitely need a well-constructed business plan (see below) and it would be useful to detail exactly how you intend to pay the money back. Some banks may be more favourable to certain businesses than others, so ask around.

Interest rates on loans vary wildly depending on the bank, the amount and the period of the loan. It is not always necessary to have an account with a bank in order to get a loan, so it is certainly worthwhile shopping around for the best rates. The cost of a loan is calculated using the *tasa annual equivalente (TAE)* which must be quoted by law. This figure is the actual rate of interest which includes all charges and varies according to the frequency of payments. The commission a bank can charge when a client pays off a loan prior to the due date is limited.

Making a Business Plan

In order to maximise your chances of obtaining a bank loan or indeed private financing of any sort, it is vital that you have a clearly presented business plan. In the UK, solicitors John Howell and Co. (The Old Glass Works, 22 Endell Street, Covent Garden, London WC2H 9AD; ☎020-7420 0400; fax 020-7836 3626; www.europelaw.com) have a lot of experience drawing up business plans in Spanish and in the format expected by Spanish banks and other institutions.

What follows is a general guideline based on information from the Official State Bulletin department (*Boletín Oficial del Estado*). Even those who have bought an established business would be well advised to make a business plan for at least the first few years. Financial planning will be much easier in these circumstances because the accounts for the last few years should be available to view and analyse.

1. Brief description of the project. Briefly describe the business activity that you are proposing (the details should be left to later sections) including the product or service offered, the need that it will satisfy, its competitive advantages and the possible risks or problems which you will have to confront.

This section should also describe the people behind the project, including their qualifications and professional experience. Banks and investors will often look more favourably on an apparently mediocre project backed by a group of experienced individuals, than on a very good idea being developed by inexperienced entrepreneurs. Describe also the level of involvement in the business of each investor, how much work or capital they will put into the business and the minimum level of remuneration that is expected for their contribution.

Finally this section will outline the structure of the business, detailing the delegation of responsibilities and describing the decision making process.

2. Description of the product or service. This section should deal in detail with the characteristics of the product or service offered.

3. Summary of market research. Include in this section an analysis of the market, a description of potential clientele, a study of the competition, a study of how the product could be distributed, the types of publicity and promotion that you intend to use, and finally the estimated price of the product or service taking into account the production costs and the amount that your target clientele will be prepared to pay.

4. Technical description of the business. This section should include precise details of the production or service process specifying those areas which will be dealt with directly by the business and those which will be contracted out. There should also be a detailed summary of all of the resources required, including a description of the required premises and installations, technical equipment such as furniture and machinery and number of projected employees. Any raw materials required and a study of who can provide them should also be included here.

5. Human resources. A detailed description of all of the projected positions which will need to be filled when the business starts operating. This should include job profiles, the necessary qualifications and experience for each position and projected salaries.

6. Marketing strategy. A description of the resources and techniques that the company will use in order to promote the business to their target population (see *Marketing Your Business*).

7. Timescale. The business plan should include a projected date for the start of business operations. This should be followed by a detailed plan for the first year, including objectives for each of the first twelve months. Finally, you should include projected goals for the long-term development of the business.

8. Legal form of the business. An important decision for the entrepreneur, and one which will affect the company's legal, fiscal and social security obligations is the type of legal entity which a company will assume, be it a sole trader, partnership or limited liability company (see *Which Business Structure?*).

9. Economic and financial analysis of the business. This is perhaps the most important part of the business plan as it allows the entrepreneur to analyse the viability of the business in some detail. It is also the part of the business plan which it is most advisable to gain specific outside help with. Town halls, the INEM (national employment agency), autonomous governments, Chambers of Commerce will all offer free help at varying levels, and the guidance of an accountant, lawyer or *gestor* may always be contracted.

a)Investment Plan: Describe the minimum investments necessary to get the business up and running including such items as launch publicity; the preparation of the business premises, the installation of telephones, computers, machinery, furniture, etc.; any necessary research; deposit on the rent or freehold price; insurance and so on.

b)Finance Plan: Exactly where the funds are going to come from to finance all of this work. For example, contributions of the company shareholders, bank loans, credit, subsidies and grants, mortgages and so on.

c)Forecast of Results: A detailed prognosis of the forecasted profits for each of the first two or three years. It is necessary to estimate profits from sales of the product or from providing a service as well as forecast the annual expenses such as purchasing raw materials, paying wages and salaries, rent and overheads such as water, gas, electricity and the telephone, transport, credit repayments, insurance, marketing costs and so on.

d)Analysis of the Break-even Point: Occasionally it can be very difficult to establish a concrete figure for the anticipated income of a company starting out. If this occurs it can be useful to also offer an analysis of your profit threshold. This is a calculation of the minimum number of sales necessary for the business to register a profit. Detail the specific incomings and outgoings that the business will have to face month by month during the early days of business, keeping in mind the possibility of deferred payments from or to third parties that the business deals with. Payment terms in Spain can be very bad and businesses may find themselves in financial difficulty if they do not have deep financial reserves.

10. Conclusions. A positive summary of the business plan aimed at selling the idea to the reader.

MORTGAGES AND SECURED LOANS

Whilst Spanish banks are often unwilling to offer loans for new business ventures, you will find them to be far more amenable if you have something to offer them as security against the loan. This could be a mortgage against the freehold of the business premises that you are buying. If you have equity such as a Spanish property you may be eligible for a secured loan. These are usually at a lower rate of interest than an ordinary bank loan. However, it is important to remember that if you use a personal asset as security for the loan, then regardless of whether a limited liability company has been formed, you are personally liable for the repayments on that loan. This is a risk that many sole traders and directors of small companies take but it is a move which should be considered carefully as staking everything on the success of a new venture can be disastrous. It is often safer, if you have formed a limited company, to borrow money against the company's assets such as the business premises.

Mortgages

The introduction of the euro and the lifting of nearly all exchange controls has allowed both residents and non-residents to obtain mortgages against their property in Spain from any bank in the world. Unfortunately, whilst fixed UK residential mortgages are fairly easy to obtain, many of the UK lenders specialising in mortgages in Spain will not deal with mortgages on commercial properties, due to the fact that the risks involved are much higher and that they require a record of income for the last three years. Even if you intend to buy a hotel or B&B, the official line from *Halifax International* is that if the property is used to generate any income at all, it will not qualify for a mortgage. As yet there are no companies aimed specifically at providing business finance specifically for the expatriate market. You may be lucky and find a UK lender who will finance your business premises but the majority of people find that they have to take a Spanish mortgage, take a loan secured against personal property in Spain, or re-mortgage their home in the UK in order to invest in the business in Spain. UK specialists in business finance such as ASC Partnership PLC (3 Park Road, Regents Park, London NW1 6AS; ☎020-7616 6628; fax 020-7616 6634; www.asc.co.uk) will be able to help you to raise finance on any UK commercial assets which can be used to fund a business venture in Spain.

Commercial mortgages from a bank or lender in Spain are available, especially if you go to one of the larger banks such as BBVA, BSCH or Barclays España (see above). If you are forming a Spanish branch of a foreign company then, according to Barclays España, the procedure will be much simpler and you are likely to get a better rate, based on the accounts and guarantee of the parent company.

If you are thinking of taking a mortgage with a lender in Spain, remember that there are fewer fixed, capped and discounted schemes operated on the Continent and terms can be more restrictive than those offered in the UK. For example, a high deposit and a maximum repayment term of twenty years is standard. You will also find that cheaper interest rates and special deals on offer usually only apply to more high-value commercial properties.

Many Spanish banks will offer mortgages on commercial property. However, the conditions relating to Spanish mortgages are often quite different to those in the UK. For example, a deposit of at least 30% is usually required with a maximum of 70% of the property value being provided as a loan (in the UK it is common for lenders to agree to 95%

or even 100%).

The Spanish method for assessing mortgages differs from that in the UK. It will be necessary to put your UK and Spanish income forward and possibly get references from your UK bank. Any other loans that you have will also be assessed. For a totally new business enterprise, banks and lenders will require a comprehensive business plan detailing company expenses and projected earnings. Note that banks such as *Barclays España* will not lend to a client who will struggle if interest rates increase by even 1%. Currently inflation and interest rates in Spain are very low and Spanish bank mortgages are being offered at less than five per cent. They are set to increase in the coming years though and whilst your repayments might be affordable at the time of purchase, a sudden rise in interest rates could leave you short. However, it is possible to get both fixed or variable interest rate mortgages, mixed interest rate mortgages and fixed repayment instalment mortgages.

COSTS AND LEGAL FEES WHEN TAKING OUT A MORTGAGE

- ○ **Valuation** of the property.
- ○ **Request of extract** (*nota simple*) – issued by the Spanish property registry showing the latest recorded details of any charges on the property.
- ○ **Bank mortgage opening fee**. This is paid at the moment of signing the deed. The fee varies depending on the bank and not all banks make a charge. This commission serves to cover the costs the bank has incurred studying the viability of the loan.
- ○ **Stamp duty** (*Impuesto de Actos Juridicos Documentdos*) at 0.5%. This must be paid when the deed is signed.
- ○ **Notary and registry**. These fees vary according to the guaranteed capital of the mortgage.
- ○ **Insurance**. Banks usually require the borrower to contract at least fire insurance to protect its interest until the loan is repaid. It is your right to choose your own insurance company, although the bank will almost certainly suggest the one that they usually deal with. The insurance fee must be paid at the time the deed is signed.

If you do obtain a mortgage in Spain, it must be formalised in a public deed of mortgage before a public notary of your choice (although the banks may pressure you to use their usual notary). The notary will ensure that the borrowers understand everything they are signing. The property must then be registered at the *Registro de la Propiedad* (property registry) with the name of the owners whom the mortgage is given to.

Second Mortgages on UK Properties

The majority of people choosing to set up in business in Spain will sell their homes in the UK and use the funds to help finance their new venture. If, for whatever reason, you are planning to hold on to your UK property, an alternative possibility for financing your business is to take out a second mortgage. Obviously, this is subject to a valuation on the UK property, and the amount you can expect to borrow varies between mortgage lenders. Your credit history will usually be checked to assess whether you will be able to manage increased mortgage payments. Remember that if you are giving up your job in the UK to start a new business in Spain, you may not be able to show the lender that you have a regular income with which to repay the mortgage loan.

The Norwich and Peterborough Building Society (www.npbs.co.uk), offer what they call a 'further advance' for people who already have a mortgage with them. This allows you to take a minimum loan of £25,001 up to 90% of the building society's valuation of your home at a standard rate of 5.74%. The loan must be repaid within the term of the original mortgage.

Useful Addresses

Commercial and Domestic Mortgages: Willow Tree Cottage, Gloucester Lane, Mickleton, Gloucester GL55 6RP; ☎01386-430000; www.commercialanddomesticmortgages.co.uk.

Conti Financial Services: 204 Church Road, Hove, East Sussex BN3 2DJ; ☎0800-9700985; e-mail enquiries@conti-financial.com; www.overseasandukfinance.com.

Easy2Loan: C/Antonio Belón, Marbella, Málaga; ☎ 952-827754; e-mail information@easy2loan.com; www.easy2loan.com.

European Mortgage Company: 10 Atlanta Boulevard, Romford, Essex, RM1 1TB; ☎01708-749494; www.europeanmortgagecompany.com.

Finanz Kontor: Avenida Alejandro Roselló 15, 5ºD, Palma de Mallorca; ☎ 971-148266; e-mail info@finanzkontor.es; www,finanzkontor.es.

First Choice Mortgage Advice: Edif. Casa Care, Belindous Campanario, Avenida de España, 29647 Mijas Costa, Málaga; ☎ 952-930459.

Mortgage 4 Spain: Apartado Correos 402, La Cala, Mijas Costa, Málaga; ☎ 952-493679; e-mail www.info@mortgage4spain.com; www.mortgage4spain.com.

Mortgage Shop: Edif. Parlamar, Avenida Gabriel Miró 21, Calpe, Alicante; ☎ 661-317707.

Mortgages in Spain: PO Box 146, Ilkley, West Yorkshire, LS29 8UL; ☎0800-027 7057; e-mail info@mortgages-in-spain.com; www.mortgages-in-spain.com.

Foreign Currency Exchange Service

Currencies Direct: Hanover House, 73-74 High Holborn, London WC1V 6LR; ☎020-7813 0332; fax 020-7419 7753; www.curren ciesdirect.com.

Part II

RUNNING A BUSINESS IN SPAIN

BUSINESS ETIQUETTE AND CORRESPONDENCE

TAX, SOCIAL SECURITY AND OTHER MATTERS

EMPLOYING STAFF

MARKETING YOUR BUSINESS

SELLING ON

Business Etiquette and Correspondence

CHAPTER SUMMARY

- Spanish businessmen much prefer to do business with people they know and like, and therefore trust, so that the contract is the formalisation of an on-going relationship.
- The Spanish are often unwilling to commit anything to paper, preferring face-to-face discussions, or conversations over the phone.
- Conducting business negotiations in a second language can cause embarrassing and even expensive misunderstandings. Even if your Spanish is fluent, there will always be cultural references and contexts that may pass you by.
- The Spanish have a lingering fear of sharing information. Companies have very flat hierarchies of only two or three tiers and in the upper echelons people are often so intent on keeping their position that they will not delegate.
- The Spanish are famed for keeping very late hours. If you are being entertained by a business associate, don't expect dinner to start before 9pm or to finish before midnight.
- In order for your business correspondence to appear more 'Spanish', and to avoid any misunderstandings, it is a good idea to become familiar with the conventions of Spanish business letters.

When it comes to Spanish business practices, it really is best to throw all of your Anglicised preconceptions out of the window. Spain has a distinct business culture which at times barely resembles its British or American counterpart and may leave the unsuspecting foreign businessman utterly bewildered. Whilst you may find Spanish customs time-consuming and frustrating, the alternative is to carry on exactly as you would in your home country, almost certainly fail and very probably have a nervous breakdown. When in Rome.....

BUSINESS ETIQUETTE

Negotiations

You may find yourself warming to Spanish business practices. They are certainly more sociable. Whereas the British tend to follow that old maxim of not mixing business with pleasure, the Spanish, in contrast, like to build up a relationship with their business partners. Spanish businessmen much prefer to do business with people they know and like, and therefore trust, so that the contract is a mere formalisation of an on-going relationship. It really is worth making the effort to develop business relationships. Peter Cobbold, who lets out property in Cataluña puts it fairly succinctly: *'Be open and honest and don't try to be greedy. People would prefer to hold onto their money or have less, than deal with someone who they did not like or who they felt was getting too good a deal out of them'.*

Business meetings in Spain are not informal. On the contrary, professional attire is expected and a handshake is customary upon initiating and closing a meeting.

You will have to learn to approach your business negotiations in a much more relaxed manner, because things may well take considerably longer. The Spanish are often inefficient because there is no structure to their meetings. Foreign businessmen and women often find that whereas in their own country they could conduct three or four important meetings in a day, in Spain one meeting may last the entire day and still prove fruitless. It is vital to go into a meeting with Spanish businessmen with an agenda of points that you wish to discuss or you may waste a lot of time.

On the other hand, the actual decision-making process in Spain is often very speedy (see box below).

Another potential frustration is that the Spanish are often unwilling to commit anything to paper, preferring face-to-face discussions or conversations over the phone. It is therefore good practice to follow up a letter with a telephone call in order to ensure a response, but there is really no substitute for a personal meeting.

> ## Improvisation is highly valued in Spanish business meetings – Richard Spellman, Ambient Media and Communications S.L., Madrid
>
> *Where the Spanish get very frustrated with foreign businessmen and vice versa during meetings comes down to the percentage of spontaneity allowed in a negotiation. Generally what happens in the UK and the USA is that decisions are not made in a single meeting. The information is taken away, evaluated and then a counter proposal is presented at a further meeting. This can take a lot of time, but generally when a decision has been made, it does go ahead.*
>
> *In Spain, the reverse is true. Spontaneity is highly valued. The ability to make a decision at a meeting, a snap judgement with no counter proposal, is highly valued. This galls the British especially, because we are not used to having that kind of decision-making freedom. The downside however, is that just as decisions can be made quickly, they can also be unmade at the very last minute.*

Business Values

In most Spanish businesses loyalty and friendships outweigh intelligence; character and amiability are rated higher than business acumen; and modesty is valued over assertiveness. The four words which are used most frequently in connection with comments on individual colleagues or clients are:

- *Valiente* – The quality most admired in business is courageous decision making. Sharing decision making is often interpreted as weakness.
- *Bueno* – This is the best compliment, if you are referred to as *un tipo bueno* you are considered clever, honourable and *valiente*.
- *Inteligente* – That the Spanish put little stock in intelligence as a business trait is shown by the fact that this is used to imply solid and boring.
- *Listo* – Sharp and not altogether trustworthy.

Language

It is important to remember that less than 30% of local managers are fluent in English. Whilst English is recognised as the international business language in Spain, on a smaller, more local scale you will have to brush up on your Spanish or even the local language. Only 74% of the Spanish population speak Castillian Spanish as a first language, and you may find it necessary to learn Catalan, Galician or Basque. Conducting negotiations in a second language can cause embarrassing and even expensive misunderstandings. Even if your Spanish is fluent, there will always be cultural references and contexts that may pass you by, so be sure not to make any assumptions.

One constant source of confusion is the use of *tu* and *usted* in business situations, especially as *'usted'* said in a sarcastic tone can be very insulting. Generally usage is based on familiarity, and most Spaniards will drop the use of the formal *usted* after an initial meeting. Note however that in the south of Spain, manners are slightly more formal than in the north and it may take slightly longer to get on to *tu* terms. One point worth remembering if you are employing Spanish staff is that to refer to subordinates as *usted* would be considered very insulting, putting them around the same level as the domestic staff.

Communication

Within Spanish companies it is not considered necessary to communicate to colleagues or subordinates anything other than what is strictly necessary for the job in hand. Correspondence, staff notice-boards and memos are conspicuously absent from all but the largest of companies.

Similarly there is not really a culture of meetings in Spain and when they do exist their function is primarily to communicate instructions. The business environment is therefore lacking in team spirit as the Spanish like to be independent and make decisions on their own.

There is a lingering fear of sharing information and people tend not to hand over knowledge to a younger apprentice, out of fear for their own job. Companies therefore have very flat hierarchies of only two or three tiers and in the upper echelons people are often so intent on keeping their position that they will not delegate. For the outsider doing business with a company, this can be useful as it is fairly easy to identify the right person to talk to, and they will usually give you an interview. On the other hand, they usually have an enormous pile of work to get through.

Business Hours

Obviously these will vary from business to business and from location to location, but there are some points worth noting about Spanish working habits. The normal business hours are 8am-1pm and 4pm-6pm, Monday to Friday. Offices generally open slightly later than in the UK, but will often remain working until 8pm with a long lunch break between 2pm and 4pm. Business discussions may even spill over into a nearby bar. From mid-June to mid-September, many offices adopt 'summer hours', especially in the hottest areas of the country, where offices are open from 8:30am to 3pm.

Lunch in Spain is by far the most important meal of the day and traditionally families would get together for a long break between 1 pm and 3 or 4 pm. Although this practice is dying out in the larger cities due to greater commuting distances and traffic congestion, it still persists in small towns and rural areas. If returning home for lunch is impractical, Spaniards will still take a long lunch break, often visiting a restaurant or café. They would never consider eating at their desk. Even drinking coffee at one's desk is considered to be unsophisticated and unsociable. Instead it is perfectly acceptable to leave the office and go to a café with a colleague. However, it would be unusual to go out for coffee or lunch with someone of a different rank.

The Spanish are famed for keeping very late hours, with young *Madrileños* often not going out in the evening until 11pm or later. Similarly, if you are being entertained by a business associate don't expect dinner to start before 9pm or to finish before midnight. Entertaining and eating out are important aspects of Spanish business life. they are used to establish personal relationships. Usually on a first business meeting, everything except business is discussed until coffee is served, when the host will move onto the real reason for the invitation. Until that moment it is best not to appear too formal.

Punctuality

It is true that procrastination and delay are an endemic part of Spanish business life. However it would be wrong to view this in a negative light, it is nothing to do with indolence or apathy, but is usually because the Spanish try to cram too many things into too short a space of time. Whilst the clichéd *mañana* attitude may still be found in the state sector, with its impenetrable web of bureaucracy, it is less obvious these days in modern, private firms. In fact the Spanish work incredibly hard, especially within middle management.

Forms of Address

The Spanish system of having two surnames is not as baffling as it first appears. Children receive both the *first* surname of their father and the *first* surname of their mother. Women do not change their names when they get married. For example, the son of Sr. José Lopez Garcia and Sra. Maria Pizarro Vega could be called Juan-Pablo Lopez Pizarro. Whilst it certainly won't cause any offence if you get this wrong it may cause some embarrassment, but in every day business correspondence there is no need to use both surnames. Official paperwork however, will require the full Spanish name.

To be addressed as *Don* or *Doña* is considered a mark of respect. Academics, lawyers and other professional people will be referred to as *Don*. This term is used before the Christian name, for example Don Eduardo or Doña Almudena.

BUSINESS CORRESPONDENCE

In order for your business correspondence to appear more 'Spanish', and to avoid any misunderstandings, it is a good idea to become familiar with the conventions of Spanish business letters:

The envelope. When addressing the envelope, the correct way is to begin with the name of the company. This is followed by Atn. (like the English Attn.) and then the name of the person. The job title follows and then the address. Note that in Spanish, unlike in English, the postcode always comes before the town.

If you wish to include your return address on the envelope, it should be written on the back, following the word *Remite:*.

ABREVIATIONS USED IN SPANISH ADDRESSES

Almd	Alameda	Avenue/Boulevard
Av/Avda	Avenida	Avenue
C/	Calle	Street
Cllj	Callejón	Alley/Passage
Cno	Camino	Road/Way
Cril	Carril	Lane
Ctra/Ca	Carretera	Main Road
Gta	Glorieta	Roundabout
P°/Po	Paseo	Avenue
Pje	Pasaje	Passage
Pl/Pza	Plaza	Place
Pllo	Pasillo	Passage
Pte	Puente	Bridge
Urb	Urbanización	Housing Estate
Ent	Entresuelo	Ground Floor
1°	1st Floor	
2°	2nd Floor	
3°	3rd Floor etc.	
cto.	Centro	Centre
dcha.	Derecha	Right-hand side
izq.	Izquierda	left-hand side

Beginning the letter. The letter should be laid out similarly to an English letter. Your own address and name, without title, should be at the top on either the left or right hand side. The addressee's name and address should be inserted on the left-hand side of the paper, above the opening greeting. The date should follow this address, and in a formal letter should be written out in full e.g. *12 de enero de 2004*.

It is customary to begin a letter with *Estimado/a*, followed by *Señor, Señora, Señorita*, followed by the surname of the person, followed by a colon. For example, *Estimado Señor Juarez:*. If you do not know the person you are writing to it is sufficient just to write *Estimado/a Señor/a* or if you would like to write the equivalent of Dear Sirs, the plural form is *Estimados Señores*. However, if you are writing to someone in Cataluña, the phrase *Estimado* is usually replaced with *Apreciado/a*. Once you have built up a good relationship with the addressee, it is perfectly acceptable to use a first name, e.g. *Estimado José*. The phrase *Querido/a* which translates as Dear, is only used when you know the addressee well.

Signing off. There are a number of potential letter endings for formal correspondence, however modern business Spanish is much less flowery than it used to be and usually sticks to the following endings:
Formal – Yours faithfully/sincerely = *Atentamente* or *Le saluda atentamente*.
Less formal – Kind regards = *Cordialmente* or *Un cordial saludo*.
More personal – Best wishes = *Un abrazo* or even *Un fuerte abrazo*.
 The ending, *Un abrazo*, which translates as 'an embrace' is often used in business correspondence where a friendly relationship exists between the parties.

E-mails. Spanish business e-mails do not generally differ too much from business letters. However, they are quite often less formal and may begin with *Estimado/a Amigo/a* (dear friend) or even *Hola* (Hi). Generally with e-mails in Spain, much of the formality is removed and people get straight to the point, as if they were speaking.

Tax, Social Security and Other Matters

CHAPTER SUMMARY

- A good accountant will save you money and keep your business abreast of changes to taxation law. They can take care of all of your accounting needs including payroll, income tax and VAT returns.
- **Payment terms:** It is necessary for small businesses in Spain to have deep cash reserves as payment terms are notoriously bad, with some companies taking up to six months to pay any money owing.
- The Spanish tax system has undergone a series of reforms designed to increase the advantage of foreign companies that begin operations in Spain. For example, small businesses receive a 5% discount on corporation tax.
- **Rates of income tax:** have been going down in Spain over the last decade and there are various allowances and deductions depending on your personal circumstances.
- All self-employed people and businesses must register for VAT (*IVA*). There is no threshold as there is in the UK.
- A sliding scale of wealth tax is payable on the worldwide assets of all Spanish residents. Wealth tax declarations should be made at the same time as income tax declarations.
- The various autonomous communities of Spain have certain powers to levy local taxes. These taxes include business tax and real estate tax among others.
- **The Canary Islands:** In order to attract investment and to compensate for the disadvantages brought about by insularity and distance from the Spanish mainland, the Canary archipelago enjoys a number of tax benefits.
- **Tax evasion:** is no longer the accepted practice it was years ago. There are severe penalties and infringements for late payments and non compliance with the tax authorities.
- Ninety per cent of Spain's population pays into the social security system and as a result receive cover for health

care, industrial injuries, unemployment insurance, old
age and invalidity.

◯ The main insurance companies offer general multi-risk
policies for businesses; these are flexible and can be
adapted to your individual needs.

◯ All public utilities (electricity, gas, water, telephone) are
widely available in Spain and are generally cheaper than
in many other European countries.

ACCOUNTANTS AND BOOKKEEPING

Sorting out one's accountancy affairs can be a complicated matter
in your native language, let alone in Spanish and with the added
confusion of an ever-changing tax regime. One piece of advice that
entrepreneurs who have made the move to Spain always give, is to get
a good accountant (*contable* or *asesor fiscal*). Most foreign businesspeo-
ple simply hand everything over to their accountant and let them get
on with the job of dealing with income tax returns and so on. If your
business is fairly small-scale then you may find that a good *gestor* will
be sufficient to look after your books and draft tax returns. However,
larger scale businesses should employ a tax consultant as well in order
to make sure they are fully informed.

An ordinary accountant is called a contable in Spain and the
asesor fiscal (literally a fiscal advisor) is the equivalent of a chartered
accountant. A good accountant will save you money and make sure
that you are kept up to date with changes in taxation law. They can
take care of all of your accounting needs such as payroll, income tax,
employees' income tax, VAT returns. They will also do your end of
year books and take them to the registry.

Accountants can be found in the Spanish Yellow Pages (*Paginas
Amarillas*), and the embassies and consulates have lists of English-
speaking accountants in your area. It is a good idea to take advice
from local businessmen as to the most reliable consultants in the area.
A list of financial services firms with English-speaking staff is also
provided below.

> **For New Businesses an Accountant is Essential – Jos Arensen, Start With Us Business Consultancy, Benalmádena**
> *One thing you definitely need for the day to day running of a business is a good accountant. When you are starting a business, your main objective is to sell. If you don't have any income, you won't have much accounting to do! So it is very useful to find someone quite small that you can trust and that has come recommended to you.*

Spanish law requires that all business enterprises in Spain keep orderly accounts that are appropriate to their activity. Your accountant will be able to advise you as to your particular business needs. It is mandatory for all enterprises to keep inventories and a financial statements book and companies with shareholders must keep a minutes book recording any resolutions adopted at shareholders' meetings. Any accounting books required must be taken to the Companies' Registry where the business is registered in order for them to be stamped and legalised.

Corporations, limited partnerships and limited liability companies must also have share or participation unit registers, which may be computerised.

The main accountancy body in Spain is the *Instituto de Auditores-Censores Jurados de Cuentas de España*, which is responsible for drafting accounting and auditing standards throughout the country. There is an office in every Autonomous Community and the contact details of your local department can be found online at www.iacjce.es. The second accountancy body is the *Instituto de Contabilidad y Auditoria de Cuentas* (see address below), which is a part of the Economics Ministry and is responsible for co-ordinating the profession and formulating national accounting charts and principles.

Useful Addresses

Instituto de Contabilidad y Auditoria de Cuentas: C/ Huertas 26, 28014 Madrid; ☎913-895600; fax 914-299486; www.icac.mineco.es.

Adesso Res Asesores: Avenida Marques del Duero 68, 1º/4, San Pedro, Marbella; ☎952-782625; e-mail adesso@terra.es.

Asesoría Económica: Calle Lagasca 79, San Pedro Alcántara, Marbella; ☎952-783139; e-mail jrc@asesecon.com; www.asesecon.com.

BDO Fidecs Insurance Management Ltd.: Suite 2C, Eurolife building, 1 Coral Road, Gibraltar; ☎+350-42686; www.bdo.gi.

Blevins Franks Financial Management: Barbican House, 26-34 Old Street, London, EC1V 9QQ; ☎020-7336 1000; www.blevinsfranks.com.

Bravo Asesoría: Avenida Condes de San Isidro 23/1º, Fuengirola, Málaga; ☎952-473062; e-mail francisco@gestoriabravo.es; www.gestoriabravo.es.

Conti Financial Services: 204 Church Road, Hove, East Sussex, BN3 2DJ; ☎0800-970 0985; e-mail enquiries@contifinancial.com; www.overseasandukfinance.com.

Delgado y Canudas Associats: Avinguda Mistral 36, Barcelona; ☎934-261550; e-mail gcanudas@retemail.es.

Gestoría Ripolles: Avenida Kansas City 12, 1ºA, Sevilla; ☎954-577558; ripolles@gestures.net; www.ripollesgaliano.com.

Spain Accountants: Marina Bay B1, C apt 11, Estepona; ☎952-791113; e-mail info@spainaccountants.com; www.spainaccountants.com.

Payment Terms

Payment terms in Spain are notoriously bad (see box below). An EU law passed in 2000 states that unless the parties agree otherwise, interest becomes automatically payable thirty days after the receipt of the invoice. In Spain however, many companies ignore this, so it is necessary for small businesses to have deep cash reserves. Indeed, throughout Europe, one in every four businesses that fail do so because of late payments. One way to relieve the cash-flow pressure is to have a *linea de descuenta* with your bank (see *Financing your business*) with which you can receive an advance on letters of credit and invoices for a small charge. This is similar to factoring.

One thing to bear in mind when paying bills is that post-dating a cheque in Spain will have no effect. The bearer can pay it in straight away and if you run your books to a very tight margin, this could lead to the cheque bouncing. If you do want to write post-dated cheques then you will have to ask your bank for a book of *Pagarés*. These are a special type of cheque which can be post-dated at no extra charge. Remember also that any cheque exceeding €3000 must be reported to the *Banco de España* and therefore may take longer to clear.

If you are on the other end of a bounced cheque, the banks will pay a partial amount of the sum. For example if your company is paid a cheque for €1000 but the client only has €500 in their account, then you will receive that amount plus the cheque back with this recorded on it. Hopefully you will be able to collect the rest at a later date. Cheques are usually not crossed in Spain so always remember to cross them.

Spanish payment terms. Richard Spellman – Ambient Media and Communications S.L., Madrid

Payment terms in Spain really are terrible. There's no payment at fifteen days. Thirty days really means forty-five or sixty; sixty days is really seventy-five to ninety; and ninety days can mean anything up to six months. Although that is ostensibly illegal, in practice the people who abuse these terms the most are the largest companies and government agencies who will pay at anything up to a year. It's shocking. You need very deep pockets and a tidy cash flow in Spain if you want to work for the big boys.

TAXATION

The Spanish tax system is extremely complicated and even many Spaniards have a lot of difficulty understanding it. With around fifteen different taxes that individuals can be liable for, levied by three tiers of government, it is hardly surprising that Spanish taxes can cause a great deal of grief to the outsider. Add to this the fact that the authorities are constantly changing tax regulations and that most taxes are based on self assessment, and you will see that it is advisable for your business to use a reliable tax advisor (*asesor fiscal*) or *gestor*.

Although Spain's taxes (especially indirect taxes) have been steadily increasing over recent decades, overall taxation remains reasonably low in Spain and still below the EU average. Indeed, income tax rates have actually been reduced over the last three years.

There are three levels of taxation in Spain: central government taxation, autonomous community taxation and local taxation. The *Agencia*

Estatal de Administración Tributaria (C/ Alcalá 9, 28014 Madrid; ☎ 901 335 533), or *Hacienda* as it is known is based in Madrid and collects government taxes via its centres in provincial capital towns.

A five year statute of limitations exists on the collection of back taxes, so if no action has been taken during this period to collect unpaid tax, it cannot be collected. The tax year in Spain is the same as the calendar year: from 1 January to 31 December.

One problem that you may have when paying taxes is Spain's cash culture. The country has a terrible problem with black money, to the extent that even accountants may advise you to make some deals in cash. Fiddling the books is fairly standard practice. Whilst it is illegal, those who take the moral option may find that their business cannot compete with other businesses that are only declaring a percentage of their income for tax purposes. Take recommendations for a good accountant and listen to his advice. Free tax advice is available from the information section (*servicio de informacion*) at your local tax office in Spain. Those offices located in resort areas usually have English-speaking staff. The tax office also provides a telephone information service open 9am-7pm Monday to Friday (☎ 901-335533).

The Modulo

Many small businesses, that have not formed an incorporated entity, find that they are obliged to start off paying their taxes using the *modulo* system. Under this system, the tax agency decides what your business income (taxed as a part of your personal income tax) should be and you are charged tax on this amount each quarter. Only the tax agency could explain the complex analysis that allows them to come up with this figure, but in the case of a bar or restaurant for example, it would take into account the number of tables, waiters, your location and so on.

It is still necessary to file an ordinary tax return at the end of the fiscal year stating actual income and any business deductions. The tax agency will then return any money owing (it is usually the case that they overestimate rather than underestimate). There are not many advantages to this system, although you do not have to present detailed quarterly statements which is helpful for small operations dealing in thousands of small transactions. After a year of this system, it is possible to change to the direct estimation system (*estimación directa*) requiring complete quarterly bookkeeping.

Moving to Spain

Procedure for UK residents. If you are moving permanently abroad, the situation is reasonably straightforward. You should inform the UK Inspector of Taxes at the office you usually deal with of your departure and they will send you a P85 form to complete. The UK tax office will usually require certain proof that you are leaving the UK and hence their jurisdiction, for good. Evidence of having sold a house in the UK and having rented or bought one in Spain is usually sufficient. You can continue to own property in the UK without being considered resident, but you will have to pay UK taxes on any income from the property.

If you are leaving a UK company to take up employment with a Spanish one then the P45 form given by your UK employer and evidence of employment in Spain should be sufficient. You may be eligible for a tax refund in respect of the period up to your departure, in which case it will be necessary to complete an income tax return for income and gains from the previous 5 April to your departure date. It may be advisable to seek professional advice when completing the P85; this form is used to determine your residence status and hence your UK tax liability. You should not fill it in if you are only going abroad for a short period of time. Once the Inland Revenue are satisfied that you are no longer resident or domiciled in the UK, they will close your file and not expect any more UK income tax to be paid.

Spain has a double taxation agreement with the UK, which makes it possible to offset tax paid in one country against tax paid in another. While the rules are complex, essentially, as long as you work and are paid in Spain then you should not have to pay UK taxes, as long as you do not spend more than 91 days a year in the UK spread over four years. For further information see the Inland Revenue publications IR20 *Residents and non-residents. Liability to tax in the United Kingdo*m which can be found on the website http://www.inlandrevenue.gov.uk. Booklets IR138, IR139 and IR140 are also worth reading; these can be obtained from your local tax office or from:

Centre for Non-Residents (CNR): St John House, Merton Rd, Bootle, Merseyside L69 9BB; ☎0151-472 6196; fax 0151-472 6392; www.inlandrevenue.gov.uk/cnr.

Spanish Tax Residence

You will become resident for Spanish tax purposes if:

- You spend more than 183 days in Spain during one calendar year, whether or not you have taken out a formal residence permit, *or*
- You arrive in Spain with an intention to reside there permanently, you will then be tax-resident from the day after you arrive, *or*
- If your 'centre of vital interests' is Spain, although this rule is hardly ever applied, *or*
- If your spouse lives in Spain and you are not legally separated, even if you spend less than 183 days in Spain.

Resident individuals are subject to personal income tax and resident entities to corporate income tax. Both non-resident individuals and entities are subject to a special Tax on the Income of Non-Residents.

Fiscal Identity Numbers: There are three types of Spanish tax identification numbers. The *Número de Identificación de Extranjeros (NIE)* is required by all foreigners resident in Spain. The number identifies you to the Spanish taxman and is required when you pay your taxes or have any dealings with the *Hacienda*, the Spanish tax office. Spanish nationals have a very similar number, the *NIF* or *Número de Identificación Fiscal*. Spanish companies must also register for the *CIF, Codigo de Indentificación Fiscal*.

CORPORATION TAX (I.S.)

The Spanish tax system has undergone a series of tax reforms designed to increase the competitive advantage of foreign companies that begin operations in Spain. There are also a number of measures designed to affect favourably the tax-paying status of small and medium-sized enterprises (PYMEs) as well as innovative firms.

Corporate taxation, or *Impuesto sobre Sociedades (IS)* only applies to companies, not sole traders or the self-employed (unless they have formed a company), that are *resident* in Spain. A company is deemed to be resident in Spain for tax purposes if it was incorporated under Spanish law, or its registered office is located in Spain, or its effective management headquarters are in Spain. Taxation of nonresident entities is regulated separately under the Nonresidents' Income Tax Law. However, permanent establishments in Spain of non residents are also subject to IS. There are some special rules applicable to permanent establishments, including tighter restrictions on what may be allowable as deductions.

Resident companies are taxed on their worldwide income both earned and unearned, including all the profits from business activities, income from investments not relating to the regular business purpose and income derived from asset transfers. Spain's current standard corporate income tax rate is 35%, although PYMEs pay only 30% and companies on the Canary Islands pay between 1 and 5 %.

Note that if losses are incurred, then they may be carried forward (if not used) for the ten immediate years following the period in which the losses arose. The company can decide how much of the losses it uses in any given period. For new companies, the period of ten years in which losses may be used starts from the first period in which it makes a profit.

The accounting year runs from 1 January to 31 December and tax is payable within 25 days of the AGM, which must be held within six months of the end of the company's accounting year.

Provisions

Under Spanish tax law, provisions are established for certain, but un-realised losses or to cover future expenses. These provisions are deductible, provided that they are properly recorded in the accounts and comply with tax legislation. These deductible provisions include, among others:

- Provisions against the value of portfolios of investment.
- Provisions against bad and doubtful debts.
- Provisions for various legal obligations and duties.
- Provisions for extraordinary repairs but only for certain sectors of industry or with the tax authorities' prior agreement.

O   Provisions for costs incurred due to inspection and repairs under warranties and for costs relating to the return of goods.

Capital Gains Reinvestment

It is possible to defer paying tax on the sale of tangible and intangible fixed assets and of investments, as long as they have been owned for at least a year and amount to at least five per cent of the company capital and that the profit is reinvested within the permitted period. This profit will not be taxed in the period of sale, or for the following three years. However, it must be paid within ten years following the year of disposal of the asset.

Tax Incentives for PYMEs

Spain's standard corporation tax rate is 35%. However small and medium-sized companies receive a reduction, and pay only 30% for the first 90,151.82 euros of taxable income and thereafter 35%. To qualify for this reduction and the following incentives, the company must have net sales (*cifra de negocio neta*) in the immediately preceding tax period, or in the case of newly incorporated companies – in the current tax period, of less than six million euros. Other tax incentives for PYMEs include:

O   Accelerated depreciation of their tangible fixed assets up to certain limits, provided that certain job requirements are met.

O   Accelerated depreciation of new fixed assets whose unit value does not exceed €600 (up to an aggregate limit of €12,000) without having recorded it for accounting purposes.

O   Entitlement to increase by a coefficient of 1.5 the maximum depreciation rates permitted by the official depreciation tables.

O   Ability to record provisions for bad debts based on 1% of such balance at the end of the tax period.

O   A 10% tax credit for investments and expenses in internet, information technology and communications.

O   A 10% tax credit for environment-related investments, subject to the fulfilment of certain requirements.

Other deductions applying to all companies in Spain, small and large, include those for scientific research, development and technological innovation, export activities, investments in items of cultural interest, investments in assets used for the protection of the environment, costs of professional training and creation of employment for disabled persons. There are usually incentives for the first three years of a small business, allowing you to reinvest any profit rather than pay corporation tax on it. This is a very good idea, allowing you to build up the company's net worth in the early years. The exact terms of tax incentives change from year to year and your accountant will be able to advise you on the current deductions.

A Handy Tax Tip. Richard Spellman, Ambient Media and communications S.L., Madrid

Here is a practical example of what you can do to help ease the burden of corporation tax on a new company. As the director of a company, it may be a good idea not to take a salary for the first months, in order to keep the company's finances looking healthier. You will have to live fairly modestly and still continue paying the autónomo *social security. As you get to the year end you can then employ yourself as a freelancer for December only and invoice the company for that amount. If that money stayed in the company, you would be paying corporation tax on it, but as it goes into your private income, you will be paying a much lower rate of personal income tax.*

This is a fairly simple tip, but one which I only learnt from bitter experience.

INCOME TAX (I.R.P.F.)

Income tax is known in Spain as IRPF (*Impuesto Sobre la Renta de las Personas Físicas*) and only applies to residents. Non-residents are taxed under a separate scheme. Those running a business and the self-employed will certainly need to file a return for income tax, no matter what their actual income is. Rates of income tax have been going down in Spain in the last decade and in the last four years, IRPF cuts have led to a 25% reduction in the tax burden.

Residents are taxable on all sources of worldwide income, both earned and unearned at a rate which varies between 15% and 45%. The total taxable income is composed of income from various sources which include:

○   Trading income from professional or business activities.
○   Income and other benefits derived from a contract of employment.
○   Investment income from property.
○   Investment income other than from property.
○   Capital gains and losses.
○   Deemed income from real property holdings for own use.
○   Income imputed from companies operating under the fiscal transparency regime.

The system has been reorganised and a vital minimum introduced (*minimo vital*). Before you become liable for income tax you deduct the minimum from your gross income and also deduct various other allowances depending on your circumstances. Up to the minute information about the minimum earnings before tax is liable can be obtained from the Spanish Tax Office website (www.aeat.es).

INCOME TAX RATES 2004

From (€)	To (€)	General Rate (%)	Autonomous Community Rate (%)	Total Applicable Tax Rate (%)
0	4,000	9.06	5.94	15
4,000	13,800	15.84	8.16	24
13,800	25,800	18.68	9.32	28
25,800	45,000	24.71	12.29	37
45,000	and above	29.16	15.84	45

Income tax is generally assessed on the household but there are no longer different tax rates for couples who choose to be taxed individually or jointly. IRPF rates for individuals start at 15% on income up to

€4,000 and rise to 45% on income above €45,000. This tax is divided between central government (85%) and the autonomous regions (15%). However, some regions offer deductions from tax due.

Allowances and Deductions

Various deductions are available from income tax totals. For example, all social security payments are tax deductible and there is a personal minimum allowance (the amount considered necessary for you and your dependants to live on). In 2003, this figure was €3,400 or €4,200 for those over sixty-five. Further allowances and deductions include:

- Professional and trade union fees.
- Legal expenses up to €300.
- A percentage of an annuity (life or fixed period) depending on your age.
- Child support payments made as a result of a court decision.
- 60% of any dividends.
- Deductions for dependents (e.g. €800 for someone aged 65-75 living with you; €1000 for someone aged over 75 living with you; €1,400 for a first child; €1200 for each child aged under three etc.).
- Disability deductions – €2,000 if the disability is between 33% and 65% and €5,000 if the disability is above 65%.
- 75% of any *plus valia* tax paid as a result of a property sale.
- 15% of the cost of purchase or renovation of your principal residence up to €9,015.
- Deductions from mortgage payments up to €9,015.
- Foreign tax deduction – if you have already paid income tax abroad you can also deduct that from your Spanish tax bill.

Tax Returns

Those whose financial situation is relatively uncomplicated can draw up their own tax return and advice on how to do this is available from the local *hacienda*. Tax return forms can be purchased from the tobacconists (*estanco*) for around €0.30 or from your local *agencia tributaria* office. There are three kinds of tax return form. Form 103 is the abbreviated declaration, form 101 is the simple declaration and form 100 is the ordinary declaration. Business and professional activities must be recorded on the last, the *declaracion ordinaria*, which is the longest and most complex of the three and will usually require the help of an accountant to complete. The fees charged by an accountant to file a tax return can vary, but you should expect to pay around €35 for a simple return and around €60 for a more complex return.

Many taxpayers or their advisers now complete income tax returns electronically using a CD Rom programme which runs on Windows. The Spanish tax authorities sell this quite cheaply and it has a number of advantages such as the fact that certain allowances are inserted automatically.

Returns should be made between 1 May and 20 June. The self-employed pay their income tax quarterly (*pago fraccionado*). If you employ any staff, it is also your responsibility to deduct your employees' income tax at source. Late filing of a tax return leads to a surcharge on the tax due (see *Penalties and Infringements* below). It is possible however, to request payment deferral.

Returns should be submitted to the district tax office where you are resident for tax purposes. Alternatively you can file the return and pay at designated banks in the area, which allows you to transfer the cash to the tax authorities straight from your account.

VAT

All self employed people and businesses must register for value added tax, known in Spain as *impuesto sobre el valor añadido (IVA)* and levy this tax on all services and goods. Unlike in the UK, all businesses must register for *IVA*, regardless of turnover. Businesses with a turnover of less than €6 million must file a quarterly return and pay tax due within twenty days of the end of the quarter. If your annual turnover is more than this you should file an IVA return monthly.

The following transactions are subject to IVA when carried out by traders or professionals in the course of business activities:

⊙   Supplies of goods or services.

- O   Intra-EU acquisitions of goods.
- O   Imports of goods. These transactions are subject to IVA regard-
       less of whether or not the importer is a trader.

The rate of IVA in Spain is normally 16%. However, there is a reduced
rate of 7% for a number of goods such as food products, water, fuel,
drugs and medicines, hotels, restaurants, transportation etc. There
is also a super-reduced rate of only 4% for basic foodstuffs such as
bread, milk, cheese, fruit and vegetables and eggs; as well as books,
periodicals, pharmaceutical products, and vehicles and prostheses for
the handicapped. In addition to IVA, special taxes are levied on auto-
mobiles, alcohol, petrol and tobacco products.

Health, education, insurance and financial services are exempt from
IVA, as is the transfer of any business, providing the buyer continues
the existing business concern, and rental of private property. Exports
are also exempt from IVA.

Businesses have a number of obligations with regard to IVA. They
must: have applied to the tax authorities for a tax identification
number, issue and deliver invoices and keep copies, keep accounts and
records of IVA transactions and file quarterly or monthly returns.

Jos Arensen, who runs *Start With Us,* a business consultancy on the
Costa del Sol points out that there is a tendency towards IVA fraud
by some shops and suppliers in Spain, who will sell you goods without
declaring any tax. However, if you wish to claim the IVA back, you will
need to have legitimate invoices showing names and tax numbers.

IVA is applied throughout Spain and the Balearic Islands. However,
the Canary Islands have their own indirect general tax (see below);
and the Spanish enclaves in Morocco, Ceuta and Melilla, have an
alternative Tax on Production, Services and Imports.

WEALTH TAX

Wealth tax (*impuesto sobre el patrimonio*) is calculated on the value
of an individual's assets in Spain on 31 December every year and is
imposed on residents and non-residents alike. Residents are taxed on
all of their world-wide assets, whereas non-residents pay wealth tax on
all of their assets in Spain. The amount payable runs on a sliding scale

from 0.2% for assets valuing €167,129, to the top bracket of 2.5% on assets worth over €10,695,996.

Liability to wealth tax is calculated by totalling the value of all of your assets including business ownership, property, vehicles, cash, life insurance, jewellery, financial investments and so on. An end of year bank statement will therefore be required showing any interest and an average balance. If you do not declare your total assets you may face a fine.

Residents will be pleased to know that there they will pay nothing on the first €108,182.18, with an additional €150,253 for a principal residence. Those with a principal residence in Spain therefore have a wealth tax allowance of €258,435.18. Very few assets are exempt from this tax, although if you have bought property with a loan or mortgage, there are deductions from your wealth tax liability. There is no allowance for non-residents.

Wealth tax declarations should be made at the same time as income tax declarations (between 1 May and 20 June) on form 714 available from the tax office. Note that if your income tax declaration shows your worldwide assets to be below the relevant limit, there is no need to make a wealth tax declaration.

PROPERTY TRANSFER AND STAMP DUTY TAX

The *Impuesto de Transmisiones Patrimoniales y Actos Jurídicos Documentados* is a tax levied on property transfers, corporate transactions and stamp duties. The tax should be paid at the Treasury Office of the corresponding community within thirty working days of the signature of the deed or the contract.

- **Corporate Transfers:** The tax is paid on corporate operations such as incorporating a company, a business merger, share capital increase or decrease. This is charged at 1%.
- **Stamp Duty:** This is paid upon signature of a public deed, of notarial documents, registry office documents and so on. The rate applied can differ depending on the circumstances and the autonomous community. It is usually 0.5% or 1%.
- **Property Transfers:** This tax is payable on the purchase, from a private owner, of property or land (but not on the purchase of

a new property). It is usually charged at a rate of 6% (although some autonomous communities charge 7%) of the value of the property as declared on the *escritura*.

LOCAL AND REGIONAL TAXES

Central government laws determine the basic aspects of local taxes. However, the municipalities have certain powers to regulate these taxes, and this may well create differences in the practical application of a tax in each municipality. In 2003 the law established two different types of local tax: 'Periodic Taxes', which include taxes on real estate, business activity and motor vehicles and 'Other Taxes', which include a tax on construction work and an increase in urban land value tax.

Business Tax

The *Impuesto sobre Actividades Económicas (IAE)* is levied annually on any business activity conducted within the territory of the municipality. This tax takes into account neither the regularity of operations nor the existence of a profit. It is calculated taking into account several factors, including the type of activity, the number of employees, the status of the activity and so on.

The good news is that in 2003, in a move to stimulate small business, the government abolished this tax for anyone with a turnover of less than €1 million per year. It is likely however, that the IAE will be replaced in the future with an alternative, in order to compensate local councils for a vast loss of revenue. The administration of this tax has also been removed from the municipalities and returned to the central Tax Agency, so it is necessary to apply to register at the *Hacienda* office.

Despite the fact that you probably will not have to pay the IAE, it is still necessary to register as you must have a tax category assigned for your business or profession.

Tax on Real Estate

The *impuesto sobre bienes inmeubles urbana/rústica (IBI)* is a tax levied annually on both resident and non-resident property owners. If you are renting business premises then you should examine your contract, but usually the landlord will pay this tax. Any owners of commercial property will have to pay.

IBI goes towards local council administration, sanitary services, social assistance, education, cultural and sports amenities and so on. The amount of IBI you will have to pay is calculated on the basis of the property's *valor catastral,* or the notional rental value. Traditionally this figure is around seventy per cent of a property's market value, but this can vary dramatically between municipalities. Local government calculates the valor catastral based on an assessment of the property including its size, access to services and roads, building and zoning restrictions in the area and the quality of the building. It is possible to appeal the valuation decision, but this should be done within fifteen days. If your valor catastral has been incorrectly evaluated, this may affect other taxes such as 'letting' income tax and wealth tax.

IBI rates are usually much higher in resort and coastal areas and in provincial capitals and large towns. The standard rate for agricultural properties (*rústicas*) is 0.3%. This rises to 0.5% for urban properties. However, rates are set locally and depend on factors such as recent improvements to public amenities and the amount of local government debt. In some towns the rate is as high as 1.7%. IBI is simply calculated by multiplying the valor catastral by the local rate.

A demand for payment is sent each year and the sum claimed must be paid by the specified date (which varies from place to place). However, many town halls do not send out bills so it may be a good idea to arrange payment via direct debit from your bank.

Other Taxes

Refuse tax. In some areas, rubbish collection charges are raised separately from the IBI. Businesses produce far more rubbish than the average house, so the tax is slightly higher. It varies depending on the location and size of the business and the amount of rubbish produced. The average charge is around €150 per year.

Tax on erection and installation projects and construction work.

This tax is levied on the actual cost of any work or construction activity requiring prior municipal permission. The tax rate is set by each municipality up to a maximum rate of 4%.

Tax on increase in urban land value. A municipal capital gains tax known as *plus valia* tax in Spain, although its full title is *Impuesto sobre el Incremento de Valor de los Terrenos de Naturaleza Urbana*. This tax is levied on the increase disclosed in the value of urban land whenever land is transferred. It does not apply to the increase in value of any *buildings* on the land and it is payable only on urban land, not rural land. Although this tax should, in theory, be paid by the vendor, the common practice is that both parties agree that the buyer pays it.

The local municipal tax office will be able to tell you before you sign a contract of sale what the *plus valia* tax will be on the property concerned. The maximum rate that this may be set at by the municipality is 30%. The tax base is the increase in land value. This tax is deductible for personal income tax purposes from the transfer value of real estate.

SPECIAL TAX REGIME FOR THE CANARY ISLANDS

In order to attract investment to the Canary Islands and to compensate for the disadvantages brought about by insularity and distance from the Spanish mainland, the Canary archipelago enjoys a number of tax benefits, including:

○   The archipelago has its own version of VAT, known as the Canary Islands Indirect General Tax (IGIC), which came into force on January 1, 1993. This is levied on goods and services supplied in the Canary Islands by traders and professionals and on imports and goods and it is much lower than VAT on the mainland. Whereas the standard VAT charge applicable to most goods and services on the Spanish mainland is 16%, the standard IGIC rate is only 5%.

○   Also of benefit to business is the fact that newly-formed and existing companies that expand, modernise or relocate their facilities can claim an exemption from transfer tax when they incorporate, increase their capital, or acquire capital goods located on the Canary Islands for three years from the execution of the public deed of incorporation or capital increase. Exemption from the IGIC is also available on supplies and imports of capital goods to these companies for three years.

○ Increased tax credits are available for investments made on the Canary Islands when certain requirements are met.

The Canary Island Investment Reserve

Reserva para Inversiones en Canarias (RIC) is an instrument aimed at stimulating self financed investment and is open to all companies subject to paying corporation tax and individuals subject to paying income tax. Profits obtained in the Canary Islands may be transferred to this special reserve up to the limit of ninety per cent of retained earnings. This gives rise to a reduction in taxable income for corporate income tax purposes in the amount provided for. For individual businessmen it means a reduction in personal income tax payable.

Appropriations to the reserve must subsequently be invested within three years in one of the following assets:

○ New or used fixed assets located in the Canary Islands.
○ The subscription of government stock up to the limit of fifty per cent of the amount transferred from profits each year.
○ The subscription of interest in the capital of companies that carry out their business in the archipelago, which subsequently make the above-mentioned investments.

The company must continue to own and actually use those assets for at least five years or for their useful life if this is lower.

The Canary Islands Special Zone

Zona Especial Canaria (ZEC) is a low tax regime which has been created with the objective of promoting the economic and social development of the islands and diversifying the production structure. The ZEC was established by the European Commission in January 2000 and will remain in force until December 2008. This legislation establishes a special tax regime for the Canary Islands Special Zone and applies to newly-formed entities domiciled in the Canary Islands and registered in the ZEC Official Register of Entities.

The tax benefits include a greatly reduced corporation tax of between one and five per cent. This is considerably less than the standard mainland income tax of 35%, or 30% in the case of PYMEs. In fact it is one of the lowest rates in the EU, the closest being Ireland at 12%. These reduced rates are not applicable on any profits exceeding certain thresholds and apply only to profits arising in the Canary islands.

ZEC entities are also exempt from transfer and stamp tax on acquisitions of assets. Finally, supplies of goods and services between ZEC entities and imports of goods by ZEC entities are exempt from the Canary Islands Indirect General Tax (the Canaries' equivalent of VAT).

There are a number of stipulations that must be observed in order to qualify for ZEC entity status. The company's office must be located in the Canaries, at least one of their directors must live in the Canaries and they must create at least five jobs within the first six months after authorisation. Companies must also make investments of at least €100,000 in the first two years in the acquisition of tangible fixed assets or intangible assets located within the ZEC.

In order to register, companies must file both an application and a report describing the activities carried out by the company, which must show viability, competitiveness and a contribution to the economic and social development of the archipelago.

INFRINGEMENTS AND PENALTIES

As recently as twenty years ago, tax evasion was rife in Spain. These days however, it is far more difficult to avoid paying taxes and there are severe penalties for infringements.

Current legislation establishes significant requirements for furnishing information to the tax authorities and there are heavy fines for non-compliance.

A delay in the payment of tax debts leads to an additional surcharge. If payment is made within three months then the surcharge is five per cent, 10% within six months, 15% within twelve months and 20% plus late payment interest after twelve months.

Failure to pay taxes to the authorities can be penalised with fines ranging from 50% to 150% of the unpaid amount. Non-monetary penalties may be applied on top of a fine and these include forfeiting the right to tax relief, to receive state subsidies and to conclude contracts with the state or other public agencies for a period of up to five years. Directors of legal entities are jointly and severally liable for fines.

If there is a fraudulent tax non-payment of more than €90,151.82, or if a state subsidy of more than €60,101.21 is fraudulently obtained then a *tax offence* has been committed. Tax offences are punishable by fines of up to six times the amount defrauded and imprisonment for between one and four years. For companies, this tax offence is deemed to have been committed by the director's or the company's legal representative.

Copies of your tax returns should be kept for at least five years which is the maximum period that returns are liable for audit by the tax authorities.

SOCIAL SECURITY

Ninety per cent of Spain's population pay into the *Seguridad Social* system and as a result receive cover for health care and maternity, industrial injuries, unemployment insurance, old age (pensions), invalidity and death benefits. The benefits are among the highest in the EU, but unfortunately, so are the contributions.

Salaried workers have the majority of their contributions paid for by the employer and the rest comes out of their salary. Unless one of the special programmes applies, employees are subject to the general social security programme. Under this programme, personnel are classified under a number of professional categories in order to determine their social security contribution. The contribution is based on the *nómina*, which is the official salary for a particular type of work. Each category has a minimum and a maximum contribution base, which is generally reviewed each year. The contribution bases for employees can be found in *Employing Staff.*

Autonomous workers, i.e. the self employed and business owners are required by law to pay into the Spanish Social Security System under the *autónomo* scheme. In 2004, the minimum contribution base for *trabajadores autónomos* was €755.40 per month and the maximum, €2731.50. In 2004, social security contributions for the self employed were set at 29.8% of the contribution base, although it is less if you choose not to have cover for short-term incapacity benefit. Self employed workers under fifty years of age are free to set their own contribution base anywhere between the minimum and the maximum. Autonomous workers aged fifty or over cannot pay contributions on more than €1,416 per month.

All self employed people, even those who work part time, must contribute to social security. If no work is done for any period longer than a calendar month, then it is not necessary to pay social security contributions for that time. For example, many small businesses close for a summer break during August.

Not only are social security contributions under this scheme higher than for salaried employees, there are also fewer benefits. For example, should the business fail, then the company directors, under the *autónomo* scheme, are not eligible for unemployment benefit. One way around this is for the company to give you a fixed contract. However, this should be discussed with a qualified accountant as it is only possible in certain circumstances such as when a director owns less than 24% of the company.

There are various levels of social security payable, depending on the amount of pension you wish to receive on retirement, but most people choose the minimum. Your social security office will supply you with a book of payment slips and payments can be made directly by your bank. It is important to note that if you have two unconnected jobs you must pay social security twice. Social security benefits are not taxed (with the exception of sickness benefits).

Further information regarding social security is available from the *Instituto Nacional de la Seguridad Social (INSS)*, Servicios Centrales, Padre Damián 4, 28036 Madrid (☎915-6888300; www.seg-social.es).

Registration

All companies must be registered in the Social Security Treasury office corresponding to the business address or head office before any work commences. You will need the original and copies of the business owner's N.I.E. and passport, a copy of the insurance policy for accident and health cover (paid for out of social security contributions), a copy of the deed of incorporation and a copy of the form from the tax office showing that you have registered for business tax. The company will be issued with a social security identification number and advised as to their social security obligations.

All employees must also be registered for social security purposes. The company director, or business owner is responsible for carrying out this requirement. This involves presenting the appropriate social security office with an application form and a photocopy of the national identity card, if the worker is Spanish, or the N.I.E. if the worker is foreign. Registration must take place prior to an employee starting work, although it cannot be done more than sixty days before.

You must also register yourself under the special autónomo scheme within thirty days of starting work. Registration should take place at the social security office corresponding to the area where the work will be done.

Benefits

Health Benefits. Social security payments entitle you to medical benefits through the Spanish National Health scheme, the *Instituto Nacional de Salud (INSALUD)*. Once registered as a member of INSALUD, you will receive an electronic social security card, a list of local medical practitioners and hospitals and general information regarding the services and charges. Registered members are entitled to general and specialist medical care, hospitalisation, laboratory services, discounted drugs and medicines, basic dental care, maternity care, appliances and transportation. Whilst you may have to pay a percentage of the cost of things like drugs and medicines, the majority of this care is totally free.

Sickness and Maternity Benefits. A worker may receive sickness pay which is a percentage of his salary depending on various factors. The self-employed may also receive sickness pay when ill at the rate of 60% of base payments for the first twenty days and then 75% thereafter as long as they can present a doctor's certificate testifying that they are unable to carry out their profession.

Maternity and paternity benefits are also both available for workers. Mothers can receive 100% of their benefit base for sixteen weeks, of which six weeks must be taken immediately after the birth. Paternity leave can also be taken for six weeks after the birth at full salary.

Unemployment Benefits. Almost all categories of employees are covered by unemployment insurance. The self-employed on the other hand, are not, unless they are medically incapacitated for work. Entitlement to unemployment benefit is based on having twelve months of contributions during the last six years and unemployment not being due to the refusal of a suitable job offer or training. Social security payments made in another EU country are taken into consideration.

The duration of the benefit varies with the amount of contributions. Regardless of previous earnings, the amount paid out to the unemployed currently stands at seventy-five per cent of the minimum wage. These benefits cease after one or two years, except in the case of families, who receive a reduced amount for two more years.

Pensions. Salaried workers and the self-employed are entitled to Spanish state pensions, which are the highest in Europe after Sweden. In 2003 the minimum pension at age 65 was €400.54 per month for a single person and the maximum was €2,029.27. Remember that just as workers receive fourteen pay packets a year, pensioners also receive fourteen payments including the two extra payments in July and December.

In order to qualify for a full pension as a *trabajador autónomo*, you must work for thirty-five years. The minimum period you must work to qualify for any sort of pension is fifteen years, for which you would receive half the full pension. Foreigners who contribute to social security for less than fifteen years receive no pension at all. However, if you move to Spain after working in another EU country, these state contributions can be transferred. Each country pays the percentage of the pension for which it is liable. UK citizens should obtain certificate E301 which shows the amount of social security contributions they have made. This can be obtained from the Department of Social Security Overseas Branch (Newcastle upon Tyne, NE98 1YX; ☎ 0191-2253963).

Should he so choose, the self-employed worker can set his salary base as high as €2700 a month and pay more into the system each month, in order to qualify for the maximum pension after thirty-five years. The pension is calculated mainly on the last fifteen years of working life and especially the last two.

Pensions are also set aside for those with permanent disabilities caused by work injury or an occupational disease, for widows and widowers and for orphans.

Private Pensions

Spain's ageing population means that a growing number of retirees are being supported by fewer and fewer workers. The future of state pensions is therefore in jeopardy, especially as they remain comparatively generous and more people receive their income from the state than from the private sector. It is estimated that by 2015 there will be over 7.5 million pensioners in Spain and the state pension fund, which has verged on bankruptcy before, may run into problems. The government is therefore trying to encourage people to pay into private pension funds in order to supplement their social security benefits. Businesses that employ a large number of people are also being leant on to provide company pension schemes.

The Spanish banks and some private companies offer a range of pension funds. It is also possible to continue contributing to a personal pension plan abroad and many of the European private pension companies have offices in Spain. However, such contributions are not tax deductible in Spain. Spanish tax-payers may normally deduct pension contributions up to a maximum annual limit of €9,015 from their taxable income.

Spanish pensions usually require a small minimum monthly payment, sometimes as low as €30. Lump sum contributions can be made whenever you like, although they must usually be more than around €600. Pensions should be index-linked so that they keep pace with inflation. Index-linked policies ensure that capital is tax free after contributions have been made for fifteen years but there is an increasing scale of tax penalties for early surrender. Some of the main pension providers in Spain are listed in the *Insurance* section below.

Businesses are not obliged to set up supplementary pension schemes for employees. Pension schemes are set up voluntarily in Spain and are deemed by Spanish law to be of a private nature. They may be set up and administered by corporations, companies, enterprises, associations, trade unions and many other bodies. If a pension scheme is set up by an enterprise for its employees, they form part of the *sistema de empleo* (employment system) and the workers covered by them participate fully in their management.

OTHER MATTERS

INSURANCE

Spain's insurance market has only really developed over the last twenty years or so, but these days there is a wide selection of both foreign and Spanish insurance companies. Some of these are listed below, but many more companies and brokers (*corredor de seguros*) are listed in the yellow pages under *Seguros*. There are hundreds of insurance companies to choose from including those who specialise in business insurance or in certain fields of business and those who cater mainly for the expatriate market, whatever their insurance needs.

Take care when choosing an insurance company. As in the UK, it can be difficult to obtain impartial advice from insurance brokers as they often work on a commission for selling a particular policy. Also a number of insurance companies have gone bust in recent years, and insurance fraud does occasionally occur. It is therefore a good idea to take recommendations and to shop around. Making a few telephone calls could save you quite a lot of money.

The type of insurance policy that you require will be very specific to your own business requirements. The main insurance considerations are:

- The building – if you own it. If you are renting, then the landlord should have insured the building (fire, lightning, explosions, water damage, electrical damage etc.)
- Its contents (theft, vandalism and damage of goods, installations, fixtures and fittings).
- Public liability (insurance against injury to third parties).
- Employer's liability (if you employ others).
- Goods in transit.
- Loss of earnings due to an incident leading to a claim.
- Professional negligence (especially for doctors, lawyers, architects etc. – see below).
- Any special cover specific to your business.

The main insurance companies offer general multi-risk policies which are fairly flexible and can be adapted to your individual needs. They may also offer special policies for certain lines of work. For example *Axa Seguros* (see below) has special policies for a number of businesses, including hotels and hostels, wine producers, mechanics and agriculture.

One difference between Spain and the UK is that professionals, such as doctors, surveyors, accountants and so on, usually arrange insurance through their own *colegio*, the body which regulates their profession. Insuring professionals is a slightly more complex matter as the policy must include clauses regarding professional negligence.

Insurance Contracts

Insurance contracts usually last for a year. The cost varies considerably depending on the level of cover required and factors such as the location of the premises. However, a figure of about €250 per year is a rough average for small businesses. It may be necessary to get your gestor to check over the contract before signing, especially if your Spanish is not perfect. This will avoid any loopholes that you were not aware of when it comes to trying to make a claim. Generally insurance companies in Spain do pay out on valid claims, but as with most bureaucratic procedures in Spain, actually receiving the money will probably take a lot of time and effort.

It is fairly common for insurance policies in Spain to be automatically extended for a further year if they are not cancelled two or three months before the expiry date. Make sure that you are aware of the amount of notice required for cancellation or you could be stuck with an unnecessary expense. There are certain conditions where a policy can be cancelled before the period of cover has expired, such as a change in the terms of the contract, or an increase in the premium. All cancellations should be made in writing and by registered post.

Making a Claim

The insurance company should usually be informed within two to five days of an incident, depending on the terms of the contract. In the case of criminal damage to the business or theft, then it is necessary to inform the local police and obtain a police report (*denuncia*) as evidence for the claim. The incident should be reported to the insurance company within twenty-four hours in such cases and they will usually send someone out to assess the extent of the damage.

Complaints

Complaints regarding your insurance policy should be directed firstly to the company itself and the larger companies will have a complaints department (*defensores del asegurado*). However, if the company does not rectify your complaint, you should contact the *Dirección General de Seguros y Fondos de Pensiones*, the body charged with regulating Spanish insurance companies and foreign companies with a registered office in Spain (Servicio de Reclamaciones, Dirección General de Seguros y Fondos de Pensiones, Paseo de la Castellana 44, 28046 Madrid; ☎913-397070; www.dgsfp.mineco.es)

Companies Offering Insurance for Businesses and Pension Plans

Axa Seguros y reaseguros: Paseo de la Castellana 44, 28046 Madrid; e-mail webmaster@axa-seguros.es; www.axa-seguros.es.
Caser Seguros: Plaza de la Lealtad 4, 28014 Madrid; ☎902-222747; e-mail comunicacion@caser.es; www.caser.es.
Direct Seguros: Ronda de Poniente 14, 28760, Tres Cantos,

Madrid; ☎902-404025; e-mail operaciones@directseguros.es; www.directseguros.es.

La Estrella Seguros: Plaza de la Castellana 130, 28046 Madrid; ☎902-333433; www.laestrella.es.

Knight Insurance: Ed. Lance del Sol, Pta I, 1a, Avda. Jesus Santos Rein s/n, Los Boliches, Apartado 113, 29640 Fuengirola, Malaga; ☎952-660535; fax 952-660202; www.knight-insurance.com. Specialists in insurance for expatriates.

Seguros El Corte Ingles: Hermosilla 112, 28009 Madrid; ☎901-122122; http://seguroeseci.elcorteingles.es.

Winterthur: ☎902-303012; fax 933-637240; e-mail winterthur@winterthur.es; www. winterthur.es.

UTILITIES

All public utility services are widely available in Spain and are generally cheaper than in northern European countries.

Electricity, telephone and water bills have a payment term of between fifteen days and a month. If not paid on time utility bills are increased by 20% and if still not paid then the phone line, water supply or electricity supply will be cut off and a reconnection fee charged. It may therefore be a good idea for any business to set up a standing order from the company account to ensure that the business remains in credit with the utility service companies at all times.

Outstanding utility bills for a business or business premises are transferred over to the new owner, so make sure that all bills have been paid up to date, before you move into a property.

Electricity

Electricity is an unavoidable overhead in any business but the charges in Spain are generally quite cheap. For example a fairly small bar or restaurant business should expect to pay around €100 per quarter, although this will obviously vary dramatically.

Having bought or rented the business premises it is necessary to register with the local electricity company by visiting their office, online, or over the telephone. The energy market was completely liberalised in 2003 and customers are free to choose their electricity provider, although in some areas there is no choice. The main providers, with offices all over Spain are Grupo Endesa (www.endesa.com), Iberdrola (www.iberdrola.es), Union Fenosa (www.unionfenosa.es) and Hidrocantábrico (www.h-c.es), all of whom offer special rates for small businesses. When registering, it will be necessary to take some identification and the contract and bills paid by the previous owner. You may also need to pay a deposit.

The cost of connection and meter installation will be somewhere between €100 and €300, depending on the power supply and region. Actual electricity consumption is usually charged per KW, although some companies allow customers to pay a monthly *cuota fija* (fixed charge), regardless of consumption. The difference is then either repaid or charged by the company at the end of the year. For small businesses this may help to control a tight monthly budget. It is more common however, to receive bills every two months following a meter reading. Additional charges on the bill include electricity tax at 4.86%, the meter rental charge, and VAT at 16%.

Many of the commercial estate agents recommend paying your electricity bills via direct debit (*transferencia*) as the queues at the local electricity companies' offices can be very frustrating. You can also pay at the local bank listed on the bill or at a post office.

Businesses with a lot of electrical appliances, or that rely heavily on computers should be aware that there are frequent power cuts in many parts of Spain, especially during periods of heavy rain. In order to avoid losing unsaved information on a computer, fitting an uninterrupted power supply (UPS) with a battery back-up, available for around €150, might be a good idea. This allows enough time to save your work after a power failure. Computers, fax machines and other expensive appliances should be protected from potential damage with a power surge protector.

Those businesses in areas where power failures are common may want to install a back-up generator in order to protect their business from being stuck without electrical equipment for days on end. Those people setting up a rural business in a very remote area may find that they have no choice but to invest in a generator as there simply is no mains electricity.

Gas

Hospitality businesses may choose to use gas appliances for cooking, hot water and heating. Mains gas is currently being introduced throughout Spain and is already available in all the major cities. In other areas however, the majority of houses and businesses still use bottled gas, which is considerably cheaper than mains gas in most northern European countries. Gas bottles known as *bombonas* are usually delivered to your door, although it is possible to collect your own from the nearest depot. The price of a 12.5kg canister is currently around €10.

The company responsible for delivering gas bottles is Repsol Butano. They require a contract with their customers, which involves a deposit of around €25 and a safety inspection of the property's gas installations. If you have a contract with them, they will continue to service and inspect all gas appliances every five years.

There have recently been reports of a number of scams surrounding gas, especially in the resort areas. For example there are a number of phoney Repsol Butano representatives who arrive without warning to inspect gas installations and then demand on the spot payments. Some of the distributors will also try to sell you unnecessary third party insurance for your gas appliances. This is a waste of money and should be avoided.

If your business does run off mains gas, then you will receive a bill every two months including VAT (*IVA*) at sixteen per cent. All utility bills can be paid by direct debit, known as *transferencia* in Spain. Upon purchase or lease of a business property, you should contact the local gas company in order to sign a contract, have the meter read and the gas switched on.

Water

Water rates are fairly minimal, although they have risen dramatically in recent years due to drought and are particularly high in the Canary Islands and parts of the Balearics. Mains water is metered and charges are calculated either per cubic metre used, or at a flat rate. After buying or leasing the business premises, you should ensure that the water contract is registered in your name and that there are no outstanding debts from previous owners. Water contracts can usually be transferred at the town hall, although in some areas private companies control the water supply. Remember to take identification such as a passport or residence permit and the contract and bills paid by the former owner, if applicable.

If your business needs to be connected to the local water supply, you will find that you have to pay a connection fee and meter installation charge, plus a deposit. In isolated areas the connection fee could be quite high, but in towns where the municipal council controls water supply it may be as little as €75. The average cost of the water itself is around €1 per cubic metre on the mainland. However, many municipalities levy a standing charge for a minimum amount of water per quarter whether it is used or not.

There are also additional water costs, depending on the area, such as the *canón de servicio*, a quarterly surcharge levied by some municipal governments and a water purification charge levied by some regional governments. There is also a small rental charge for the water meter. Water bills are paid quarterly. Note that VAT is charged at a reduced rate of 7% on water.

Telephone and Internet

Telefónica (www.telefonica.es), Spain's equivalent to BT, was privatised in 1998 and although it has lost its monopoly in Spain, it still retains a powerful hold on the telephone service. To get a telephone line installed at your business, you will need to go to the local Telefónica office (the address of local offices can be found in the Yellow Pages – *las paginas amarillas*). Take along your passport or *residencia* and proof that you own or lease the premises.

It currently costs around €150 for the initial connection fee and around €10 per month (plus *IVA*) for line rental. This standing charge will need to be paid bi-monthly and connections should not take more than a few days to install. It is possible to buy or rent handsets.

If you are taking over the account of a previous owner, you will need to arrange for the telephone company to close the existing telephone account and send a final bill to the previous occupiers of the premises. A new account will then be opened in your name from the day that you take possession of the property. There is a charge made for this service.

Call charges in Spain are higher than those in the UK. Since deregulation in 1998 competing telephone companies have offered alternative services to Telefónica and there is scope for using these other companies' services, especially for long distance and international calls. Some alternative companies, that may offer better packages for your business are **Retevisión** (www.retevision.es), **Jazztel** (www.jazztel.com), **Telforce** (www.usewho.com/telforce/), **Aló** (www.alo.es) and **Uni2** (www.uni2.es).

Peak rate is from 8am-5pm Monday to Friday and 8am-2pm Saturday as well as all day Sunday and during holidays. Different telephone operators offer different tariffs, which are subject to change due to the competition between the companies, so it is worthwhile shopping around for the best deal for your business.

Mobiles. As in most of the EU, demand for mobile phones has rocketed in Spain in recent years and many businesses rely on them. Self-employed tradesmen who are constantly on the move often only use a mobile for work purposes. Mobiles are also ideal as your first phone when you move to Spain as the connection charge is cheaper than a landline and the number remains the same wherever you are.

Before buying a phone it is a good idea to compare the various offers available. The three major networks have special services for businesses of all sizes and due to a price war between them in recent years, tariffs have fallen dramatically. The main Spanish providers are **Movistar** (www.movistar.es), **Amena** (www.amena.com) and **Vodafone** (www.vodafone.es).

The Internet. When you install your phone lines, you might want to connect to the internet with the Internet Service Provider owned by the telephone company. This usually allows you a free internet connection with calls at local rates. The telephone companies also have discount tariffs for heavy internet usage called *tarifa plana*. These charge a flat rate irrespective of usage. However, businesses that need regular internet access, or communicate mainly via e-mail will want to take advantage of an ADSL broadband connection. Broadband is now universal in most urban areas and fairly cheap to install (around €180). Line rental works out at around €35 per month for a standard 256k bandwidth.

Employing
Staff

CHAPTER SUMMARY

- Spain's unemployment rate has fallen dramatically in recent years, although it is still one of the highest in the EU. The Spanish labour market is characterised by a submerged 'black economy' and many workers are forced to work long hours in poor and sometimes dangerous conditions.

- It is obligatory for companies to register any vacancies, whether skilled or unskilled, permanent or short-term, full time or part time with the National Institute of Employment (INEM).

- **Employers in Spain:** are forced to pay *pagas extraordinarias* to their workers: extra payments of the monthly wage, usually made in the summer and at Christmas.

- **Social security payments:** are split between employer and employee, but it is the company that pays the lion's share.

- Workplaces with more than ten employees are required by law to appoint workers' delegates with powers to negotiate on behalf of the companies' employees.

- From the outset of business activities, employers are obliged to minimise the risk of occupational hazards.

- **Employment contracts:** can be made either for an indefinite term or for a specific duration. Under a short-term contract, the employer is liable for only a small redundancy payment when dismissing a worker.

  - The government provides certain incentives to encourage long-term employment contracts.

  - Although the situation is gradually changing, the cost of redundancy and the fines for unfair dismissal are still among the highest in Europe.

FINDING STAFF

SPANISH LABOUR MARKET

In the last few years, Spain's unemployment rate has fallen from twenty per cent to approximately ten per cent and a steady creation of jobs has been maintained. Although Spain still has one of the highest levels of unemployment among European countries, it is now much closer to the overall EU rate.

In terms of regional variation, Navarra, the Balearic Islands, Aragon, Rioja and Catalonia have the lowest unemployment rates at around 6.5%, whereas Andalucia, Ceuta and Melilla and Extremadura present the highest unemployment rates, sometimes exceeding 20%. Spain has the highest unemployment rate for young people in the EU, around 25%, and women too are high at 15%.

The service sector employs the greatest number of workers, although it has a high level of seasonality due to the tourism and catering sectors. Construction also continues to register a continued increase in employment after a few years of strong expansion and a period of stability.

Over the past two decades, a new trend has emerged in Spanish society, showing a preference for university education over technical training courses. As a result of these changes, Spain has an excess of professionals with university degrees and a clear deficit of technical and specialised professionals. Therefore, whilst the majority of the unemployed are unskilled, there is also a significant number who are university graduates.

The Spanish workforce has seen both an increase in salaries and an improvement in working conditions over the last ten years. However, the introduction of temporary contracts, which the unions described as *'basura'* or rubbish contracts, did erode some worker security but new government incentives for indefinite contracts are helping to counter this.

The black economy. This is another salient feature of the Spanish labour market. Recent estimates suggest that there are around 500,000 illegal workers in Spain. This positions Spain's 'black economy', or *economía sumergida* as one of the largest in the developed world. A combination of the influx of illegal immigrants, willing to accept low cash payments for unskilled work and unscrupulous employers demanding very low wage labour have created this thriving illegal economy. The problem is exacerbated in Spain by the employer's high social security obligations. Taking on an illegal worker may make the difference between profit and loss. As a result, it has been estimated that the turnover of this black economy makes up around 20-25% of the official GNP. Illegal workers are often forced to work very long hours in poor and sometimes dangerous conditions.

Employers who are new to Spain sometimes attempt to pay their workers cash-in-hand in order to either pay lower wages or avoid heavy social security payments. Be warned, this is not recommended. Recent years have seen a clamp down on illegal labour and labour inspectors now make regular checks. Every year they find hundreds of cases of unregistered employees, especially in the coastal bars and restaurants. Fines *start* at €3000 irrespective of whether you are employing Spaniards or foreigners and companies are fined for each illegal employee. Another risk is that if you do use illegal labour you will have no redress should a labour dispute arise. This fact that has been exploited in the past by less-than-honest expatriate workers in order to blackmail employers, safe in the knowledge that with such high fines it will be far cheaper to pay them off than to involve the authorities.

RECRUITMENT

Although recruitment in Spain is still largely conducted through informal networks with many key posts never reaching the job pages, it is obligatory for companies to register any vacancies, whether skilled or unskilled, permanent or short-term, full-time or part-time with the INEM, the National Institute of Employment (*Instituto Nacional de Empleo*). The INEM are a useful free source of information regarding the labour market and will advise businesses on the correct recruitment procedures to follow, including regulations for drawing up contracts.

National Institute of Employment. Jobs must be registered on an official form in any employment office, although preferably the one which corresponds to the business address. In order to find your local employment office, visit the INEM website (www.inem.es) and click on *Direcciones y Teléfonos*. The employer must indicate the following to the local employment office: what the work entails, type of contract, and the place, date and procedure of the selection process.

Having consulted its database, the employment office will send the employer a short list of suitable candidates for interview. Sometimes the employment office will carry out a series of tests on candidates in order to gauge their professional ability. All services provided to the employer by the INEM are free.

Private Placement Agencies. It is also possible to direct your employment needs to private placement agencies who will attempt to find suitable employees to meet your needs. These are non-profit making organisations who may only charge fees relating to expenses arising from the services provided. However, these private agencies are highly restricted and kept subordinate to the INEM and according to the Spanish Labour and Social Affairs office, it is likely that the next few years will see a greater liberalisation of private agencies. The INEM keeps a record of all of the authorised work placement agencies.

Temporary Employment Agencies (ETT). If you are looking for short-term workers, Spain has many Temporary Employment Agencies. These are private companies that facilitate temporary employment by contracting workers themselves and then transferring or lending their services to other companies. The databases of such agencies, known as ETTs in Spain are generally extensive, but have a high turnover rate and are therefore not always up to date. They may also have difficulty filling positions in certain professional categories. However, one advantage is that they do offer to replace a worker in cases of non-satisfaction of the client. Their names and addresses can be found in the Yellow Pages under 'Temporary Employment Agencies' or online at http://www.mtas.es/empleo/ett-OIA/inicio.htm.

Human Resources Consultants. If you are looking to fill a very specific position then it may be useful to use the services of an HR consultant. They offer a highly specialised service, recruiting professionals for permanent vacancies. HR consultants also usually offer a guarantee of replacement during the first three months. Their fees are fixed in relation to the salary of the position to be filled and the level of difficulty in finding candidates. These consultants can be found via the chambers of commerce, town halls, telephone directories or through the HR managers association, *Asociación Española de Dirección de Personal* (AEDIPE), C/ Moreto 10, 28014 Madrid; ☎914-200612; fax 914-200894; www.aedipe.es.

The Media. Finally, the media in Spain is a useful recruitment tool. There are more than a hundred newspapers published in Spain. The most important ones, which have distribution throughout Spain and overseas are *El Pais* (www.elpais.es) and *ABC* (www.abc.es), *El Mundo* (www.elmundo.es) in Madrid, and *El Periodico* (www.elperiodico.es) and *La Vanguardia* in Barcelona. All of these have a daily section dedicated to job offers, although most job offers are advertised in the Sunday editions. The regional and local newspapers also have a Classifieds section where it is possible to advertise positions. Local and regional radio and even television stations have programmes that will advertise positions for your business.

The internet has specialised websites offering CV databases at a fairly low cost and a search that can be done very quickly. However, the main disadvantage of these is that the contact is impersonal and not always kept up to date.

General Rules of Recruitment

In the past it was necessary for any foreigner starting a business in Spain to employ at least one Spanish national in order to receive a business licence. Whilst Spain's entry into the EU has led to the demise of this stipulation it is probably advisable to have at least one Spanish employee to assist in serving Spanish clients. Even if you are starting a tourism related business on the coast, it is worth remembering that just as many Spaniards spend their holidays at the beach as foreigners.

Minimum Age. It is illegal to employ anyone under the age of sixteen under any circumstances. For workers aged between sixteen and eighteen, there are certain protective measures. For example, they may not work overtime or at night and they may not work in certain hazardous or unhealthy activities or jobs.

Non-Discrimination. Discrimination in hiring or within the workplace based on sex, marital status, age, race, social status, religion or political ideology, union membership or language is prohibited by the Spanish Workers' Statute. It also prohibits discrimination due to physical or mental handicaps if a candidate is otherwise suitable for the job. In 2002 new laws were passed to confirm the principal that men and women have professional and salary equality. Direct discrimination, harassment and sexual harassment are all strictly prohibited because they violate the principal of equal treatment of men and women.

EMPLOYMENT LEGISLATION

Employing staff in Spain is subject to many regulations and what follows is merely a general overview. Any specific queries relating to the obligations of the employer should be directed to the Spanish Ministry of Labour and Social Affairs at one of the addresses below. The *Ministerio de Trabajo y Asuntos Sociales* also produces an annual 'Guide to Labour and Social Affairs' which is available in English for €14. It is also available in Spanish online at www.mtas.es/Guia2003/portada.htm.

Useful Addresses

Spain: *Ministerio de Trabajo y Asuntos Sociales*, Agustín de Bethencourt 11, 2.º, 28003 Madrid; ☎913-632300; fax 913-632373; www.mtas.es.

UK (accredited in the Republic of Ireland): Labour and Social Affairs Advice Bureau, 20 Peel Street, London W8 7PD; ☎020-7221 0098; fax 020-7229 7270; e-mail spanlabo@globalnet.co.uk.

Labour, Social Security and Social Affairs Sections, Brook House, 70

Spring Gardens, Manchester M2 2BQ; ☎0161-2373736; fax 0161-2287467.

United States: Labour and Social Affairs Advice Bureau, 2375 Pennsylvania Avenue, N.W., Washington D.C. 20037; ☎202-728-2331; fax 202-822-3731; e-mail claswash@erols.com.

Canada: Labour and Social Affairs Advice Bureau, 74 Stanley Avenue, Ottawa ON K1M1P4; ☎613-742-7077/613 742-8257; fax 613-742-7636; e-mail laboral@docuweb.ca.

WAGES AND HOLIDAYS

Spain has a statutory inter-industry minimum wage, which is established every year by the Government. In 2004 it amounted to €6,447 for persons over 18 years of age, including twelve monthly and two extra payroll payments. However this is quite low and most employees are paid more.

British employers are often very surprised to learn that their employees are entitled to fourteen months' salary for working only eleven months of the year. According to Spanish custom and law, at least two extra payroll payments must be made each year, one at Christmas and the other usually in July. These *pagas extraordinarias* were originally designed to ensure that workers had a little extra money for their Christmas and summer holidays and whilst they may indeed seem extraordinary to foreign employers they are universally acknowledged and eagerly anticipated.

In addition, workers are entitled to a month's vacation, as well as 14 paid public holidays. The worker must disclose holiday dates at least two months in advance, though it is very common for staff to take their annual holiday in August. As a result many local amenities, especially in the larger cities, close for all or part of August, of particular note when dealing with bureaucracy. At this time the roads are jammed with Spaniards dashing back and forth to the costas. Public holidays differ from year to year and from region to region, but generally an autonomous community will designate twelve national holidays and two local ones, such as an individual town's fiesta. During public holidays very few businesses, other than bars and hotels will be open.

NATIONAL PUBLIC HOLIDAYS

1 January	*Año Nuevo*	New Year's Day
6 January	*Epifanía*	Epiphany
March/April	*Viernes Santo*	Good Friday
March/April	*Domingo de la Resureccion*	Easter Sunday
April	*Lunes de Pascua*	Easter Monday
1 May	*Fiesta del Trabajo*	Labour Day
15 August	*La Asunción*	Feast of the Assumption
12 October	*Día de la Hispanidad*	National Day
1 November	*Todos los Santos*	All Saints' Day
6 December	*Día de la Constitución*	Constitution Day
8 December	*Fiesta de la Hispanidad*	Feast of the Immaculate Conception
25 December	*Navidad*	Christmas Day

For the rest of the year however, your employees should be hard at work, unless of course they get married, give birth, move house, are seriously ill, have union duties or unavoidable public and personal duties, or suffer the death or hospitalisation of relatives and so on, in which case they are entitled to a paid leave of absence. This can vary in length depending upon individual circumstances. A woman is entitled to 16 weeks maternity leave, although the Spanish Social Security system will pay much of her salary throughout this period.

The maximum working week is 40 hours, calculated on an annualised average basis. The large majority of people work Monday to Friday from 9am until 2pm and then from 4.30pm for another three hours. However a number of businesses are adopting the foreign company approach and operate from 9am to 5:30 or 6pm with an hour for lunch.

A minimum one and a half days off per week is mandatory, usually Saturday afternoon and all day Sunday, or all day Sunday and Monday morning. Workers under 18 are entitled to two uninterrupted days off per week.

Overtime must be voluntary and cannot exceed eighty hours per year, unless it is compensated with time off within four months from the date in which the overtime was worked. There is an official 40% pay increase for overtime, with double time for Sundays and national holidays.

SOCIAL SECURITY

One of the most crippling costs of employing staff is the payment of their Spanish Social Security contributions. Whilst these contributions are split between employer and employee, it is the boss who pays the greater share. This is on top of having to pay his own contributions (see *Tax, Social Security and Other Matters*).

All new employees must be registered immediately with the social security authorities. It is illegal to hire workers without having registered them for social security. It is also necessary to register their employment contract with the Spanish Institute of Employment (*INEM*) within the next ten days.

Social Security covers complete health care, accident and disability insurance, unemployment payments and the worker's retirement pension from the State.

Special social security programmes exist for agricultural workers, seamen, self-employed workers, civil servants and military personnel, coal miners and students. For everybody else there is a general social security programme. However, within the general programme the following professions qualify for special treatment: artists, railway workers, sales representatives, bullfighting professionals, professional football players.

Unless one of the special programmes applies, employees are subject to the general social security programme. Under this programme, personnel are classified under a number of professional categories in order to determine their social security contribution. The contribution is based on the *nómina*, which is the official salary for a particular type of work. Each category has a minimum and a maximum contribution base, which is generally reviewed each year.

SOCIAL SECURITY BASES FOR GENERAL CONTINGENCIES 2004

Group	Professional Category	Minimum Base	Maximum Base
1	Engineers and graduates	799.80 Euros/month	2731.50 Euros/month
2	Technical engineers and assistants	663.60 Euros/month	2731.50 Euros/month
3	Clerical and workshop supervisors	576.90 Euros/month	2731.50 Euros/month
4	Unqualified assistants	537.30 Euros/month	2731.50 Euros/month
5	Clerical officers	537.30 Euros/month	2731.50 Euros/month
6	Messengers	537.30 Euros/month	2731.59 Euros/month
7	Clerical assistants	537.30 Euros/month	2731.59 Euros/month
8	Foremen classes 1 and 2	17.91 Euros/day	91.05 Euros/day
9	Foremen class 3 and craftsmen	17.91 Euros/day	91.05 Euros/day
10	Labourers	17.91 Euros/day	91.05 Euros/day
11	Workers under 18 years of age	17.91 Euros/day	91.05 Euros/day

SOCIAL SECURITY BASE FOR PART TIME CONTRACTS 2004

Group	Minimum base (per hour)
1	4.01
2	3.32
3	2.89
4 to 11	2.67

The minimum contribution base, in practice, means that if you are paying an employee the absolute minimum wage, you will still have to pay contributions based on the minimum base of around €537.

Contributions are set for general contingencies in 2004 at 28.3% of the salary. An employee's contributions are in the region of 4.7 % and the employer's contributions are much higher at around 23.6%. However, the calculations are complex, with each of the percentages varying dependent on salary changes. As an employer, you must pay the contributions for each employee and you must also deduct the 4.7% contribution from their salary. This will be recorded by the Social Security General Treasury.

EMPLOYEE REPRESENTATION

Employees are represented by company committees or by employee delegates depending on whether the number of employees exceeds fifty. These representatives have a right to information on the employer's financial situation and to copies of the business's annual report.

Workers' Delegates. Work places with more than ten employees but fewer than fifty, require workers' delegates. Between one and three delegates are elected from within the workforce by a majority vote of the entire workforce. Delegates have a number of powers and responsibilities, including the right to negotiate company or workplace agreements, the right to information or consultation on financial, commercial and labour matters; responsibility for supervising and monitoring compliance with regulations on labour matters, social security, employment and health and safety; and the right to take administrative and legal action.

The Workers' Committee is an organ of representation in enterprises or workplaces with fifty or more employees and its purpose is to defend and promote employees' interests at work. The committee has between five and seventy-five representatives, depending on the size of the enterprise or workplace, who are elected by the employees and hold their mandate for four years. In contrast to the situation in many other countries, the committee's role is largely one of opposition, rather than of involvement in joint management. Whilst not union-based, the committees have been influenced and sometimes dominated in the past by trade unions.

Trade unionism in Spain is marked by its low membership and lack of funds. Spain has around 15 million workers but only 2 million of these are union members. However, agreements with the unions are legally binding.

Prevention of Occupational Hazards

The general framework for health and safety at work was established in 1995 and regulates the obligations or duties of employers and employees in relation to risk prevention. Increasingly stringent regulations on the prevention of occupational risks are being implemented in Spain.

Employers of any kind are responsible for the health and safety of their employees. From the outset of business activities, employers are obliged to remedy situations of risk and plan preventative action. This includes the obligation to perform risk assessments, adopt measures in emergency cases, provide protective equipment and to ensure the health of the employees.

In companies with more than fifty employees, a health and safety committee must be established and consulted regularly on procedures. However, in smaller companies it is necessary only to have a 'prevention service', for which the employer should nominate one or more workers. In companies with fewer than six workers, this role can be assumed directly by the employer. Safety representatives should monitor the compliance with regulations on the prevention of occupational hazards and be consulted on any employer decisions regarding such matters.

Failure to comply with these obligations may give rise to substantial fines by the Ministry of Labour and Social Affairs.

HIRING AND FIRING

TYPES OF CONTRACT

In Spain, a contract may be made verbally or in writing, although in certain cases such as part-time, temporary and training contracts lasting more than four weeks, the contract should be made in writing. Spanish labour law will usually regard the relationship between employer and employee as legally binding regardless of whether there is a written contract, and the worker is protected from dismissal even if your business is heading towards bankruptcy. Therefore it is vitally important that both parties understand the contract. Generally, the employment contract will include the following points:

- Details of the employer and the employee.
- The length of time that the contract is valid for.
- Type of contract.
- Professional category.
- Description of work conditions, the work centre, working hours, work schedule.
- Duration of holidays.
- Level of compensation for dismissal.

Employment contracts in Spain can be made either for an indefinite term or for a specific duration. This has not always been the case but anger amongst Spanish businessmen at the government's rigid protection of the worker's right to job security, led to a series of measures in 1994 and 1997 designed to create a more flexible labour market. The difficulty and expense of dismissing workers was creating real problems for seasonal businesses such as hotels, and was actually making bosses reluctant to take on extra employees for fear of being stuck with them through difficult periods. The government therefore made provisions for hiring workers on short-term contracts as well as the standard indefinite contracts.

Under a short-term contract the employer is liable only for a small redundancy payment when dismissing a worker. In general, contracts are made for an indefinite term and there must be specific circumstances to justify temporary hiring. Unless a temporary contract takes one of the legal forms shown below, it will be deemed to be permanent.

Short-Term Contracts

Contract for a specific project or service. The time period for this type of contract is uncertain and depends on the length of the project or service. This type of contract should clearly and precisely set out what work needs to be done. Its termination entitles the employee to receive an indemnification of eight days of salary per year worked.

Casual contract due to production overload or backlog. This type of contract may only last for a maximum period of six months, or twelve months if extended. Again the project should be set out clearly in the contract and its termination entitles the employee to eight days of salary per year worked.

Contract to substitute employees entitled to return to their job. This type of contract must name the employee being temporarily replaced and the cause of his or her substitution, and may only last until the return of the replaced worker.

Two further short-term contracts exist for training purposes:

- **Work experience contract.** This type of contract may last for a minimum period of six months and a maximum period of two years and is only open to recent graduates. The salary for such a contract must be between 60% and 75% of the salary of a worker holding an equivalent post. Once the term of the contract has expired, the same person may not be hired again under the same type of contract in any company.
- **Trainee contract.** This contract allows young people to acquire the theoretical and practical training necessary for a certain work post. It is specifically for workers aged between sixteen and twenty-one who do not have the qualifications necessary for a work experience contract and may last between six months and two years. The employer must ensure that

a trainee spends a minimum of 15% of his or her working hours undertaking theoretical training. Again, an individual may only work this type of contract once.

Incentives for Indefinite Contracts

Whilst businesses have been happy to take full advantage of such short-term contracts, the trade unions are less enthusiastic about what they refer to as *basura* or 'rubbish' contracts offering the worker little security.

In an attempt to counter trade union criticism and to reduce unemployment, the Spanish government offers incentives to encourage long-term employment contracts. These incentives are available to the employer if an already existing temporary contract is transformed into a permanent contract or if the permanent employee is from any of the following disadvantaged groups:

- Young people aged sixteen to thirty.
- Unemployed women.
- Women in sectors where they have traditionally been under-represented.
- The unemployed aged over 45.
- Unemployed workers who have been registered as job-seekers at the National Employment Institute (INEM) for at least six months.
- The disabled.

The use of such contracts entitles the employer to tax benefits and subsidies of up to 75% on the employer's social security contribution. It also reduces the amount of severance pay for improper dismissal to thirty-three days salary for each year worked, rather than forty-five.

Part-time Contracts. Employment contracts may be made full-time or part time. The part-time contract is defined as a contract in which the number of hours of work has been agreed with the worker per week, month or year and is less than that of a full time worker in the same work place, performing similar work. Part-time workers have the same rights as full-time workers.

DISMISSALS AND LABOUR DISPUTES

One of the most troublesome and expensive aspects of employing staff in the past has been firing them. Traditionally it was almost impossible to dismiss a worker for any reason other than gross incompetence without facing a large redundancy sum and possible legal action. Although the situation is gradually changing, the costs of redundancy and the fines for unfair dismissal are still amongst the highest in Europe. This has long been a bone of contention amongst Spanish employers and many choose to settle out of court due to the court's reputation for finding in favour of employees.

An employment contract may be terminated for certain reasons which usually do not give rise to a dispute such as mutual agreement, death, retirement, or a contract ending. However, Spanish law also regulates three principal grounds for dismissal of an employee – Collective layoff, Objective causes and Disciplinary action.

Collective Layoff. This category allows employers to dismiss a group of workers through a specific administrative procedure. Dismissals will only be possible if the Labour Authorities approve them by an administrative ruling. An employer may dismiss at least ten workers in a company with under a hundred employees, 10% of employees in companies with between a hundred and three hundred workers and more than thirty workers in companies with three hundred or more employees. The entire payroll can be dismissed under this category if the business ceases entirely. The procedure for such dismissals includes the obligation of granting a period of consultations with the workers' representatives or with the employees directly.

In such cases the employer must pay his dismissed employees twenty days of salary per year worked, up to a maximum of twelve months salary.

Objective Causes. An employer may dismiss a worker for a number of objective reasons such as the known ineptitude of the worker, the inability of a worker to adapt to the changes of his job, intermittent absences from work or a need to cancel posts due to economic, technical, organisation or production reasons. In these circumstances the employer should serve at least thirty days of advance notice in writing, or at least pay the salary of the notice period.

If an employee is dismissed for an objective cause, they are entitled to twenty days of salary per year worked, up to a maximum of twelve months salary. The worker may appeal this decision.

Disciplinary Action. If there is a serious and wilful breach of the contract by the employee, the employer may fire a worker without compensation. Such breaches of contract include repeated and unjustified absenteeism, insubordination or disobedience, physical or verbal abuse towards the employer, wilful diminution in the ordinary job productivity or habitual drug or alcohol abuse which adversely affects job performance. The employee must be given written notice of dismissal, stating the causes and effective date of dismissal. Again, the worker may appeal this decision.

Any dispute over a labour issue should be taken to the Labour Courts, the *Magistratura de Trabajo*, who will sit in judgement, although a conciliation hearing must first be held between the worker and the employer to attempt to reach an agreement. The Labour Courts will classify a dismissal as fair, unfair or null.

If the Labour Courts rule that a dismissal is unfair then the employer must either re-instate the worker or pay an indemnification of forty-five days of salary for every year worked, up to a maximum of forty-two months of salary.

The labour courts will pronounce a dismissal null for a number of reasons, including failure to comply with the formalities for objective dismissals, its cause being a form of discrimination and/or implying a violation of fundamental rights. In such cases the worker must be immediately reinstated and paid any due salaries.

Senior Executive Contracts. Special rules apply to certain categories of employees, most notably senior executives, who exercise independent management authority. The terms of employment for such executives are subject to fewer constraints than those for ordinary employees and as such they can be dismissed without cause. Executives must serve notice at least three months in advance and are entitled to an indemnity of seven days' pay per year worked, up to a maximum of six months' pay. The senior executive may also freely cancel his contract, as long as he serves three months of advance notice. However, if a senior executive is dismissed for objective causes or disciplinary reasons and the dismissal is judged to be unjustified then, he or she is entitled to twenty days' pay per year worked, up to a maximum of twelve months' pay.

SPECIAL LABOUR LAW CONSIDERATIONS WHEN BUYING OR SELLING A BUSINESS

Certain labour law provisions are particularly relevant when acquiring or selling an ongoing business in Spain.

When a business is transferred, the employees are also transferred and the new employer takes on all of the former employer's labour and social security rights and obligations, including pension commitments. The employees must be informed in advance of the proposed date of transfer, reasons for the transfer, the legal, economic and social consequences of the transfer for the employees and any measures which are envisaged for the employees. There is also an obligation to arrange for a period of consultations with elected employee representatives if new labour measures are adopted.

Another important consideration is that when a business is transferred both the seller and the buyer are jointly and severally liable for labour claims which arose prior to the sale for a period of three years afterwards.

Marketing your Business

CHAPTER SUMMARY

o The majority of businesses will find that not one marketing method, but a combination of several yields the best results. The Spanish attitude to marketing is to start local and then build up spheres of influence.

o Digital printing in Spain is very cheap and there are numerous graphic designers in the larger cities and coastal resorts.

o If your target audience is the expatriate and residential tourist market, then advertising in one of the many English-language newspapers printed along the Spanish coast is essential.

o Radio advertising can be a fairly cost-effective way of reaching a wide audience and all sorts of businesses choose to advertise on local radio.

o Trade directories are often out of date because people change jobs rapidly, so the only way to ensure that you target the right person is to call in advance.

  o The Spanish will almost always give you the name of the right person to contact.

o **Trade fairs:** are the only occasions when people from the same sector get together and they are therefore useful for networking and building up personal contacts.

o The ubiquity of the internet has led to a growing trend for tourists to plan part or all of their holidays on-line, so it is a good idea to advertise on tourism websites.

  o Many sites will list your business for free or even review your services.

o These days having a website is fundamental for many businesses. A good website acts as a permanent and highly-accessible worldwide showcase for your business.

The aim of marketing is to let your potential customers know firstly that the business exists and secondly how they could benefit from using your products or services. This is a major consideration for any new business. It can take a long time to establish a reputation and steady client base and many businesses struggle in the early years as a result. The right marketing tools will, however, help to ease the burden.

There are various methods of marketing available to businesses in Spain. Clearly the most suitable method of promoting your business depends very much on the goods or service that you offer and your target audience. For example, many bars and restaurants in coastal areas will find it adequate simply to have an A-board or displays outside the premises, announcing their main selling points. On the other hand, larger companies will need to make use of media advertising, and more direct marketing techniques such as mailshots. The key to successful marketing lies in finding the most effective method for *your* business at the lowest possible cost. A comprehensive guide to marketing methods in Spain, *'Guia de los Medios de Comunicación de España'*, is available for reference at the Information Centre of UK Trade and Investment (Kingsgate House, 66-74 Victoria Street, London SW1E 6SW; ☎ 020-7215 8000).

The majority of businesses find that not one marketing method, but a combination of several yields the best results. Philippe Guémené, who runs the Crocodile Park in Torremolinos, summed up his marketing strategy quite nicely: *'I see marketing as like trying to hit something on the beach. If you throw a handful of pebbles, then one of them is sure to reach'*.

The trade association responsible for the marketing and advertising industry in Spain is the *Asociacion Española de Anunciantes* (Paseo Castellana 121-8, E-28046 Madrid; ☎ 915-560351; fax 915-970483; www.anunciantes.com).

Good marketing is essential – Richard Spellman, Ambient Media and Communications S.L., Madrid

It is important to remember that your marketing budget comes out of your bottom line and this can be very painful. However, the business does need to be marketed well otherwise nobody will know that you are there. There is a lot of competition in Spain in some areas – for example, half of the registered bars in Europe are in Spain – so it is necessary to have something which makes your business stand out.

The Spanish attitude to marketing is to start local and then build up spheres of influence. Don't attempt to take on the whole country at once because you will spend all of your time travelling and get nowhere. You need to build up a power base that is local or at the most regional. When you have that, you can move on.

Word of mouth and personal contacts are the best marketing tools that you can possibly have. If you gain a reputation for giving good value for money, it will be greatly appreciated here in Spain. The Spanish are very price conscious.

When advertising in Spain, remember that everything here comes in through the eyes, it is very visual. There is no subtle text, they don't mind saying we are the best, we are the biggest etc., even if it's nonsense. Advertising standards authorities here have a very laissez-faire attitude.

MARKETING METHODS

Advertising

Directories. A good place to start is to ensure that you are included in the appropriate business directories. The Spanish version of Yellow Pages is published in each province and provides details of local businesses (*Paginas Amarillas;* ☎906-365024; www.paginasamarillas.es). Euro Pages (☎900-131131; www.europages.es) is also a useful tool for businesses with a more international perspective. It contains information on some 150,000 suppliers. In some areas there are also English-language business directories. The English Speaker's Telephone Directory (ESTD; ☎956-776958) for example, is produced annually and contains business listings for the Costa del Sol and Gibraltar.

Printed Material. Advertising your business can take many different forms but it is always useful to have something printed which can be handed out to potential clients or distributed as leaflets, posters and flyers. Digital printing in Spain is very cheap and there are numerous graphic designers in the larger cities and coastal resorts. A full colour glossy brochure will need the experience and professionalism of a designer and printer, but simple leaflets or business cards can be designed on any home computer and then simply taken to the local copyshop or printshop for mass production.

Once printed, it is necessary to find the best methods of distribution. In the coastal resorts, many bars, hotels and tourist related businesses employ reps to distribute pamphlets and flyers in the streets or take them to hotel lobbies and tourist information centres. It can be quite expensive to employ your own marketing reps and a more cost-effective alternative is to employ the services of a company that represents a number of businesses. For example in the Costa del Sol area, companies such as Promarketing S.L. (C/ Murillo Bracho 3, 29620 Torremolinos, Malaga; ☎ 952-383140; fax 952-387566; e-mail info@promarketing.es; www. promarketing.es) offer a service which ensures that hotels, travel agents, car rental offices, tourist information centres and any other places with a proliferation of tourists are well stocked with your leaflets. Their representatives make regular tours of the area and ensure a regular supply of promotional material. Such a service is invaluable to any tourist attraction or service.

Media. The pages of the English language media in Spain are filled with advertisements for every imaginable expatriate service in English. If your target audience is the expat and residential tourist market then advertising in one of the many newspapers printed in English along the Costas and in the larger cities seems to be essential. The main newspapers are detailed below, but you should also look out for the various free papers which spring up from time to time in the main cities and coastal resorts.

The costs involved in advertising in an English language newspaper can vary depending on the publication's circulation and the size and type of advertisement. Rates in the Costa Blanca News, which is read weekly by around 100,000 residents and tourists, currently range from 30 cents per word for small ads, to €350 for a quarter page display advertisement, to €1,350 for a full page. A full-page advertisement in the Costa del Sol News or Weekly Post, costs €690 and the equivalent advertisement in the Majorca Daily Bulletin costs around €800. It is usually possible to take advertisements in a variety of sizes, ranging from an eighth of a page upwards.

Those businesses aiming at a Spanish market may well choose to advertise in one of the local newspapers. Most newspapers publish free supplements, often listing local attractions. However, the Spanish are not a nation of newspaper readers despite the rebirth of the free press after Franco's death and it may be more sensible to advertise in the appropriate trade magazine, of which there are many. Remember that in something as visual as an advertisement, if the Spanish is not word-perfect, then your business will probably be rejected out of hand.

Those aiming at the expatriate market may also find radio advertising to be a useful method of reaching a large audience. Local expatriate radio is only able to survive through the medium of advertising, but unfortunately the quality of advertising in Spain is still fairly amateur. Nevertheless, the English and other foreign-language commercial radio stations in major cities and resort areas do reach a large audience and are worth investigating. Stations include Central FM, Coastline Radio, ONDA Cero International, Global Radio, Octopus FM and Spectrum FM.

All sorts of foreign business owners choose to advertise on local radio, from bars and restaurants to removals companies. A station such as Octopus FM on the Costa del Sol (98.3FM; Avda. Los Boliches, Los Boliches, Fuengirola, Malaga; ☎952-667742; fax 952-667720; e-mail info@octupusfm.com; www.octupusfm.com), will offer you the option of having the advert simply read out by an in-house presenter at no extra charge or outsourcing ad production to a local company for around €50, or to a UK company for around €120. Airtime rates vary from station to station and depending on the number of daily plays required, but on average you should expect to pay around €500 a month for five daily plays of a thirty second advertisement. In winter the same deal might be available for as little as €200. Some stations also offer businesses the opportunity to sponsor an hour of airtime at a negotiable rate.

English Language Newspapers

Barcelona Metropolitan: ☎934-514486; www.barcelona-metropolitan.com. Free monthly magazine.
Costa Blanca News: Edificio Ensenada, 2nd Floor D, Calle Dr. Perez

Llorca 9, 03500 Benidorm, Alicante; ☎965-855286; e-mail smallads@costablanca-news.com; www.costablanca-news.com. Weekly newspaper published on Fridays.

Costa del Sol News: CC Las Moriscas Local 13, Avda. Juan Luis Peralta, 29639 Benalmádena, Malaga; ☎952-449250; fax 952-568712; www.costadelsolnews.es. Weekly newspaper published on Fridays.

Weekly Post: Edificio Ensenada, 2nd Floor D, Calle Dr. Perez Llorca 9, 03500 Benidorm, Alicante; ☎965-855286; e-mail smallads@costablanca-news.com; www.costablanca-news.com. A sister paper to the Costa Blanca News which comes out on Saturdays. Also covers the Costa Blanca area.

The Majorca Daily Bulletin: San Feliu 25, Palma de Mallorca, Mallorca; ☎971-788400; e-mail editorial@majorcadailybulletin.es; www.majorcadailybulletin.es. On sale in Majorca, Menorca, Ibiza and Formentera.

Sur in English: Diario Sur, Avda. Dr. Marañón 48, 29009 Malaga; ☎952-649600; www.surinenglish.com. Weekly newspaper covering the Costa del Sol area.

Tenerife News: Apartado 11, 38412 Los Realejos, Tenerife; tel. 22-346000; fax 22-344967; e-mail info@tennews.com; www.tennews.com. Fortnightly newspaper with a readership of around 50,000.

Direct Marketing

If you have done a comprehensive study of the market before going ahead with establishing the business (See *Procedures for Starting a New Business*), then you should have a fairly good understanding of your potential clientele. Databases and sector guides can be bought from marketing companies, the addresses of which are available from the Association of Direct and Interactive Marketing Agencies (*Asociación de Agencias de Marketing Directo e Interactivo*, Avda. Diagonal 437, 5a Planta, 08036 Barcelona; ☎ 932-402720; fax 932-012988; e-mail info@agemdi.org; www.agemdi.org). Some of the better chambers of commerce will also be able to furnish you with such information, often free of charge.

Wasting money on ineffective advertising is a sure-fire road to bankruptcy. Make sure you target your marketing at the right sector, be it the transitory tourist trade, the residential expatriate market, the Spanish market, the young, the old and so on. Selective advertising not only improves marketing efficiency but also allows you to be very precise in your material, creating the impression of professionalism amongst your target audience.

Mailshots. The mailshot is usually a package consisting of a brochure and a standard letter of introduction with a short, simple sales pitch. The disadvantage of this kind of advertising is that the response rate is traditionally very low, although it remains a very popular method of publicising businesses.

Unless you intend to send enormous numbers of mailshots, it is advisable to send them to specific target groups (see above). Having compiled a list of organisations that might need your product or service, it is necessary to address your information to the correct person. In Spain particularly, letters which do not pinpoint a specific person, or e-mails directed to 'info@...' will simply go straight into the bin. Trade directories are often out of date because people change jobs rapidly, so the only way to ensure that you get the right person is to call in advance. This can be quite difficult, especially if your Spanish is fairly elementary. Sometimes though, this can work in your favour as there is a tendency to assume that all foreign calls must be important. The Spanish are very generous and will almost always give you a contact name.

It is always a good idea to follow up a targeted mailshot with a phone call. As a general rule, the Spanish are unwilling to commit anything to paper and prefer to do business over the phone or in person.

E-MAIL MARKETING

New Spanish regulations expressly forbid the use of 'spamming', i.e. unsolicited and indiscriminate advertisements sent by e-mail. Should you wish to use e-mails, the Spanish will appreciate it if you include a remove notice, allowing them to be removed from a mailing list if they reply to the e-mail. The standard Spanish remove notice reads:

En (name of your company) *mantenemos nuestro compromiso de privacidad sobre los datos. Bajo el Decreto S.1618 aprobado por el 105 Congreso esta carta no puede ser considerada SPAM mientras incluya la forma de ser anulada. Si no quiere recibir más información de* (name of your company) *conteste a este mensaje con Asunto: baja. Muchas gracias por su atención.*

Trade Fairs and Exhibitions. The best way to establish your business within a particular sector is to visit a trade fair. These are held with great regularity in Spain and for all sorts of trades. They are the only occasion when people from the same sector get together and they are therefore useful for networking and building up personal contacts. As mentioned earlier, the importance of personal relationships in Spanish business should not be underestimated.

It is not necessary to take a stand at the fair, which can be quite expensive. At an early stage it is adequate to talk to as many people as possible and hand out business cards. The Spanish are very good about giving you a hearing and a well prepared visit to a trade fair may help to drum up a great deal of business.

Spain has a good selection of trade magazines and periodicals covering a wide-range of sectors. Information about forthcoming local trade fairs and exhibitions should be listed in these. Otherwise, details of fairs in the major cities can be found at the following web addresses:

- Madrid: www.ifema.es
- Barcelona: www.firabcn.es
- Bilbao: www.feriaint-bilbao.es
- Valencia: www.feriavalencia.com

A search facility for trade fairs in Spain is also available on the website: www.spainbusiness.com.

INTERNET MARKETING

Recent years have seen a tremendous increase in internet usage throughout Spain, largely due to lower call charges and cheaper computers becoming available. As a result, over 65% of all small and medium-sized businesses in Spain have some sort of internet presence, be it advertisements or their own website.

Registering your business with an online directory can therefore be a very useful method of attracting business. Directories which offer internet access such as *Paginas Amarillas* (www.paginasamarillas.es) and Euro Pages (www.europages.es) are very accessible and fairly cheap to register with.

If your business caters to the tourist trade, there are many opportunities to advertise with, or at least be listed by, one of the many websites devoted to informing the public about places to stay, things to see and do, nightlife and so on. The ubiquity of the internet has led to a growing trend for tourists to plan part or all of their holidays online and tourism websites receive thousands of visitors every day. Even a regional website such as www.andalucia.com purports to receive 50,000 visitors every week. Many of these websites also have directories of all sorts of businesses from doctors and estate agents to antiques dealers and dating agencies, catering mainly for the expatriate scene. Many sites will offer to list your business for free or to review your business online. Others sell advertising space.

Most of the English-language newspapers and many regional Spanish newspapers (see above) also have an online classifieds section where you can advertise your business or service.

Useful Websites

General tourist and expat sites:
www.spanishforum.org
www.idealspain.com
www.tourspain.co.uk
www.tuspain.com
www.travelinginspain.com
www.aboutspain.net

www.spainforvisitors.com
www.typicallyspanish.com
www.spainexpat.com.

Regional sites
www.andalucia.com
www.granadainfo.com
www.ibiza-spotlight.com
www.madridman.com
www.planetbenidorm.com
www.xbarcelona.com

Creating Your Own Website

For the majority of businesses today, having a website is absolutely fundamental and if managed well is a cost-effective method of attracting business. Many people are put off because they don't have the technical knowledge themselves and are worried that employing others to manage the website will be horrendously expensive. In fact, after the initial set-up costs, the expense of monthly maintenance of the site is marginal and pales in comparison to the potential rewards a well-designed site will bring. A good website acts as a permanent and highly accessible worldwide showcase for your business.

It is particularly important to have a website if your business is tourist related. One of the major problems with targeting visitors to Spain is that every week or every fortnight, your target population changes completely. With print media, radio or television, it can be very costly to continue paying for weekly advertisements throughout the entire season. On the other hand, with a website the information is permanently available to your target clientele anywhere in the world. Potential customers, planning their holiday activities in advance, can find information about your business and perhaps even book online. For those letting out property, a website is absolutely vital. According to Mike Stickland of Stickland Web Studio, such businesses receive around two thirds of their bookings online.

Having a website is essential. Peter Deth – Happy Diver's Club, Marbella

The internet is the most important advertising or marketing tool that we have. More than fifty per cent of our customers have seen our website, so we spend a lot of money on maintaining and updating the website to keep it looking fresh. I am not a web designer so I employ a webmaster, someone who knows how to bring my website to the top of the search engines. We now have fairly high ratings on all of the search engines, but we put a lot of effort into it. I would rather spend more money promoting the website than on print media because it is far more important. We spend around €100 a month on the website, but I would be happy to pay double that because it brings in so much business.

The most important consideration for any website is accessibility. If the site does not appear near to the top of the seven major search engines, then people simply won't find you. Obviously, the more obscure your business is, the greater chance your website has of getting a higher rating. One way to guarantee a higher search-engine rating is to pay one of the major search engines to position the site. However, this can be expensive and is not altogether necessary. A good web designer will register your site with all the major free search engines and construct your site in such a way that it will achieve as high a position as possible. This is done by strategically placing the words that people are likely to search with on the first page of the site and by creating hidden 'keywords'.

The layout of your website comes down to personal preference. However, a typical site includes the following:

- Home Page. This should be well presented and contain the title, logo, a description of the business complete with likely search words, contact details and links leading to the other pages.
- The Business. The second page should have a full description of the business, complete with pictures if applicable, and the main selling points. If you plan to offer a discount for online bookings, this information should be clearly displayed here.
- Location. It is a good idea to have a printable map of the area complete with a clear description of how to find the business.

○   Contact Page. Information regarding enquiries and bookings should be detailed here. Many property rental businesses use online booking forms.

Making the site visually attractive is imperative. Some of the more economical web designers use templates with unoriginal graphics, which will look cheap and put people off. However, if your website is too 'flashy' then it may not be user-friendly or download quickly. Research shows that if a website takes longer than eight seconds to download then people will look elsewhere. Remember that if you are aiming at a Spanish market then nothing will deter people more than poorly translated Spanish. Make sure you use a reputable translator if your own Spanish is not word perfect.

A final consideration is the 'domain name'. This is the address of your website, which typically takes the form *www.yourname.com*, or possibly *.co.uk* in Britain, or *.es* in Spain. Having a memorable domain name will improve your accessibility and hence the effectiveness of the site.

Costs. Set up costs can vary enormously. A bottom-of-the-range site may cost no more than £79 to get up and running, although it is possible to spend anywhere up to £2000. If you aim to spend around £500-£600 then you should be able to come up with an attractive and highly ranked site.

Once a website is running, then the hosting costs can be as little as £5 a month. Maintenance costs will depend on how often the site needs to be updated. For the majority of businesses, the site will not need to be updated with any great regularity and website designers usually charge around £30 per hour for their services.

Finding a Website Designer

There are literally hundreds of freelance designers who will be happy to give you a quote for a website. Some of these who specialise in businesses in Spain are listed below, but an internet search for designers in your local area should produce a good selection. Most websites have a link to their designer at the bottom of the homepage, so it is a good idea to contact those designers who have created sites which appeal to you and may be suitable for your own business.

Stickland Web Studio, 83 North Trade Road, Battle, East Sussex
 TN33 0HN; ☎01424-775021; e-mail mike@sticklandweb.co.uk;
 www.sticklandweb.co.uk.

Pro Digital Media Internet Design Agency; ☎952-885985; e-mail
 sitelink@website-designers-spain.20m.com; http://website-design-
 ers-spain.20m.com.

Peppercorn Ltd., UK office: 1st Floor, 16 Church Street, Amp-
 thill, Bedfordshire, MK45 2EH; ☎0870-0660400; e-mail
 design@peppercorn.co.uk; Spain Office: Camino Laurel 4, Las
 Camillas, Alcaidesa 11315, La Linea; ☎956-797100; e-mail
 diseno@peppercorn.co.uk; www.peppercorn.co.uk.

Mas Adelante; ☎647-533833; e-mail info@masadelante.com;
 www.masadelante.com.

Venga Venga Worldwide Web Weavers; www.vengavenga.com.

Selling On

CHAPTER SUMMARY

○ Any business needs to allow itself some time for preparation before selling. Entrepreneurs must set the right price, get the accounts in order and ensure that the business looks as attractive as possible.

○ All employees must be informed in advance of the proposed date of transfer, reasons for the transfer, and the legal, economic and social consequences of the transfer for employees.

○ Businessmen re-selling a leasehold business usually price the business merely by charging what they paid in the first place, plus a little extra if they feel that they have increased the value of the business.

○ The easiest way to sell on is to employ the services of a registered agent. Agents deal with all matters including advertising the property and accompanying prospective buyers to view the business.

○ Buyers usually put down a 10% deposit with an arrangement to pay the balance within an agreed time period.

○ If you are selling a business with freehold premises, the two aspects must be treated separately. The sale of the property will be dealt with by a notary public, whereas the sale of the business's intangible assets are a private agreement between vendor and purchaser.

○ **Capital Gains Tax** is incurred every time a property, business or stocks and shares change hands. The taxable amount is the difference between the acquisition and the transfer values.

    ○ Short-term gains are added to any other income and taxed as part of IRPF (income tax).

    ○ Plus Valia tax is commonly paid by the purchaser rather than the vendor.

There is a thriving market for resale businesses in Spain and if you have made a success of your business and your efforts have crystallised into a valuable asset, then it may be time to sell on. Entrepreneurs choose to sell a business for many reasons, including wishing to invest the capital into a new project. Whatever your reason, the procedures involved in selling are fairly simple and you should be able to demand a reasonable price for your business.

The costs involved in selling a business are minimal but will include:

O   Capital gains tax.
O   Fees to professional advisors (lawyers and accountants).
O   Business agent's fee.
O   Any liabilities not being assumed by the buyer.

PREPARING THE BUSINESS FOR SALE

Any business needs to allow itself some time for preparation before selling. Issues such as setting the right price for a business, getting the accounts in order and ensuring that the business looks as attractive as possible will take a good deal of forethought and hard work. Nevertheless, it will save you time and money if you get these things right at the outset.

Business records can be a very effective tool for luring potential buyers. It can take time to prepare the books in such a way as to show maximum profitability and ideally you should start preparations a year or more in advance. The most recent financial year's results are critical when a buyer is evaluating a business. Most small businesses operate in such a way as to minimise tax liability, for example receiving tax credits by reinvesting any profit immediately. Unfortunately accounting practices that minimise tax liability can also minimise the apparent value of the business. As a result, there is often a conflict between running a company the way an owner wants to and making the company attractive to potential buyers. Consultation with an accountant or *asesor fiscal* will help you to reflect optimum performance. Financial records should be compiled neatly and clearly for ease of viewing.

Good financial statements do not eliminate the need for making the company aesthetically pleasing. The premises should always be clean, the inventory current and the equipment in good working order. Presentation plays a crucial role when selling a business, so a lick of paint here and there, the replacement of old and faded decorations, fixtures and fittings are all important.

Certain labour law provisions are particularly relevant when selling an ongoing business in Spain. When a business is transferred, the employees are also transferred and the new employer takes on all of the former employer's labour and social security rights and obligations, including pension commitments. The employees must be informed in advance of the proposed date of transfer, reasons for the transfer, the legal, economic and social consequences of the transfer for the employees and any measures which are envisaged for the employees. There is also an obligation to arrange for a period of consultations with elected employee representatives if new labour measures are adopted. It is important to keep your employees on side as the loss of any key employee could be crucial to the success of the new owner and hence the deal.

Some businesses might even consider preparing a business presentation package to show to potential buyers. Such a document would usually include:

- A history of the company and details of the current owners.
- Three to five years' financial records.
- A description of how the company operates, including details of any suppliers and/or distributors.
- A description of the facilities and personnel if applicable.
- A review of marketing practices and details of the competition.
- An explanation of insurance coverage.
- A discussion of any pending legal matters or liabilities.

Pricing the Company

Determining the value of a business is a process fraught with potential differences of opinion and difficulties. Unlike in other countries, there is no set format for pricing your business. As described in *Acquiring a Business or Business Premises*, the Spanish use a very informal system of evaluating a business based on the price of similar businesses in the area. Demand for resale businesses is high and sadly, the ability of foreign entrepreneurs to recognise that a business is overpriced is often low. It is for this reason that even owners that have been running their business at a loss are still able to sell at a similar price to their initial purchase price.

For those entrepreneurs reselling a lease which they have bought previously, the trend is to charge the same amount as they paid for the business, plus perhaps a little more if they have invested a lot of money or been successful in building up a regular clientele. This should be demonstrable in the business accounts. If you wish to get back the amount that you originally invested, remember to include the agent's fee (usually between 5% and 10%) and the landlord's transfer fee (written into the contract, usually between 5% and 20%), in the price. You will of course be liable for capital gains tax on the difference between the purchase and sale value.

Those who are selling on a business which they themselves have built up from scratch will have greater difficulties in assessing the value of their business and it may well be worth employing the services of an accountant or asking the agent to evaluate the business. Starting with an assessment of the value of other similar businesses, you should then factor into the calculations a number of other variables including:

- Pecent profit history.
- General condition of the company (e.g. the facilities, the accuracy of books and records etc.)
- Market demand for the particular type of business (including an evaluation of the competition).
- Economic conditions of the area.
- The intangible assets of the business such as client base, location, reputation, years in business, licences and so on.
- Future profit and expansion potential.

A further consideration when pricing the business is the amount of cash that you will personally require for the next stage of your life. Many business sellers want enough cash to repay all of their personal debts, such as their mortgage, personal loans, credit card debts etc. Additionally, they may be looking to invest the profits from the sale into a further business venture. Whatever your personal needs, be sure to estimate the amount that you need from the sale before fixing a price.

SELLING THE BUSINESS

If you decide to sell the business as either a leasehold or a freehold, or just the premises, the procedure is fairly simple. You may sell privately but most people employ the services of a registered agent (many agencies are detailed in *Acquiring a Business or Business Premises*), who will deal with all matters including advertising the property and accompanying prospective buyers. Agents will also deal with the legal technicalities of the sale such as contracts, signing before the notary (for a freehold), paying necessary taxes on the property and so on. Using an agent ensures the smooth progress of the sale and relieves the client of much of the usual worry and concern relating to the sale.

It is possible to advertise the business for sale through several estate agencies and only pay commission to the one that makes the sale. Estate agents in Spain operate much more openly than in the UK and often share their contacts within a network. Usually they have an agreement to split the commission between them, regardless of who actually sells the business.

Commission rates vary between the various agencies, so it pays to shop around. As a rough guideline, expect to pay around 5%-10% of the sale price to the agency. The more valuable your business, the lower the rate of commission. The commission is usually accounted for in the asking price so although it appears that the vendor pays the agent's commission, in fact it is the purchaser who bears the actual cost. If you bought the property through local estate agents, it could be useful to ask them to deal with the vending process as they will know the business and the property.

Although the purchaser of a business should always seek legal representation, it is not always necessary for the vendor. Nevertheless, it may be advisable especially if you are selling a business which you have built up from scratch and wish to add any special clauses. For example, some vendors may wish to include a clause protecting their rights to open up another similar business and their rights to take clients with them. Unless the buyer specifically demands clauses regarding these issues in the contract however, your rights will not be affected. Even if such practices are specifically prohibited in the sale contract, the Spanish often get around the problem by obtaining a business licence in someone else's name! A list of English speaking lawyers dealing with Spanish commercial law is included in the chapter *Procedures for Starting a New Business*. Alternatively, the nearest embassy or consulate will have a list for the local area.

When it comes to striking a deal with a prospective buyer, they will usually put down a 10% deposit with an arrangement to pay the balance within an agreed time period. As mentioned previously, if the buyer pulls out at the last minute or does not complete payment, then he will lose his deposit. However, if the vendor pulls out of the agreement having accepted a deposit, it is usual for the vendor to have to pay twice the amount of the deposit back to the prospective purchaser.

Selling a Freehold Commercial Property or Freehold Business

The Spanish make a clear distinction between the business premises and the business itself, no matter how apparently intertwined they may appear, for example, in the case of a hotel. If you are selling a business with freehold premises, then you must treat the two aspects separately. The sale of the property will be dealt with in the deeds executed by a public notary. The sale of the often intangible business assets are a private agreement between vendor and purchaser.

Freehold properties on urban land will be liable for *plus valia* tax upon transfer. Although this should in theory be paid by the vendor, it is more likely that the purchaser will pay this tax unless a clause is added to the contract of sale and a sum is withheld for the payment of the tax. If you paid the *plus valia* tax when you bought the property freehold, make sure that it is paid by the purchaser when you come to sell, otherwise you will have paid it twice.

There are a number of documents that you will need to present to the notary when it comes to selling on a freehold or a freehold business. As far as the notary is concerned, the business aspect is part of a private contract between the two parties and he will not enter into this aspect of the sale. The documents that must be presented are therefore only those related to the actual property. These are:

○ The *escritura*: You must present a copy of your title deeds to the property which you will have received when the property was filed with the *Registro de la Propiedad* (the property registry office). This details any charges, mortgages etc that are listed against the property.

○ Last receipt of payment of the *Impuesto sobre Bienes Inmeubles – IBI*. It is now a legal obligation to produce this in order to prove that the real estate tax has been paid on the property to date and that the property is registered with the local authorities for tax purposes. This receipt will also show the *valor catastral* – the value of the property as assessed by the local authorities.

○ The *Referencia Catastral*: This is the file number of the property as kept by the *Catastro* (Land Registry). The Catastro has a record of the physical characteristics of the property.

○ Copies of the transfer tax, stamp duty and *plus valia* tax that you paid on the property when you bought it.

○ Declaration of income tax. Your tax status may be required by the notary and the purchaser.

CAPITAL GAINS TAX

Capital gains tax is incurred every time a property, business or stocks and shares change hands. It should not be mistaken for the local tax known as *plus valia* ('capital gain') tax which is described below.

Taxation of Spanish capital gains is fairly complex and it is an issue which should always be discussed with an *asesor fiscal* prior to selling off assets. Non-residents are taxed at a flat rate of 35%. However, for residents, capital gains tax applies to all of your world-wide gains, whether for valuable consideration or for no consideration. Gains from assets held for less than a year are treated as income. Short-term gains are therefore added to any other Spanish income and taxed accordingly in the year in which the gain was made. Capital gains from the transfer of assets held for more than a year are taxed at 15%. There is no tax-free minimum.

Certain allowances are made for assets which have been held for a long period of time. For example, assets bought before 31 December 1994 are granted far more generous allowances. In such cases, the capital gain is reduced by a given percentage, depending on the type of asset, for each year that the asset was held prior to 1996. This inflation relief does not apply to capital losses.

The capital gain is calculated as the difference between the acquisition and transfer values, as legally defined, of the items transferred. For example, a capital gain on property, commercial or residential, is calculated on the net gain in the declared purchase price (as shown in the *escritura*) of the property when bought and the price that it fetches when subsequently sold. There are certain allowances available on this tax for the cost of conveyancing and any improvements made to the property. Gains are generally only taxed when a gain is crystallised, for example, upon the sale of an asset.

Capital losses may be offset against capital gains. However, short-term losses may only be offset against short-term gains, not long-term gains. Similarly, long-term losses can only be offset against long-term gains.

UNDER-DECLARATION

As mentioned in *Acquiring a Business or Business Premises*, there is a heavy cash culture in Spain and vendors are often advised by their accountants to under-declare the sale price in order to ease the burden of capital gains tax. The remainder of the sale is then paid for in cash. Although a common practice in Spain, this is highly inadvisable, not to mention illegal and the Spanish government is constantly looking for ways to crack down on cash purchases.

Plus Valia Tax

Plus Valia is a municipal capital gains tax, known fully as *Impuesto sobre el Incremento de Valor de los Terrenos de Naturaleza Urbana*. This tax is levied on the increase disclosed in the value of urban land whenever land is transferred. It does not apply to the increase in value of any *buildings* on the land and it is payable only on urban land, not rural land. The common practice is that both parties agree that the buyer pays this tax.

The local municipal tax office will be able to tell you before you sign a contract of sale what the *plus valia* tax will be on the property concerned. The maximum rate that this may be set at by the municipality is 30%.

A declaration must be made by the vendor (or purchaser) within thirty days, but in practice the *Ayuntamiento* (Town Hall) usually calculates the tax based on the property values obtained by the notary.

FURTHER READING

Guides to Business in Spain

A Guide to Business in Spain (ICEX, 2003); €27.05 (including postage). Available from ICEX (Instituto Español de Comercio Exterior, Departamento de Asesoría Jurídica y Administración, Paseo de la Castellana 14-16, 28046 Madrid; ☎913-496100; fax 913-496120; e-mail icex@icex.es). Alternatively the guide is available to view online at www.investinspain.org. A very useful source of information, but aimed more at large business and industry.

Cómo Crear una Empresa (Boletín Oficial del Estado; 2002) €3.00. Part of the *'Conoce tus derechos'* (know your rights) set of booklets issued by the Official State Bulletin. Fairly simple but in depth look at the options and solutions available to entrepreneurs.

Crea tu Propia Empresa: Estrategias para su Puesta en Marcha y Supervivencia (McGraw Hill; 2003); €17.00. A Spanish-language guide for first-time entrepreneurs dealing with the key aspects of business and the processes involved in business start-ups. Very good section on business financing.

Doing Business with Spain (Kogan Page, 2001); £40.00. Aims to help international companies take advantage of the Spanish market. Needs updating.

Guide to Labour and Social Affairs (Ministry of Labour and Social Affairs; 2004); €14.00. A list of all of the employment and social security regulations. Published in English and available from Labour and Social Affairs Advice Bureau, 20 Peel Street, London W8 7PD; ☎020-7221 0098; fax 020-7229 7270; e-mail spanlabo@globalnet.co.uk

Tu Propia Empresa: Un Reto Personal. Manual Util para Emprendedores (ESIC Editorial, 2003); €16.00. Very good, Spanish-language, general analysis of the processes involved in starting a new company in Spain.

Legal and Accounting Guides to Spain

The Blevins Franks Guide to Living in Spain (Blevins Franks, 2003);

£6.99. Useful financial guide to Spain by international financial advisers, Blevins Franks.

You and the Law in Spain (Santana Books, 2003); £19.95. Fourteenth edition of the very helpful and readable guide to Spanish law for foreigners.

Living in Spain

Buying a House in Spain (Vacation Work Publications, 2003); £11.95. Comprehensive guide to buying property in Spain with full coverage of the various regions.

Driving Over Lemons: an Optimist in Andalucia, Chris Stewart (Sort of Books, 1999); £6.99. Marvellous autobiographical account of an English couple who make the move to Andalucia to live a simple rural life amongst the villagers.

Live and Work in Spain and Portugal (Vacation Work Publications, 2002); £10.99. A detailed survey of the opportunities for living and working in Spain and Portugal.

No Going Back: Journey to Mother's Garden, Martin Kirby (Time Warner Paperbacks, 2003) £6.99. Comic account of a family moving to a small mountain farm in Catalonia and turning it into a viable small-holding business.

The Spanish and Life in Spain

The British on the Costa Del Sol, Karen O'Reilly (Routledge, 2000). A sociological study of the phenomenon of mass British culture in Spain, detailing the day to day realities of expatriate life.

The Rough Guide to Spain (Rough Guides, 2002); £13.99. The best handbook to Spain with very good background on Spain's history and culture.

The Spaniards; A Portrait of the New Spain, John Hooper (Penguin, 1987). One of the best overviews of the changes in Spain since Franco's death.

The Xenophobe's Guide to the Spanish (Oval Books, 2002); £3.99. An irreverent look at the beliefs and foibles of the Spanish.

GLOSSARY OF TERMS

Abogado: Lawyer.

Academia de Ingles: Private English academy or school.

Agencia Tributaria: Spanish Tax office, also known colloquially as the *Hacienda*.

Alquiler de Temporada: Short-term rental contract.

Alquiler de Vivienda: Long-term rental contract.

Agente de la Propiedad Inmobiliaria (API): Qualified and licensed estate agent.

Agrícola: Agricultural.

Alojamiento Rural: Rural Accommodation.

Asesor Fiscal: A fiscal advisor – the equivalent of a chartered accountant.

Autónomo: Full title is *trabajador autónomo*. Refers to somebody who is self-employed. This entails a special social security regime.

Ayuntamiento: Town Hall or local council.

Boletín Oficial del Estado: Official State Bulletin department of the Spanish government.

Cajas de Ahorro: Spanish savings banks.

Cámaras de Comercio: Chambers of Commerce.

Carnet Sanitario: Health and hygiene certificate which anybody who handles food must hold.

Catastro: Land registry.

Certificado del Desembolso Efectuado: Certificate stating that the minimum capital necessary to incorporate a company has been deposited into a bank account in the company name.

Certificado Médico: Medical certificate.

Certificacion Negativa del Nombre (CNN): Certificate documenting that nobody else holds your company name.

Cesión: The official term for buying the goodwill and fixtures and fittings of a business whilst renting the premises. Known also as a *traspaso*. The exact terms of the cesión must be stated in the contract.

Código de Identificación Fiscal (CIF): Company tax identification number required by all incorporated entities.

Colegio: Professional association.

Comunidad de Bienes: A business that is not an independent legal entity and belongs to two or several proprietors who assume unlimited responsibility.

Comunidades Autónomas: Spain is divided into seventeen Autonomous Communities each with its own regional assembly. Each also has its own flag, capital city and president. Central government retains overall control of such matters as foreign policy and defence.

Contable: Accountant or bookkeeper.

Cortijo: Term used in Andalucia for a farmhouse, usually with a plot of land and outhouses.

Cuenta Propia: 'Working on you own account' – a term for self-employment.

Departamento de Desarollo Rural: Department of Rural Development – there is one in each of the seventeen autonomous communities.

Dirección General de Política de la PYME: Organisation dealing with the promotion of small and medium-sized businesses in Spain.

Empresario Individual: Sole trader.

Entidad Estatal de Seguros Agrarios (ENESA): Organism in charge of state-subsidised agricultural insurance.

Escritura: Deed (either a title deed or a deed of incorporation).

Estudio de Mercardo: Market research.

Federación Española de Empresarios de Camping y Centros de Vacaciones (FEEC): Spanish federation of campsite and holiday centre owners.

Federación Española de Hosterlería (FEHR): Spanish federation of hostelry.

Fianza: Deposit.

Finca: Term used in much of Spain for a farmhouse, usually with a plot of land and outhouses.

Gestor(es): Professional that helps guide people through the labyrinth of Spanish bureaucracy.

Gestoría: The office of *gestores*.

Gestoría Inmobiliaria Propiedad España (GIPE): Type of estate agent that is less qualified than an API.

Giros en Descubierto: Overdrafts.

Hacienda: Ministry of the Economy. Often used to describe the local tax office, the *Agencia Tributaria*.

Impuesto de Actos Juridicos Documentdos: Stamp duty.

Impuesto de Transmisiones Patrimoniales: Transfer tax.

Impuesto sobre Actividades Económicas (IAE): Municipal tax on business activities.

Impuesto sobre Bienes Inmeubles (IBI): Tax levied annually on the owners of real estate.

Impuesto sobre el Patrimonio: Wealth tax.

Impuesto sobre la Renta de las Personas Físicas (IRPF): Income tax paid by individuals.

Impuesto sobre Sociedades (IS): Corporation tax paid by companies.

Impuesto sobre el Valor Añadido (IVA): The Spanish version of Value Added Tax.

Inmobiliario/a: Property or real estate.

Instituto Cameral de Creación y Desarollo de la Empresa (INCYDE): Found in certain Chambers of Commerce, INCYDE offers free advice and personalised assistance to people wanting to set up a company and also to those who wish to set up as self-employed.

Instituto de Crédito Oficial (ICO): Official credit institute.

Instituto Español de Comercio Exterior(ICEX): Spanish Institute of Foreign Trade.

Instituto Nacional de Empleo (INEM): National employment institute.

Instituto Nacional de Salud (INSALUD): Spanish national health institute.

Libro de Reclamación: Complaints book. Many regional authorities insist that small businesses that deal with the public have a complaints book and a notice announcing that it is there.

Licencia de Apertura: Opening licence issued by the municipal council. Required for all business premises.

Linea de Descuenta: Literally a 'Discount Line', which allows the businessman to get an advance on any money owed, similar to 'factoring' in the UK.

Local(es): Business premises. Estate agents refer to a *local* if there is no business for sale with the premises.

Ministerio de Agricultura, Pesca y Alimentación (MAPA): Spanish Ministry of Agriculture, Fisheries and Food.

Masia: Term used in Cataluña to describe a farmhouse in a rural area, usually with a plot of land and outhouses.

Memoria de Actividades: Literally: activity report. A written explanation of the business activity you intend to carry out.

Micro Empresas: Businesses with less than ten salaried employees.

Ministerio de Trabajo y Asuntos Sociales: Ministry of Labour and Social Affairs.

Módulo: A tax system designed for small businesses. The tax agency decides what your business income (taxed as a part of your personal income tax) should be and you are charged tax on this amount each quarter.

Numero de Identificación de Extranjeros (NIE): Tax identification number required by foreigners who wish to run a business.

Numero de Identificación Fiscal (NIF): As above but for Spanish nationals.

Nómina: Official salary for a particular type of work, on which the social security base is calculated.

Notario: The *notario* is a public official in charge of officially registering certain events such as property purchases and the incorporation of a company.

Oficina de Extranjeros: Foreigner's Office, where applications for residence permits should be made.

Pagas Extraordinarias: Extra payments of a month's wage in the summer and at Christmas.

Pagarés: Literally 'I will pay' – a special type of cheque that can be post-dated.

Paginas Amarillas: Spanish yellow pages.

Punto de Asesoramiento e Inicio de Tramitación (PAIT): New automated technology which is not yet widely available. Helps entrepreneurs to set up an S.L.N.E. quickly and easily.

Pequeña y Mediana Empresas (PYMEs): Small and medium-sized businesses.

Plan Integral de Calidad del Turismo Español: Spanish tourism integral quality plan 2000-2006. Aims at regeneration of the mature tourism sector and the development of alternative tourism in Spain.

Plus Valia: Municipal capital gains tax on the value of land.

Préstamo: Loan.

Régimen Especial Agrario: Special social security regime for anybody working in agriculture.

Registro de la Propiedad: Property registry.

Registro Mercantil Centro: The companies'/mercantile registry where all companies must be registered before they can begin trading.

Reserva para Inversiones en Canarias (RIC): The Canary Island Investment Reserve.

Seguridad Social: Social security

Sociedad Anónima (S.A.): The equivalent of a British public limited company (plc) or an American corporation (Inc.). This is the most widely used form of business entity in Spain and is used for investments in major projects.

Sociedad Colectiva (S.C.): General partnership. The simplest of the commercial entities. It is essentially an independent legal entity owned by two or more general partners, all assuming unlimited responsibility for the company.

Sociedad Comanditaria: Similar to the General Partnership but ownership is divided between one or more general partners who assume unlimited responsibility and one or more limited partners whose liability is limited to the amount of capital contributed but who play no part in managing the company.

Sociedad de Responsibilidad Limitada (S.L.): The most common form of business entity for smaller enterprises.

Sociedad Limitada Nueva Empresa (S.L.N.E.): A specialised version of the S.L. designed to be set up quickly and at a lower cost.

Sucursal: Branch.

Tarjeta de Residencia/Comunitaria: Residence Card/Community Card.

Trabajador Autónomo: Self-employed worker.

Traspaso: Literally 'transfer'. A term used for a business purchase where the goodwill of the business is bought but the business premises are rented. Officially called a *Cesión*.

Transferencia: Direct debit.

Turespaña: The Spanish Tourist Board.

Ubicación: Location.

Unipersonal: A limited company formed with only one owner/shareholder.

Valor Catastral: The value of property as assessed by the local authorities.

Ventanilla Unica Empresarial (VUE): 'One-stop shop for business'. A department of some Spanish Chambers of Commerce combining all of the departments necessary for entrepreneurs to establish a new business.

Zona Especial Canaria (ZEC): The Canary Islands Special Zone is a low tax regime which has been created with the objective of promoting the economic and social development of the Canary Islands.

ACRONYMS

See Glossary for English explanations.

API: *Agente de la Propiedad Inmobiliaria.*

BBVA: *Banco Bilbao Vizcaya Argentaria.*
BOE: *Boletín Oficial del Estado.*
BSCH: *Banco de Santander Central Hispano.*
CIF: *Código de Identificación Fiscal.*
CNN: *Certificacion Negativa del Nombre.*

DGPYME: *Dirección General de la Politica de la PYME.*

EIB: European Investment Bank.
EIG: Economic Interest Grouping.
ENESA: *Entidad Estatal de Seguros Agrarios.*
ENISA: *Empresa Nacional de Innovación.*

FEEC: *Federación Española de Empresarios de Camping y Centros de Vacaciones.*
FEHR: *Federación Española de Hosterlería.*

GIPE: *Gestoría Inmobiliaria Propiedad España.*

IAE: *Impuesto sobre Actividades Económicas.*
IBI: *Impuesto sobre Bienes Inmuebles.*
ICEX: *Instituto Español de Comercio Exterior.*
ICO: *Instituto de Crédito Oficial.*
INCYDE: *Instituto Cameral de Creación y Desarollo de la Empresa.*
INEM: *Instituto Nacional de Empleo.*
INSALUD: *Instituto Nacional de Salud.*
INSS: *Instituto Nacional de la Seguridad Social.*
IRPF: *Impuesto Sobre la Renta de las Personas Físicas.*
IS: *Impuesto sobre Sociedades.*

IVA: *Impuesto sobre el Valor Añadido.*

MAPA: *Ministerio de Agricultura, Pesca y Alimentación.*

NARIC: National Academic Recognition Information Centre.
NIE: *Numero de Identificación de Extranjeros.*
NIF: *Numero de Identificación Fiscal.*

PADI: Professional Association of Diving Instructors.
PYMEs: *Pequeña y Mediana Empresas.*

RIC: *Reserva para Inversiones en Canarias.*

S.A.: *Sociedad Anónima.*
S.C.: *Sociedad Colectiva.*
S.L.: *Sociedad de Responsibilidad Limitada.*
S.L.N.E.: *Sociedad Limitada Nueva Empresa.*

UTE: Temporary business association.

ZEC: *Zona Especial Canaria.*

Complete guides to life abroad from Vacation Work

Live & Work Abroad

Live & Work in Australia & New Zealand...................................£10.99
Live & Work in Belgium, The Netherlands & Luxembourg.....£10.99
Live & Work in China..£11.95
Live & Work in France..£10.99
Live & Work in Germany..£10.99
Live & Work in Ireland £10.99
Live & Work in Italy £10.99
Live & Work in Japan £10.99
Live & Work in Russia & Eastern Europe £10.99
Live & Work in Saudi & the Gulf £10.99
Live & Work in Scandinavia £10.99
Live & Work in Scotland...£10.99
Live & Work in Spain & Portugal...£10.99
Live & Work in the USA & Canada £10.99

Buying a House Abroad

Buying a House in France...£11.95
Buying a House in Italy £11.95
Buying a House in Portugal..£11.95
Buying a House in Spain £11.95
Buying a House on the Mediterranean £12.95

Starting a Business Abroad

Starting a Business in France...£12.95
Starting a Business in Spain £12.95